There's Enough Woman Left to be Your Lady

Junious Epps Jr.

Copyright © 2003 by Junious Epps Jr.

There's Enough Woman Left to be Your Lady
by Junious Epps Jr.

Printed in the United States of America

ISBN 0-9705305-3-6

Library of Congress Control Number: 2002090303

Epps, Junious Jr.
There's Enough Woman Left to be Your Lady

1.Women issues 2. Christianity
3. Motivational self-help. 4. Interpersonal conflict.
5. Human life cycle.

All rights reserved. No part of this publication may be reproduced or transmitted in any form or by any means without written permission of the publisher.

Unless otherwise indicated, Bible quotations are taken from the King James Version.

Xulon Press
www.XulonPress.com

Xulon Press books are available in bookstores everywhere, and on the Web at www.XulonPress.com.

Introduction

Woman! From the day that she was extracted from Adam to her deception in the Garden of Eden she has been an integral part of man. However, seeking her rightful place as a ruler among God's creation hasn't been without pain, suffering, and rejection. Providential illumination poignantly details how the blood of Jesus searches the hearts of women with faults, jealousy, brokenness, vindictiveness, and pain. He saw the whoredom of Mary Magdalene, the woman with an issue, the resurrection of Jarius' daughter, the woman bent over for eighteen years, and the woman at the well, as having separate entities of temperament, misgivings, suspicions and problems.

Like so many women of the world who love glitter, glamour, and glory, these women of the Bible had a misplaced sense of moral wealth that robbed them of spiritual and moral values. The love of Jesus majestically reconstructed broken foundations of immorality, death, love, and heartbreak in each of their lives and shows the path to salvation, deliverance, and wholeness to modern day women of God. Brokenness in the presence of God is His opportunity for healing, deliverance, and total restoration in women ministry, fellowship, teaching, evangelization, marriage, and for anyone that's in need of a spiritual blessing.

History must constantly strive to include "Herstory." All true stories for women as well as men are nothing but ghost stories, if mankind repeats the same growth and experience over and over again without knowledge of what has "gone before."

It's my hope that women everywhere will find peace, quiet, solitude, faith, and deliverance after reading about their sisters of the past that walked and talked with Jesus, and that they go from the wilderness of ecclesiastical discrimination to their inheritance in the ministry that God is calling them into. Although Eve has mingled with dust of the earth long ago, the problems that she caused mankind will never shake the foundation of Christ's love for her and all other women.

CONTENTS

1. SHE MUST BE A SPECIAL LADY 9
2. MY WORLD IS EMPTY WITHOUT YOU 19
3. WHEN YOUR WELL RUNS DRY 35
4. RESPECT 45
5. WHAT YOU WANT DO FOR LOVE 73
6. JEALOUS LOVE 91
7. WOMEN ARE A RARE JEWEL 103
8. A STRANGER IN PARADISE 119
9. JUST A TOUCH FROM THE MASTER'S HAND 137
10. WHAT TO DO WHEN YOU HAVE BLOWN IT 179
11. I HAVE A PROBLEM 193
12. A LOVE LIKE YOURS DON'T COME KNOCKING EVERYDAY 201
13. SURGERY WITHOUT PAIN 217
14. DRINKING FROM DEEPER WELLS 261
15. WHAT GOOD AM I WITHOUT YOU? 273
16. I AM WORKING MY WAY BACK TO YOU 281

1

She Must Be A Special Lady

*God created all things and on the sixth day said, "Let us make man in our image, in our likeness, and let **them** rule over the fish of the sea and the birds of the air, over the livestock, over all the earth, and over all the creatures that move along the ground. So God created man in his own image, in the image of God created he him; male and female he created them." (Genesis 1:26-27) "And Adam said this is now bone of my bones, flesh of my flesh: she shall be called Woman, because she was taken out of man." (Genesis 2:23)*

Man is the crowning glory of God's creation, and God is the missing link in man's existence. God and man are interlinked spiritually and physically, and are not indistinguishable like other animals. The mysterious chemistry between man and animals comes from the fact that God created both from the dust of the ground, but man sits in the middle of God's creative hierarchy. Man was made lower than the Angels were, and a little higher than the animal kingdom. This means that man has just enough angel in him to not be a beast, and enough beast in him to not be an angel. The first man Adam had a pure, loving, intimate, relationship with the Lord without sin. Man was alone, but he was not absolutely alone because there were the animals, and more importantly there was God. Yet, God said that Adam was incomplete without a "helper." The Hebrew word "helper" is translated *"ezer kenegdo."* It means "duplicity." Much like cloning the idea is to be a counter-part to oneself. Therefore, God created woman because He said, "That it's not good for man to be alone." The word "helper" is an unfortunate translation because it implies a hierarchy, as though the woman exists only to help the man. What value then did God and Adam place upon Eve? We can observe that woman and man were made "suitable" corresponding to or like each other, neither inferior nor superior. Woman and man were to share equally in the dignity of creation and in the fundamental privileges of the covenant of grace. Both man and woman could walk with the Lord in the garden, and know His fellowship and love. The first woman, our mother Eve knew God and understood what God required of her. She could love, worship, and obey her Maker. When she was involved in those activities she was most fully a human being. Both man and woman complete and complement one another. Adam and Eve's creation is rooted in the divine image of personality, intellect, emotions, and moral likeness to God. No other created being has this image. Yes, woman is different from man, yet there's beautiful equality and harmony in the idea of woman being an equal counterpart in God's plan for creation. In addition, woman's differences from man cause God to deal with her in unique and exciting ways. For example, her emotions are different from men due to hormonal levels. A woman's emotions may cause her to react with laughter one minute and tears the next minute. At certain times of the month she may be as strong as iron or dealing with depression. It is easy for a woman to "feel" insecure or guilty about her emotions. Especially, since for years a woman's emotions have been associated with weakness. If we think about it maybe the woman needed all this emotional ability and sensitivity because of her highly diversified role. The woman named Eve must have been a special lady because she was sitting at the top of Gods creation in handcrafted beauty.

Adam and Eve were also married in splendor. At the worlds first wedding music from Morning Stars (Angels) filled the sky. The scent of the Garden of Eden's perfumed flowers engulfed the air. Perfect temperatures were forecast for all mornings eternal. Bright colors and foliage of green was entwined in the grass, and the sky was used as a blanket to cover them. Fields illuminated with every variation of color in a crayola color box dazzled their eyes. The colors of the new world bounced brightly off the sides of the universe as Adam took the hand of the flawless, immaculate daughter of God and said, *"This is bone of my bone, and flesh of my flesh."* Adam had gone all the way down to the skeletal frame of the woman in describing his relationship with Eve. He had finally found someone that understood him, loved him, and could fellowship with him. She would become his partner, lover, confidant, and friend. That's what every woman should be for her husband. Adam took a solemn vow to cherish for all eternity the most perfect woman of all time. It was not a sexual union of marriage, but one consummated in love and unity. It reaffirmed what God had intended. The two became one flesh. They were naked and unashamed because they were one in body, mind, and spirit.

When a man sees his woman as being a part of him and touches the woman's mind he gets her interest. When he touches her heart he gets her love, but when he touch her soul he gets passion beyond his wildest dreams. Put all three together and he has found his soul mate for life.

At the conclusion of the marriage ceremony God presented to the world Mr. and Mrs. Adam. As a wedding present God had given them lifetime rights over all the earth. Adam and Eve's residence was not an ivory mansion, but a garden eastward in Eden located at 777 Paradise Rd. The roof of their house consisted of earth and heaven with its overhead canvas of powder blue, and with a dash of white clouds sprinkled here and there to enhance its backdrop. Never was any roof so curiously framed, ceiled, and painted. The sun, moon, and stars were used as electric light. The green-carpeted earth was their richly inlaid floor. The fruit of trees was their grocery store, and shade from its leaves was their retirement villa. Yet, trouble in the form of a snake and tree stripped them of their robe of innocence and left them stark naked in sin. Subtlety took away their opportunity for eternal happiness. Satan knowing that Eve had half the strength to resist temptation without Adam by her side, took the form of a snake, lodged in a fruit tree, and chose a time when Eve was alone to converse with her. He told her that she would find pleasure and wisdom in the core of the fruit. Eve listened too long to Satan. She gave her body over to lust of the flesh, and enticed Adam to also eat with her. After committing spiritual adultery with the Devil, Adam and Eve hid from God and each other behind the trees. (Genesis 3:7–8) Given the obvious parallels between these two acts of concealment, what does this imply about Adam and Eve's marriage after they ate the fruit? It implies that the underlying cause of their sin was selfishness. They both wanted to know what powers lie in the knowledge of good and evil, but fell from God's grace in the process. The

There's Enough Woman Left to be Your Lady

same hands that held Adam, held the fruit, which held the fate of the world. Eve's hand's caused separation among her, Adam, animals, God, and billions more people to follow. The first family was sentenced to perpetual agony. When God expelled them from the paradisiacal garden every form of sin entered the world and destroyed everything. All kinds of ugly things that God never intended began to happen. Man and woman began to find fault, and blamed one another for their downfall. The fall drastically distorted God's intention for man and woman. Sorrow, wretchedness, and eviction from Paradise are what they paid for a moment of luxury. They could no longer be naked and unashamed. A perfect God took a perfect woman from the side of a perfect man to be his companion in a perfect home, but she rebelled against God's government and authority. Curiosity, pride, and disobedience caused Eve to taste of the fruit forbidden by God. Forbidden fruit for Eve was so beautiful and delicious that she invited her husband to partake of it. Eve had a powerful influence over Adam that's how she enticed him to eat the forbidden fruit. Her daughters (women) also have regal influence and great power over men for good or evil. The average woman doesn't realize the tremendous strength and power that she has to influence people. Women have an unyielding, relentless ego. When they get it their mind to do something it becomes embedded in their conscious, and they will stop at nothing to achieve their purpose. Inquisitiveness has destroyed millions of families and people, especially women, and has carried countless numbers into ruin. Some women have dislocated their hips, shoulders, necks, and backs, by trying to pluck fruit from a tree that's either too high for them or beyond their reach. Millions of Adams and Eves eat fruit from trees that don't belong to them, and they end up with indigestion. The fruit that Eve plucked and ate set the universe reeling and staggering under the weight of crimes, wars, and diseases. The consequences of that one sin have shut prison doors, and opened medical hospitals laced with diseases. Insane asylums have been overflowing with despondent and sometime incurable patients. Eve's curiosity has caused mankind to witness scores of misery across and around the world. Man has heard wailing and crying from starving children in Third World countries. He has watched plagues rise from one corner of the world and catch a ride on airwaves, ships, and airplanes to bring famine, sickness, and despair of heart to sick and dying nations. He watches nightly on television the terror of bullets and bombs that has ripped apart and claimed the lives of innocent people. Disease, death, murder, drought, famine, war, racism, slavery, and the subjugation of women would be daily news. Men would treat women as property, and would deny them the right to study the written word of God. They would be prohibited from exercising their spiritual gifts that were given by God to help rule and subdue the earth. Women would suffer the indignities of being treated as sex objects, and valued only if they produced male children. They would be used as expendable objects of male desires in polygamous marriages. They would be granted no right of divorce, and yet they could be abused and discarded. Over the centuries, women's weaker muscular strength, coupled with the dependencies generated by increased pains in childbearing, would make them increasingly subjugated by men. The curse of Eve's sin would put woman under subjection to man. However, in the creation of female, we see that woman was created to be Adam's helpmeet. A "doormat," "people pleaser," "servant," or "slave" was certainly not what God had in mind for Eve. To fully appreciate the value of women men need to understand God's original intention. Both the male and female were created in the image of God, and were given the role of leadership and dominion. God intended that Adam and Eve both should multiply and rule over the earth. He said, "Let *them* have dominion." (Genesis 1:26-28)

There is a distinction between the created roles of man and woman. Man and woman were created from different materials. Adam was created from the dust of the ground, which links him to the world, while the woman was created from the rib (side) of man, which links her to the man. That's how she became known as woman because she was taken from the *"womb"* of man. It's this difference that's the basis of the Apostle Paul's argument in 1 Corinthians 11:12, *"For as woman came from man, so also man is born of woman. But everything comes from God."* After Adam woman was the first of everything in human lineage, but God made profound differences between men and women. The way in which man and woman were created determines the role differences they are to play. Woman's task in ruling is smaller than man's, and man's task in reproduction is not as great as woman's, but they are both united in this work. The use of masculinity has operated as if women alone are responsible for their sexual behavior, reproductive health, and childbearing. Both male and female has a primary role in reproduction, but only the woman has a larger and more important role, which is bearing children, and nursing them. God has created her physically and psychologically for that task. Eve's disobedience to God's commandments doesn't mean that a woman in every area of life is a second-class person. Despite male subjugation and domination, God has used many powerful women. Even more so, the Lord Jesus Christ gave his life to set men and women free from the curse of the law that holds us accountable for sin. *"Christ redeemed us from the curse of the law by becoming a curse for us, for it's written: "Cursed is everyone who is hung on a tree."* (Galatians 3:13) Jesus was cursed and hung for everyone so that the order of creation could be restored to a right relationship with God. The power of his death over the curse is beautifully set forth in Galatians 3:28. *"There is neither Jew nor Greek, slave nor free, male nor female, for you are all one in Christ Jesus."* Eve's death has brought no respite or perfection to womanhood. Jesus Christ died so that all mankind would be set free from sin, racial class differences, and gender divisions. He set males and females free from the curse so that they could be restored as gender equals and one flesh. Before the fall Adam and Eve ruled together with distinctive gender differences that were much more than mere cultural conditioning. There was no confusion, and no sin, only perfect agreement. It's after the fall that confusion, sin, disagreements, pride, struggles for power and rule emerge. God is not leaving things the way they were after the fall! Yes, the Bible say that it's not good for man to be alone, but it doesn't say that it's not good for woman to be alone. Women are not an adjunct, or an addendum to a man's masculine edition. They're not something that God threw in to even out humanity. A man's masculinity is not dependent upon subordination and dominance of a woman, but rather it's depended on his own strength, and the strength that he gets from a woman. He need someone who has just enough "testosterone" to know where her man is coming from in his relationship with her, and the male must have just enough "estrogen" to be feminine enough to know the needs and expectations of his woman. Those needs are his pillars. The woman corresponds to the man in that she like him is made in God's image. Successful men know that happiness in romantic relationships is not due to luck. That's because anointed women's choices in men are consistent, and they use reliable principles of God's word along with having a game plan to hook a man. That's the Adamic/Edenic covenant passed down from God in the Garden of Eden to man. Successful wives are cheerleaders and ego builders. They send roots of love and devotion deep in the ground that gives men a strong foundation for relationships, family, and marriage. They know that a man seek attention by way of strength. His self-esteem is rooted in his ability to make love, sustain his job, and to provide for his family. They also know that he needs a wife that will make him feel confident, important, worthwhile, in charge of his home, and compliments him, not one that competes with him. Woman is an independent creature that was intended to live, walk, act, think, and to fight her battles along side her husband, but Eve foolishly gave up those rights when she plucked and ate the fruit with her hands without consulting Adam.

"Every wise woman buildeth her house, but the foolish plucketh it down with her hands." (Proverbs 14:1) This section gives us insight into a woman who combines feminine strength and wisdom to be an unequalled wife, mother, worshipper, businesswoman, and minister with a homeward orientation. Her life is filled with abundant joy and fruitfulness. A good wife is a blessing not only to her husband, but also to her family and those around her. She causes the affairs of her family to prosper. By her wisdom bills are paid, grocery and food are provisioned, the children are well educated and maintained, and the husband has comfort in the home. She look upon the house as her own to take care of, although she knows it's her husband's right to rule the house according to the will of God. A foolish woman that has no fear of God or respect for her husband and family will tear her house down. It will be as if she tore it down with her own hands; and the husband couldn't do anything about it. Every spiritually wise woman should make her own plans, and be her own architect and supervisor, while maintaining a family and home guided by the spirit of God. She should achieve her family and her own destiny, while using the Lord as her overseer. A man's job is to help support a woman by sharing his time, love, understanding, finances, and physical help. If he doesn't want to do that it would be better that a woman was alone. A woman reverts

to a "doormat" role and image when she supports a man that will not work or reciprocate her affections. Or when she waits and watches for her man and rarely rejects him, even when he comes to her covered with the smell and signs of another woman that he has spent time with.

2

My World Is Empty Without You

It's said that this is a man's world. In this man's world women are viewed as cheap, exploited for their beauty, and down played for their brains. About 2500 years ago, a brave young woman saved her nation with her beauty and brain. Her Hebrew name was Hadassah, which means "Myrtle," but we know her by her Persian name, Esther. The book of Esther is a tale of exploitation, intrigue, and deliverance, but it's more so about sexual harassment. Esther's story begins with a drunken king named Ahasuerus. For six months he showed off the wealth and splendor of his kingdom. The alcohol flowed freely. At the end of his boastful display he began a great banquet. He spared nothing, and shared freely. To top it all off, the whole celebration was to close with that he treasured most in all his kingdom; his queen. The Queen was to come before the king in the closing hour on the last day of the feast, wearing the crown that the king had provided for her, and arrayed in the finest royal garment to show the people and his prince's her beauty. On the seventh day of feasting and drinking, when Ahasuerus was in high spirits, he commanded that his Queen, a beautiful woman named Vashti, be brought before him wearing her royal crown so that the he could show her off like all the other wealth of his kingdom. In a radical act of rebellion Vashti refused. She would not be treated like a piece of meat that men would ogle and lust for.

Ahasuerus was a great king. He was not accustomed to anyone disobeying him, especially a woman. In Persian society even Queens had few rights. The king was furious and consulted his advisors to decide what to do. (Esther 1:16-22) Then Memucan (one of the seven Princes) replied in the presence of the king and the nobles, "Queen Vashti has done wrong, not only against the king but also against all the nobles and the peoples of all the provinces of King Ahasuerus. For the queen's conduct will become known to all the women, and so they will despise their husbands and say, "King Ahasuerus commanded Queen Vashti to be brought before him, but she would not come." This very day the Persian and Medianite women of the nobility who have heard about the queen's conduct will respond to all the king's nobles in the same way. There will be no end of disrespect and discord. Therefore, if it pleases the king let him issue a royal decree and let it be written in the laws of Persia and Media, which cannot be repealed, that Vashti is never again to enter the presence of King Ahasuerus. Also let the king give her royal position to someone else who is better than she. Then when the king's edict is proclaimed throughout all his vast realm, all the women will respect their husbands, from the least to the greatest." The king and his nobles were pleased with this advice, so the king did as Memucan proposed. He sent dispatches to all parts of the

There's Enough Woman Left to be Your Lady

kingdom, to each province in its own script and to each people in its own language, proclaiming in each people that every man should be ruler over his own household. King Ahasuerus and his advisors were afraid that women would rise up from their exploited position. They were in no mood to let women make any decisions. (Esther 1:19-22) Vashti on the other hand was in no mood to be made as a showpiece. She knew that as a Persian woman her beauty was to be hidden from others and seen only by her husband. Therefore, she refused to come to the banquet. The King should not have sent for her to come into his presence when he was drunk. In his state of mind he was using her beauty to further his pride and arrogance. He dishonored himself as a husband and made himself look small as a king. If this falling out had been within their home it may have been settled and forgotten, but it happened in public. Therefore, the king was embarrassed. He felt that she was a bad influence upon all the families of the kingdom. He also felt that her actions would embolden other wives to dominate, and disobey their husbands. Vashti may have unwittingly been the first recorded woman claiming equal rights and sexual harassment by a male in authority. Even so the exploitation of women continued. Ahasuerus deposed Vashti from the throne and divorced her when she attempted to maintain her dignity. He began searching for another wife. He called for all the beautiful young virgin girls of the kingdom to be brought to the capital city. Their mind, soul, personality, likes, or dislikes did not matter. The only thing that mattered was beauty. Each woman was given beauty treatments, and schooled in proper manners befitting a queen. Then one by one they were brought to the palace to spend the night with the king. All of these young virgins except the one who was chosen to be the king's new Queen would be used and forgotten. One named Esther excelled them all. Esther was an orphan who was adopted by her cousin Mordecai who raised her as his own daughter. Esther wasn't flirtatious enough to come before the king with artificial beauty. She won the honor of becoming queen by natural and spiritual beauty. Against all odds, a young woman dragged away from home against her will became part of the king's harem, and later his Queen. In one respect, this was a great honor, but how would any woman feel to be taken from her home simply because of her beauty, and be given a one-night tryout where she would be accepted or rejected? Once accepted, how would she feel to be in a relationship with a man who controlled her total life, had other wives, and did not love her, but only her beauty? Since the fall of humanity, women in many societies have been treated with similar injustice and unkindness.

Esther concealed her national and religious identity. When Mordecai learned of Haman's (the Kings number one man) plot to kill all of the Jews he approached Esther and asked her to talk to the king. It had been more than a month since the king had called for Esther because he had many women and likely more than one Queen. Mordecai was asking Esther to risk her life. The king's law was that anyone who approached him unsummoned would be put to death unless the king held out his gold scepter. Not even a Queen could approach the throne without risking her life. Esther's response to Mordecai, *"Go, gather together all the Jews who are in Shushan, and fast for me. Do not eat or drink for three days, night or day. My maids and I will fast as you do. When this is done, I will go to the king, even though it's against the law. And if I perish, I perish."* (Esther 4:16) She loved her people so much that she was willing to save their lives, and risk her life to approach the king. What do we see about this young woman of faith? Esther believed in fasting and prayer, and was counting on God to help her. She used her God-given intelligence to devise a plan that would rid her people of its enemy forever. She was a brave, godly patriot who defined herself when she said: "And if I perish, I perish." Like the former Queen Vashti, Esther was no longer going to let the king extort her natural beauty, but she was going to let him see her clothed in the beauty of Holiness and serving the great Jehovah-Jireh, *"The Lord will provide."* Much could be accomplished in the kingdom of Jesus Christ if more women lived in the beauty of Holiness like Esther, who moved from the position of being an exploited pretty face young girl to become the deliverer of God's people. She risked her life to do God's will. Esther provides lovely examples of true beauty, courage, and spiritual maturity. Specifically, she knew when to overlook, when to confront, how to make a respectful appeal, and when to remain silent. Though obviously intelligent and gifted, she did not promote her own agendas, but was firmly fixed on the Lord's purposes. She had unshakable faith in the Lord, strong gifts in biblical peacemaking, and she rose above the sinful prejudices of her time to plead for the lives of her people. She dared to approach the king, to speak face to face with him and to be taken seriously. Esther is a great example of faith, ingenuity, and courage. After all, most women will not be called upon to save an entire nation or negotiate with a king bent on destroying their family. In Genesis, Song of Solomon, Ephesians, and Revelations, women represent the church, both in and out of Bible prophecy. What would happen to the church today if it refused and openly rebelled to be washed in Jesus blood, sanctified, and to wear the royal crown and clothes provided from the best that the King could provide? If the church refuses to show her beauty to all in the final climax of the battle between good and evil, and to show that she is changed, beautified, and prepared by grace to live in a sinless kingdom, where would we be? If King Jesus' own Queen (the Church) refuses to obey Him, then surely there will be no New Jerusalem! Women are not slaves, hirelings, or subordinates to men. They are queens. A woman doesn't need attendants, royal clothes, or a processional, for she is crowned by the grace of God. She has been crowned spiritually by God to cheer up despondent and sick people, wipe tears from the eyes of her children, and give hope and help to her Adam. A woman's nobility and queenly walk is inspired by her exercising the obedience that she has now come to respect in God and her Adam. A good woman is like gold and diamonds. She's rare, precious, high in value, located in rock deep in the earth, hard to find, and gives off brilliant rays of light from her own illumination. If she will dig deep into the mine of her heart and soul, she will see that it breathes and gives her life. She has won the right to rule in her own domain because she is continually atoning for her mother's (Eve) transgression by being obedient to God's word. Women are truly sorry for Eve's role in the garden, and they seek to minister and be a blessing daily to spiritually and physically sick people. Women make and maintain close friendships every day. When those friendships include loyalty, respect, and genuine affection, they are truly beautiful. All friendships between women are beautiful and dangerous in very different ways. Women naturally turn to one another for solace, support, and spiritual sustenance, yet are encouraged at every turn to dismiss and compete with one another. Sadly, many women today don't know how to enjoy thriving, intimate relationships with another woman. They are more likely to be catty, petty, combative, and competitive, instead of accepting one another. What could be an area of great strength becomes an area of weakness. Just like women biblical heroines, all women of God are called to be peacemakers. However, instead of living as peacemakers and showing themselves to be daughters of God, many Christian women speak with and relate to their husbands and family like unbelievers. Some women have used their tongues for evil in the household and have

There's Enough Woman Left to be Your Lady

severely wounded the tender young mind of their children by saying negative things about the father. A woman should understand that she will always be the closest parent to a child. First of all she carried the child for nine months and shared its growth, pain, and sustenance. Before and after deliverance she bonds with the child. Most children always give reference to their mother and God for all that she and He have done for them. Male children also rather talk with their mother instead of the father because mothers seem to understand them and are more compassionate. But if the mother is a sharp tongued, ranting, raving, uncontrollable complainer, or is against anything that he seeks to accomplish, she will become a thorn in his flesh and he will remove her out of his life. Society responds to words of kindness, tranquility, and love from a woman of God. Loving words also " magnify" a man, and cause him to grow morally and spiritually. The Bible declares, "Power of life and death is in the tongue." A woman's tongue can exalt or destroy a man, but if she knows what to say and when to say it she can be of great help to her man, especially minister's wives. Inevitably all pastors' wives face a kind of loneliness that is known only to them. A pastor's demanding schedule is frequently demanded of others, and it robs his wife of private time with him. When he does allot time for her, phone calls or meetings often interrupt even that time. Being the pastor's wife in a smaller church has unique joys and challenges, but the pastor's wife can't hide in any size church. She's more visible, feels more needed, and often feels more vulnerable. She may hope she won't see a particular critic each Sunday, but generally the critic seems to make a clear path straight to her. She may also feel that she and her children are always "on display," and that may cause her to become over-involved in church activities. When questioned why she does so much, she may say, "Someone has to do it." She's also probably more aware of the problems and struggles of the Pastorship, and carries more of the weight of her husband's disappointments and fears. On the positive side, she has the opportunity to be more involved in the lives of each family in the church by participating more intimately in their spiritual growth and personal crisis. She may experience the fulfillment of having had an integral part in a child's salvation, a mother's repentance, or a husband's interest in spiritual things. She may also have more opportunity to develop her own gifts and serve in areas of interest. The pastor's wife feels the need for friendship, but she must choose friends carefully and establish boundaries, that allow her to have levels of friendship without possessiveness on the part of any member. Minister wives should learn not to depend on just one person in the church to meet all their needs for friendship. The hearts of many minister's wives have been broken by betrayed friendships with one or two members. If a minister's wife wants to develop new friendships she should make sure to look beyond the women on staff and other minister wives. Consequently, it's important for the pastor and his wife to maintain friendships outside the church with people that know them from elsewhere, are not involved in the church business, and will love them no matter what. A pastor's wife attitude is important in his work. It also shows how God is important in the home, and she encourages other women to search for the same importance. By taking the position of "a fellow traveler on the journey of life" a pastor's wife gives all the women in her church the freedom to be real, and to admit there are struggles, failures, and losses. It's important for a "First Lady" to guard her husband's ministry with fierce loyalty. If she doesn't, not only will her relationship with members be affected, but his ministry can also be damaged. Often a Pastor's wife can't counsel a close friend, or talk about personal things to another woman that belongs to her husband's church, because it could compromise confidentiality, and decrease her husband's effectiveness as a minister. She also has to refrain from freely giving out comments since an innocent remark could become ammunition later in a dispute. She must not talk as if she and the pastor have no problems, or they have all the answers. It brings disillusionment to church members, who will criticize her because they do have problems without answers. The mouth was designed to speak blessings not cursing. Instead of faithfully "blessing and never cursing" or "doing good even when treated unjustly," some Christian women often attack through unwarranted gossip. Others use vicious words disguised as "prayer requests" to ask God's vengeance on someone. They also use spiteful actions such as having meetings, writing letters, and making phone calls to confront and rebuke those that are outside of their inner circle, and who are the focus of their anger. Regardless how long the Pastor and his wife have been at a church they are still considered "new" and "outside" people among members. Members whose roots go back to many generations think that it's "their" church and that pastors come and go. There will always be criticism of the pastor's wife. Criticism hurts, but God can use the criticism for growth, if she allows it. Some people may think it's unfortunate that a minister's spouse must use extra caution while speaking and forming friendships, but that's one of the costs of ministry.

In every culture in which men are dominant, girls and women are encouraged to hold males in higher esteem than females, to value relationships with men over relationships with women, and to see one another as competitors rather than allies. Abiding friendships between women are dangerous because jealousy, betrayal, and envy between women are considered normal, but they threaten the social order in which men come. When women put themselves and their girlfriends first, men get nervous. The other reason that friendships between women are dangerous is that it opens up the possibility of a world of hurt. All love relationships involve vulnerability and the possibility of pain. When women dare to trust one another in friendship, the vulnerability of pain can be intense. Rejection or betrayal can cut like a knife and leave lasting scars, but where there is a relationship, there will be conflict. Friendships and family relationships are frequently marked by ongoing conflicts, and a fight or flight mentality that avoids vulnerability and true, abiding love. Women often sing the blues while struggling with judgmental, harsh, and bitter hatred towards people that are close in their lives who have rejected, abandoned, or attacked them, especially in mother and daughter conflicts. Some women are jealous of their daughter, and are often trapped in adolescent games of competition and gossip involving a daughter. They therefore, try to focus their attention on dressing, dating, and outshining their daughters in everything. This shows a lack of maturity and causes the daughter to lose respect for the mother. Hatred for a mother has caused some women years of pain, but they must realize that they're not hurting the mother. They're hurting themselves and are in bondage to her, because of the hate held in their heart against the mother. God will release them from that when they forgive their mothers. To try to win a conflict by overpowering a relative, partner, or friend, or holding in anger is not healthy for any relationship. A woman shouldn't allow emotional pain to be an excuse to remain bitter, angry, and unhappy. It can't help her to grow spiritually. Although many friendships cross religious, ethnic, and color lines there are valid and invalid reasons that women seek friendships with other women of different racial backgrounds. Some want to prove that they are not racist; especially within black and white female relationships. For some white women the idea of having black women friends seems to make them more genuine and in "style." Yet, friendships between black and white women are complicated by the effect of racism. Because racism is entrenched in the daily lifestyle in this country, its effects can undermine friendships in both subtle and obvious ways. The effect that racism has on black and white women who are trying to construct relationships with one another can be truly devastating. Sometimes, the very basis of the friendship is marred by unspoken racial overtones such as language or culture. In the course of a friendship, white women who think of themselves as non-racist are sometimes surprised to find themselves having thoughts or feelings of racial prejudice, and they react with denial or defensiveness. Therefore, interracial women friends must be ever respectful of the other person's feelings, and not always feel the need to say everything that comes to mind. No woman should assume that everything that occurs to her to say is going to be ok. Yet, too often white women make the mistake of condescending their thoughts, and expecting their black friends to help them overcome their prejudice. White women raised in what they see as their God-given right to speak their mind, often don't realize that what they think are simple differences of opinion are really rooted in differing racial perspectives. Some resist or resent any hint that their whiteness influences their opinions, but will insist that only black people are biased about race. Therefore, when congregated together some white and black women will skirt around racial issues as if they are walking on eggshells. Relationships can be poisoned by racism even when both people are acting in good faith and doing their best. A white woman raising her voice against a black woman can unwittingly evoke memories of superiority that can leave both black and white women hurt and angry. When confronted with the fact of their racial privilege, many white women often become silent, blush, cry, stammer, or fall apart. Black women sometimes perceive this as a "front." The peculiar position of white women complicates matters further because white men created racism to relegate minorities and white women to a particular position within the racist white system. However, white women benefit from racism, but they are also oppressed not only by sexism, but also by the power that white men use to keep them in control. White women blind themselves to their own pain just to continue to enjoy a racially privileged society and lifestyle. These "sisters" must remove the blinders from their eyes and be open to seeing not only racism, but also sexism. White men used the myth of the black male rapist as a justification for white women to fear black males, and for his legitimate use of violence against black men. That gave white women a wide range of power over black men, but also made it more impossible for white women to do anything about the men who were really raping them: white men. White women refusal to accurately identify their rapist sabotages and distorts their will to resist becoming abusers. Being silent about their abusive treatment advertently causes them to become the oppressed as well as the oppressor. A white woman can appropriately identify both as female and as white, but she can't liberate herself while oppressing black women without losing an important connection with womanhood and with humanity. All women must trust their own ability to be a good friend without being overly confident. Friendship cannot arise if they're watching every word that's being said. Still, people shouldn't be so careful that they end up awkwardly accepting racial bias in any form.

 Friendships come and go in our lives. Women can be best friends for years with another woman, and somehow destroy the relationship. The loss of a dear friend as a result of unresolved conflict, and the friend having no desire to reconcile, is one of the most painful broken relationships a woman can encounter. It's most painful because it separates both physically and spiritually. The place where a woman

There's Enough Woman Left to be Your Lady

stands spiritually has everything to do with her attitude toward herself. Some women at times place a sign around their necks advertising that they're seeking a friend, although not intentionally. These types of women place themselves in a position of negative vulnerability, and opening themselves up to relationships of "bondage." Women today are in bondage, as well as many others of years past were. They're being kept, controlled, manipulated, used, brutalized, and crushed emotionally as well as spiritually at times by so called "friends." Bondage comes in many forms and from many places, and is often a guest in women lives for so long they think it has a right to be there. Satan feeds off their vulnerability. By feeling so vulnerable, the first person that makes them feel adequate tempts them to give in to flesh, and they create sin for themselves. This is often how women become in bondage to blasphemers, thieves, prostitutes, drugs, and criminals. For years some women have lived and worked in a twilight world of nightlife where sex, drugs, bullets and glass were flying all over the bar, followed by the arrival of blaring squad cars sirens. During those years they seldom thought about God because sin loves darkness rather than light. There is a healthy balance in spending time with others, but once a woman gets sucked into this way of life she doesn't want to mix with clean good-living people. Some women hold on to bad relationships, and often love people that don't love them. They hang on to men or women friends that don't show the same love and affection that they do. Some women also make excuses for people that otherwise are not sympathetic to them, and refuse to believe that these people are selfish. They are naïve and lack the courage to change. Therefore, people take advantage and drag them down, and keep them from reaching the height of their success. When the world outside is unkind and darkness hovers, it often finds them alone with four walls. Peering through the window of lost time they realize that their life is filled with gloom so day after day they stay locked up in their room. Looking at their world outside of a cold, empty, and lonely room their teary eyes light up the faltering rain, and causes them to want to drift away. Yet, her smile is her makeup that brings forth spring and summer fragrance. It showers blessing upon all that come in contact with her. Women fear rejection, and are often cautious with trusted friends, but trust need to be earned. However, some women don't realize that each of her "trusted" friends has assimilated into her being some of the very fiber of which she has become. They brought out the best and the worst in her. Yet, they loved her enough to confront, challenge, and to console her throughout her endeavors. They encouraged her in her strengths and helped her overcome her weaknesses. Therefore, she should be open to positive vulnerability. Vulnerability hastens bonding in the spirit. When the special friendships you thought would last a lifetime are broken or lost, the wounds may require more than just loving care in order to heal. You may have to grieve for a lost friendship. Grieving may take weeks, months, or even years. A lot depends on how the friendship ended. Don't take on a load of guilt, but admit the relationship has ended. The pain you are feeling is real and hurts, but allow yourself to feel the pain. It will intensify as you realize the relationship has ended, but the way past the pain is to go all the way through it. Acceptance is the positive side to rebuilding. Don't start the "if only" game. Just suffer and grow. Sometimes hurting people hide so others will not suspect their fear, but emptiness can be replaced by inner fullness and strength. Avoid unhealthy conversations as you go through this painful process, and check yourself to avoid withdrawing or "coping" mechanisms such as staying busy. Busyness may delay the healing process and can also be very tiring. Women also need to think about those that they love however awkward they may seem, and let them know that they love them by the expression of their hearts. Sometimes friends are more likely to express love to one another than family members are. Close friendships require an interest and love for other people. It also requires letting go of idealistic expectations and unrealistic demands. Some friends grow apart because they easily give up on each other when wrongs occur, and their relationship become rocky. Instead of showing grace through loving confrontation and forgiveness, they regularly move on to new relationships. Good friends are good forgivers. Former friends need to deal with the intense pain of deception. They should come to terms with the broken relationship and learn to forgive. If a woman is seeking inner freedom, forgiveness is not an option; she simply must do it. It enables her to start healing and to see others' failures through the eyes of mercy. As she reflects on the friends of her life, she must realize that some were in her life for only a season. Yet, she should remain in "open" season with her love for others. A woman should realize that she might never know why some relationships ended; therefore, she should reflect on the positive blessings and the impact a friendship made on her life during the happy times. Even as she makes new friends she should think positive. If someone wants to share personal information about his or her life, but seems hesitant, she should lead the way by opening up first. However, she should only tell as much about her personal life that she wouldn't mind hearing repeated. Proverbs 7:11 in speaking of a contentious woman said, *"She is loud and stubborn; her feet abide not in her house."* The apostle Paul said, *"Let them be discreet, chaste, keepers at home, good, obedient to their own husbands."* Why? *"Because otherwise the word of God will be blasphemed."* (Titus 2:5)

    Christ loves to have his spouse stay at home. That is, to be with him in the faith and practice of his ministry, and not running and repeating things that were told them in confidence. Christian women shouldn't be given to wander and gossip. It's a precious gift to your friends when they personally discover that you cherish confidentiality, and hold their secrets close to your heart. Stress takes place in growth, but you must learn to deal with it. To avoid stress, a godly woman should sit quietly for five minutes a day without telephone, television, or radio interruption. It should be just her, Jesus, and the stillness, making peace. She should increase the time until she become comfortable with herself, the quiet, and the Lord. She should keep a prayer notebook and think of ways that she will purpose to serve someone each week (including an enemy), and then she should devote herself to covering each person in prayer. At the end of each week, she should record how she feels about these people and whether she's seen any specific answers to her prayer requests. When conflict threatens your heart and your church, seek to be first about raising the prayer banner in your life and in your church. If you are one that is right now involved in a "bondage" relationship or have been wounded emotionally, physically, or spiritually, the beginning of your freedom comes in admitting to the Lord, and to yourself the truth of your pains and struggles. You must tell Him that you are in need of help. If you have owned your part in a conflict and others refuse to do the same, give them grace, pray for them, and if necessary, distance yourself from the overflow of their bitter root of sin until they allow God to do healing in their heart. Broken relationships can provide a platform for growth. Use it as motivation to grow, and it will change any crisis into an opportunity. Finally, realize that going through a broken relationship leaves you with a choice to stay bent over with bitterness or a desire to get better. Bitterness will only destroy you and never the person you are angry at. Which one will you choose?

3

When Your Well Runs Dry

Have you ever had a wilderness experience? Wilderness means wildness. It's something undeveloped or untamed living in silence. Your wilderness experience could be a time when everything seemed to dry up in your life and you couldn't hear God's voice. He spoke, but He was shouting to you in that silence. God speaks to us in the wilderness of our soul. Throughout the exodus from Egypt to the Promised Land of Canaan, the generation-long wilderness wandering of the children of Israel causes the people to walk through a desert, and they're complaining that there's no water. Think about that. The reason there is no water is because it's a desert. The word desert means "deserted." Nothing of value is there. In order to get to the Promised Land, we have to go through the desert. If you don't want to go through the desert, you're going to have to give up the

Promised Land, because you have to go through the desert to get there. You can try to map your way out to avoid the desert, but you won't get to the Promised Land that way. You have to decide whether you think getting to the Promised Land is worth going through the desert, or taking your chances with Pharaoh. Before the nation of Israel could go into the Promised Land they had to go through a painful, bloody, and personal circumcision. Circumcision requires losing your old way of life. The process of spiritual circumcision may mean a cutting off or loss in areas that have been a part of our lives in order to draw us to the Savior. God requires each of us to be painfully circumcised in heart before we are allowed to enter and receive the blessings that await each believer in the Promised Land. Consequently, like the people of Israel, we must wait until we are healed before we begin to be effective in our calling. If we launch out too early, we will be ineffective and may risk infection and disease. We will not be at our full capacity. We all have to ask ourselves; whether getting to the Promised Land is worth going through the desert. No one really wants to go through the desert that we often find ourselves in the middle of. But at some point we become convinced that we cannot get to the Promised Land except through that way and complaining will not solve the problem. Some people are habitual complainers. You know who are complainers. When you see them coming you rush and wish you could head in the opposite direction. You know they are going to sap you of strength and bring clouds into the sunshine of your day. In Exodus chapter fifteen through seventeen there is a recurring theme: "Israel Complains." In these chapters we have the account of the Israelites moving into the desert of Shur. For three days they are unable to find water. Finally, they come to Marah where there is water, but the water is bitter. The people are discouraged and frustrated. They murmured and struck out at Moses asking, "What shall we drink?" Moses turned to the Lord and we read that the Lord "showed him a piece of wood." This tree or piece of wood was taken by Moses and thrown into the bitter water. The water suddenly became sweet. We don't know what chemical property was in the tree that caused the water to lose its bitterness, but we do know that the sweetness of God gave them drinkable water. After forty-five days into the Exodus journey, the food and provisions were getting kind of scarce. The people were hungry and becoming a little concerned. They came to Moses and said, *"Would to God that we had died by the hand of the Lord in the land of Egypt, when we sat by the flesh pots, and we ate bread to the full. For you have brought us forth into this wilderness, to kill this whole assembly with hunger."* (Exodus 16:3) These people had decided that it wasn't too bad after all to have been in slavery. They were happy that they had food, a place to stay, and someone to tell them what to do. They were ready to go back into slavery to avoid having to go through hardships to secure their freedom. It's amazing what some people will give up in order to please the flesh. The Israelites had begun lusting for meat, but the grace of God is seen in the provision of bread that was in the form of a wafer, and a great flock of quail. It was grace heaped up and overflowing. It was only after the people have seen the grace of God both in the giving of His Spirit, and in the sending of the quail that judgment falls. It falls because there has been no repentance to Moses by those who are the closest to him, which were his brother and sister.

Exodus 17:1-7 states that the Hebrew people are foot-weary as they start traveling again. Walking in large mass from slavery to freedom, they begin to get cranky. The occasion for their crankiness varies; lack of water, shortage of food, and discontent with Moses, but their response to adversity is becoming boringly predictable. The people tempted the Lord by saying, "Is the Lord among us or not?" Again they had come to a place where they thought that they were going to find water, but there was none. So, what do they do? They turn on Moses once again. First, they complain to Moses, who responds by chastising them, telling them that their complaint is an evidence of a lack of faith in God. In return, the people criticized Moses and his ability as a leader, saying that it was his fault that they were out in the middle of nowhere without food to eat or water to drink. Moses is getting a little frustrated, and tired of the constant criticism, therefore he turns to the Lord and asks what he should do. The Lord answered Moses, *"Go on before the people. Take with you some of the elders of Israel and take in your hand the staff with which you struck the Nile, and go. I will stand there before you by the Rock at Horeb. Strike the Rock, and water will come out of it for the people to drink."* (Exodus 17:5) So Moses did this in the sight of the Elders of Israel. Finally, God, showing more grace than most of us would be able to muster responds by providing for the people's need. It's a pattern that's repeated over and over again. God performs a miracle, but forever identifies this as a place where the Israelites tested, or quarreled with Him. Moses called the place Massah "testing," and Meribah "grumbling." The names Massah and Meribah are found several more times in the Bible and always it denotes a place of grumbling and hardening of heart. Later on in the wilderness wanderings Israel returns to this place. The people again argued with Moses, but this time it was in the desert of Zin concerning water and food. Moses and Aaron came in from the presence of the assembly to the doorway of the tent of meeting, and fell on their faces before the Lord. Then the glory of the Lord appeared to them; and the Lord spoke to Moses, saying, *"Take the rod; and you and your brother Aaron assemble the congregation, and speak to the rock before their eyes, and it shall give forth his water. You shall thus bring forth water for them out of the rock and let the congregation and their beasts drink."* (Numbers 20:8) The instructions of the Lord were very explicit. Moses was to go and <u>speak</u> to the rock. On the previous occasion in Exodus 17:6, God had told Moses, *"I will stand before thee there upon the rock in Horeb; and you shall smite the rock, and there shall come water out of it."* Moses was to strike the rock only once with the rod. Why the change? Why is he merely to speak to it now in Numbers 20:8? Evidently, this is a test of Moses' obedience. The Rock is a type of Christ. (1 Corinthians 10:4) Therefore, when Moses struck the rock twice in anger he was also striking God. (Numbers 20:11) It's from God that we receive rivers of living water, and we receive those waters because He was struck once on our behalf at Calvary. His sacrifice was once and for all. He doesn't have to be sacrificed repeatedly. To approach Him now, we need only speak to Him in prayer. Disobeying God cost Moses entry into the Promised Land. That was something that he probably regretted. Regrets and guilt plague everyone in this life. All women could each come up with a list of ten things that they wish they could have done or said differently, even in the last year. The more they think about those things, the more depressed, and angrier they become. There are good times and hard times in the Christian life. Some of the hardest times come from the people we love. The deeper your love for the person, and the more of yourself you have invested in that person, greater is the hurt when he or she turn against you. When a spouse tells you that he or she doesn't love you any more, and wants a divorce. A sister or brother turns against you over money or an inheritance. A child says they never want to speak to you again. A wife, husband, or long time friend suddenly turns on you and spreads false rumors or tells your secrets to others; these are defining moments that can cause deep hurt and pain. Each of these situations has a common element; someone you love and care for inflicts the wound. Sometimes when hurtful words come from someone we love, they are not meant to hurt us, they are meant as a cry for help. A spouse may become distant because of physical changes in his or her body or feelings of inadequacy on a job, and may feel guilty for not doing his or her part. She or he may find that "putting his or her partner down" is a way of feeling better about their own inadequacy. From a spiritual and sociological stance we need to work at really listening to the heart of a love one that's upset, and ask the question, "What is the real problem?" Moses felt a similar kind of hurt when he first confronted Pharaoh, and the Hebrews accused him of doing more harm than good. He experienced it again when the children of Israel were out in the dessert and they accused Moses of trying to kill them. That had to hurt. What must have really hurt worst, was the fact that his brother Aaron and his sister Miriam publicly criticized him and challenged his leadership. The professed reason for this negative talk is that Moses married a Cushite (Black) woman from Ethiopia. (Numbers 12:1) God had given strict instructions to the Israelites that they should not marry anyone from the land of Canaan. This was based on religious reasons not race, but he didn't forbid marriage from outside of Israel entirely. Moses probably talked things over with the Lord before he ever got married. The racial "concern" over the wife of Moses is not the real issue. It was a smokescreen used to mask an undercurrent of jealousy and sibling rivalry. Both Miriam and Aaron had a difficult time accepting their "little brother's" leadership." They asked, "Has the Lord spoken only through Moses? Hasn't he also spoken through us?" In the midst of this family feud, the Spirit of the Lord came down in a pillar of cloud and intervened. God stood at the doorway of the tent, and He called Aaron and Miriam to account. When they both came forward, God said, *"Hear now my words: If there is a prophet among you, I the Lord shall make myself known to him in a vision. I shall speak with him in a dream. Not so, with my servant Moses, He is faithful in all my household. With him I speak mouth to mouth, even openly, and not in dark saying, and he beholds the form of the Lord. Why then were you not afraid to speak against my servant, against Moses?"* (Numbers 12:5-8) What does this have to do with Moses marriage? Was Miriam jealous of his new wife because it diminished her influence on her brother? Was she really a racist? Miriam didn't care at all about whom Moses married, but she did care about her "power base." Up until this time Miriam and Aaron had a great deal of power in the land. With 70 additional leaders appointed by Moses, Miriam was feeling edged out. She saw her influence diminish and she didn't like it. She felt as if she had been cheated and she was angry. It appears that the real problem may be jealousy. When jealousy rears its ugly head it makes people selfish at work, home, and in the church. Preachers, Teachers, and Evangelists, start being protective about their ministry, area, and pulpit. It makes it difficult for them to teach others. They become blind to serving the Lord. They forget that it's God's will to use them in whatever way He sees fit. Jealousy makes a person overly sensitive. A jealous and insecure person will overreact to things that seem to threaten their position. In order to be instructed women must be soft, pliable, and be able to listen without feeling threatened by those who speak. They need to realize that they cannot always be on center stage, and that sometimes it's better to say nothing than to tear down someone else. It was stated, *"Now Moses was a very humble man, more humble than anyone else on the face of the earth."* The basic meaning of the Hebrew root word for humble is "to be bowed down." One could be bowed down by force (subdued) with care and trouble, or with submissiveness (humbleness). We live in a world of hurting people who has been bowed down by the brunt force of life. All around us there are people who are simply living from day to day with no hope for tomorrow. They see little purpose in life and their goal is to get as much as they can before they die. These folks don't need us to feed their despair, and they don't need us to turn away and talk against them because of their attitude. They need us to infect them with the good news of Jesus Christ, and to live with joy and not just talk about it. Perhaps you such as Moses have tasted bitter water in your wilderness hike. You may have been convinced when you look at the world and the wounds it causes, the lives it distorts and destroys, and the hearts that has been broken. Have you ever had some unexpected event happen in your life that caused great fear? Sudden calamities can result in great fear unless you know who or what's behind the event you fear. But your fear can turn to joy when you know whom or what you're confronting. Many times we have events in our lives that appear to be ghosts. It may be a period in your life when you have lost your marriage, finances, business, and nearly your mind, but these were the ghosts that instilled fear and great turmoil in your life. When you first started out for Heaven you may have had some dark hours of conviction. The mountains quaked and devils tormented. All the sins of your life came before you, and they were perhaps the darkest hour you ever saw. You may have wanted to go back, but a voice inside you said; "You must go on. You have to drink of the bitter cup, and carry this cross." All of God's creations have to traverse the desert, and be pounded by the sandstorms of misrepresentation, and abuse. Yet, God will lead you to a totally new calling in your life, and will demonstrate to you that He was behind the storm that led to these new discoveries. Although you may have obstacles in your way you have to swim the river, climb the mountain, and walk your way home to glory. The events and emotions that you go through are real. Yet, you have to hold fast to the reality that nothing can touch you without passing through God's blender of life. Although God has all kinds of ingredients of life mixed in together, he allows only that which is necessary to touch you. If anything unnecessary does touch you God has a purpose. Seemingly life-threatening events can be turned into one of great miracles. God turns them from being a place of fear, to a place of miracles, but you may not know it for a while. God wants each of us to walk in his healing grace. There are battles that we may have to fight on our way to the Promised Land. The people of Israel fought only two battles when they were coming out of Egypt, but in the Promised Land they fought 39 battles. Each of us must be prepared to give our lives to sustain the freedom to enjoy the benefits of living in the Promised Land. However, we must also be prepared to wage war against the enemy of our souls. Make sure the Lord has provided the needed healing to your circumcision experience before you enter the Promised Land. After your desert experience God will reveal His true purposes for these events. Blessed be God that the day of transgression will soon be over, and then we will be where the wicked shall cease from troubling and the weary shall be at rest.

4

Respect

Every detail of a woman from her hair down to the finely crafted curves of her body screams "I am woman," but Jesus said, *"Whosoever **look** on a woman to lust after her has committed adultery with her already in his heart. If thy right eye offend thee pluck it out, and cast it from thee; for it's profitable for thee that one of your members should perish, and not that thy whole body be thrown into hell."* Matthew 5:28-29

With that one word *"look"* Jesus condemned in the most forceful way possible, all forms of pornography, and the entire enterprise of commercializing the female body in advertising and entertainment. Imagine how much wrath is being stored up in heaven against the billion-dollar business of doing precisely what the Son of God prohibits, namely, enticing men to look upon women not as persons, but as objects of sexual pleasure. Some men use the freedom of masculine dominance as a tool to oppress women. They oppress women through pornography, and verbal sexual harassment. The media does its share by advertising and brainwashing women into believing that they have to be thin and sexy. Women on the other hand benefit from political correctness. This is the idea that only correct, non-offensive words should be spoken even when they are being exploited, and only agreeable, happy, images of them should be seen. By this analysis freedom of speech doesn't benefit women, only men. What is clear from Matthew 5:28 is that Jesus Christ means to rescue women from this attack on their personage. Throughout his ministry Jesus showed that the kingdom he came to establish would include men and women from every race and nation. He was the fulfillment of an ancient promise made to Abraham. God told Abraham that his descendants would be as numerous as the stars in the sky, but that's not all. He also said that one of his seeds would bring blessing to all the nations of the earth. In Genesis 3:15, God also told the serpent that the Seed of the woman would bruise his (Satan's) head. Jesus was that Seed to which God referred to Abraham and the serpent: He is the seed that brings about spiritual birth. Spiritual birth comes only through the miracle of God's power to heal and forgive. God's "birthing" power works through seeds of faith, witnessing, and evangelization, but they must be good living seed that's fertile and reproductive in order to produce ecclesiastical life. All believers are His, and the seed of Christ shall endure forever.

The U.S Constitution and the Bill of Rights made provisions for "Separation of church and state." Two hundred years after the Bill of Rights was drafted, we still have strange notions that religion is purely a private matter. Faith and public life, is popularly supposed to have nothing to do with each other. Therefore, we tend to silence our beliefs. Most people would never give a religious reason for supporting or opposing any kind of public policy decision.

There's Enough Woman Left to be Your Lady

The vast majority of people believe that the church is for taking care of people's private spiritual needs, and that the government will return the favor, and keep its nose out of church business. Today our view of separation of church and state is entirely foreign to Jesus' way of thinking. Almost two thousand years ago, faith, and public life were a lot more closely related than they are now. In fact, they were inseparable. The Roman government pretty much allowed the Jewish people to practice their faith without much interference, as long as they did not challenge Roman authority. Herod, the Roman governor was concerned with the radical social changes that a "storefront" preacher named Jesus was promoting. What Jesus preached was radically different from what life was really like in Palestine under Roman rule. This rabbi's teaching was so powerful and influential that Herod wanted him dead. Jesus' behavior throughout Luke's gospel broke every religious rule: Jesus ate with outcasts, worked on religious days when he was supposed to rest, treated women as equals, and taught that the poor should be fed, housed, and clothed. He was not content with the social status quo. Jesus said that this kind of care for others, equality, and fellowship were signs of God's love to mankind based upon the rules of Theocracy. Judaism was a tolerated religion. If Jesus had simply been a good Jewish citizen Herod would have had no reason to want Jesus dead, but Jesus challenged the social order of his day, its injustices, and rigid class structure. He also sharply criticized a class of pious, learned, and influential Jewish scholars called Pharisees. His scathing and inflammatory remarks about their hypocrisy, love of money, and their complicity with a corrupt occupying government were enough to make the Pharisees want to bring Jesus up on charges. Despite his stinging criticisms of the Pharisees, Jesus at least must had their respect. After all the Pharisees listened to Jesus teach in the synagogues, and as Luke tells us, several of them had invited Jesus to dinner in their homes. This seems to indicate that the Pharisees viewed Jesus as a social, intellectual, professional colleague equal to them. Religious liberty is a precious right, and it's one that everybody is not granted. Even without this protection, Jesus spoke fearlessly against the social status quo of his day. Christians are called to be like Jesus, to follow his example, and we have a legal structure that allows us to do so, both as individuals and as a church community. The question we need to ask ourselves is this. Why, as Christians in a free society, are we so reluctant to follow the footsteps our Lord, and speak against the injustice of minorities, children, disenfranchised people, and women with the same courage that Jesus had? Jesus cared for women therefore, he could relate to their bodily pain and suffering. He knew that as women travail in birth that he also had to suffer pain while giving birth to the New Testament Church. It would bring on labor pains even unto death, but he would not abort the plan of salvation. Jesus could attest to the weakness of women who use their body as sexual objects. The typical Jewish genealogy didn't include women, but here are four women names on the list that should surprise us: Tamar, Rahab, Ruth, and Bathsheba. Just as in our culture, for better or for worse, most women take their husband's name, so in Jewish culture the legal rights ran through a man. So to find four women mentioned is surprising. Even more surprising is the fact that three of these women were non-Jews and one of them was married to a non-Jew. Tamar was an Aramean. Rahab was a Canaanite. Ruth was a Moabite. Bathsheba was the wife of Uriah the Hittite. Why did Matthew choose to talk about these Gentiles? He could have picked Abraham's wife, Sarah, or Isaac's wife, Rebecca. To the Jews selecting Gentiles to show Christ's lineage was like polluting the pure waters of Jesus' ancestry. But if we know anything about Jesus, we probably aren't that surprised. Even the Christmas

There's Enough Woman Left to be Your Lady

story about Jesus' birth reveals that Jesus came for the Gentiles as well as the Jews. When the angels said to the shepherds, *"Peace on earth, good will toward men."* (Luke 2:14) They weren't just talking about goodwill towards Jewish people they were talking about all of God's creation in whom He was pleased. Although Christ came from a spiritual and human lineage of royalty he still had scandals tied to his family tree. The scandal of Jesus' genealogy is not about his right to rule, but rather about His right to choose whom He desires to share his kingdom. The scandalous family tree of Jesus is not just about why he came it's also about how he works. Jesus' earthly grandmother that hailed from David's lineage, whose name was Rahab, had been a woman of notoriety that had repented and reformed. (Joshua 2:1-24) When we first meet Rahab in the Bible, she is a professional lady (prostitute) of the night. Rahab is also called a harlot in the New Testament where both her good works and faith are praised, and to teach us that the greatness of sin is no hindrance to God's pardoning mercy, if we truly repent in time. (James 2:25) Rahab became biblically famous when the Israelites were in search of a home. After having wandered around the wilderness for forty years, Joshua sent spies into the Promised Land to search out the people and the landscape. They came into the city of Jericho, and somehow these "nice, innocent guys" ended up in the red light district at Rehabs house. It was providential because Rahab protected them and later came to be a follower of God. Rahab trusted God. She went against her countrymen because she knew that God had given her native land to the Israelites, and she could not hinder them from possessing it. God blessed her by saving her family from destruction, and allowed her to marry within the Jewish race. Rahab married Salmon with whom she produced Boaz. Boaz begot Obed of Ruth; and Obed begot Jessie; Jessie begot David and the line went all the way out until it came to Joseph of whom was born Jesus who is called the Christ." (Matthew 1:5-16) Still, whenever Rehabs name is found in the Bible, she is called "Rahab the harlot." (Hebrews 11:31, and James 2:25) Sometimes, even after a woman has straightened out her life her past still haunts her. Rejections hurt. Have you ever been excluded from something that you really wanted to be a part of? There is a built-in need for all of us to belong somewhere. The family that Jesus came to create doesn't turn away anyone for the color of his or her skin, past sins, or the size of a person's bank account. Jesus came for all manners of people. His genealogy tells us that. To Gentiles his genealogy isn't much of a scandal. We'd expect God to act without prejudice, but there is something more here. As you look closely at these women and their stories, you can see that they're not the kind of people you would expect to be in the bloodlines of the Son of God. They were outcasts, and sinners, but Jesus still treated them with respect. Don't get me wrong; men are no different than the women in the family tree of Christ. Jacob was a liar. David and Solomon were philanderers and womanizers. Manasseh was an idolater, just to name a few. Jesus came from a long line of sinners. Their stories make that clear, especially in Genesis 38:6-30. In that chapter Judah had chosen Tamar as a wife for his son. His son died and left her childless. The law required that another son should marry her so she could have children, but the son refused. So Tamar, desperate to have a child, concocted a scheme where she dressed up as a prostitute, put a veil over her face, and waited by the roadside until her father-in-law, Judah, strolled by and paid to have sexual pleasure with her. Twin sons were conceived. One of them was Pharez, who became a forefather of Jesus. It doesn't stop there. Ruth of the Old Testament book of Ruth wasn't a harlot. The only fault that the Bible ascribes to her is that she was a Moabite. The Moabite race was a product of incest. They were children conceived by Lot while was living in a cave with his two daughters after the destruction of Sodom and Gomorrah. His daughters were afraid there would be no one left to marry them and give them children so they got their father drunk, seduced him, and both girls got pregnant by their father. One of the girls named her son Moab. God's law said that none of the descendents of Moab could ever enter the house of the Lord. (Deuteronomy 23:3) The Jews found the Moabites repugnant. Although Ruth married Boaz and took on Jewish culture, she was still a descendent of incestuous people. The fourth woman mentioned was Bathsheba the wife of Uriah. Her story is not pretty either. She had an affair with King David. They had tried to keep it a secret, but their union had produced a child. David had her husband killed, and then married her to cover it up. Their illegitimate child died in infancy, but they had another son, Solomon, who became the next link in the royal line of scandal. There's another woman of question in Jesus' genealogy; his earthly mother Mary. She was a young, unmarried, pregnant girl who had created quite a scandal. She and her fiancé said that the Holy Spirit impregnated her. Who could believe the Son of God would come from an unwed mother and an invisible father? Would you believe them? But this is where Mary's story intersects with the stories of Tamar, Rahab, Ruth, and Bathsheba. Despite the scandals surrounding their unions, God chose them and their offspring to continue the royal line, and He did the same thing through Mary. By including them, we're reminded that God in his grace works in the most unusual, even scandalous ways, and through the most unlikely people. What a story to have in Jesus' family tree! Try explaining that to your children! Put these stories together and the genealogy of Jesus have prostitution, incest, adultery, and murder. This is not the Bible Hall of Fame; it's the Bible Hall of Shame. You see, most of us have a misconception about the Bible and Christian faith. We think the Bible should be a book of virtues; a book of role models that we should emulate in order to be good Christians. We have ideas that God is at the top of a ladder calling down to us: "Do good, live right, and praise me." So we muster up all the spiritual will power we possibly can, and we try to climb the ladder hoping to reach God by our works. God doesn't reward by work but by faith. The message of the family tree of Jesus shows something about why he came. He came to rescue those kinds of people that we find in his genealogy: weak, broken and sinful people. The scandal of Jesus' lineage reminds us that our God is a God of grace and mercy. He doesn't stand at the top of the ladder and tell us to perform. He knew that no one could climb up that ladder. So he sent Jesus down the ladder to live the life you and I couldn't live; and to die the death you and I should have died. He invites us to ride on Jesus' shoulders as he climbs back up the ladder. That's why the angel said to Joseph, *"You shall call his name Jesus, for he shall save his people from their sins."* (Matthew 1:21)

Jesus was called a "friend of sinners." (Luke 7:34) He came to seek and to save those that are lost. It's bad news for some, and it's good news for others. Some of us have a spirituality of self-reliance and self-sufficiency. No matter how much we may talk about the grace of God, we're still trying to climb the ladder; still trying to emulate the heroes of the Bible. The Gospel of Jesus Christ confronts us over and over again with the utter inadequacy of our own willpower. It shatters the myth that we can pull ourselves up by our own spiritual bootstraps. The fact is that we can't add a single inch to our own spiritual stature. It used to be that women had less pressure from societies to be somebody or live up to someone else expectations. For thousands of year's women roles have been to be quiet, submissive, and pregnant. When a man has certain expectations of whom and what a woman is it causes mixed emotions in her life.

There's Enough Woman Left to be Your Lady

Women are taught from the womb to the tomb on how to be a lady. They are taught how to sit and play in a dress, be feminine, and how to display charm. They are taught that a woman doesn't suppose to come on to a man and to limit their choice of hairstyles, makeup, clothes, and boyfriends. Nice girls are considered to be those that are still a virgin. Girls that rebel against traditional standard, and are known to be sexually active are labeled sluts or whores. The Bible has lots to say about a whorish woman, yet prostitution is one of the world's oldest professions. In some locations it's considered a public service. Prostitution is a world where women don't have the time to be thinking about what men should or should not be doing to them. They are only concerned with surviving. Some women have resorted to prostitution to feed them and their kids, but that doesn't make it right. Often on missionary journeys Jesus met many people of diverse backgrounds, but mostly whom he met were women that were shut up in prisons of self-interest and doubt. The pressures of life had burdened some of them until they adopted personalities that were not able to keep up with the demands of social living. These women had denied and evaded reality for so long that they began to have personality, and functional disorders. Their world around them became disorientated, and parts of their mind and body began to malfunction. Some of these women had become catatonic, paranoid, regressive, and unresponsive to any type of aid or love, but Jesus came to give them health. The word health is taken from the root meaning, *"heal."* It represents the wholeness of a person. The greatest gift that God has given to any person except salvation is health. Jesus did not care where a person had been, or what they came in contact with, he just wanted to know where they wanted to be spiritually. To be effective in his ministry Christ carried with him twelve men who were to learn from him what to preach and how to preach. There also were certain women who attended his ministry that ministered to him of their substance. Perhaps they could have been considered his patients for he had healed them of evil spirits and sickness. Some of them had been afflicted in the mind and some in the body. He had been to them a powerful healer, and they were bound in gratitude to serve him and his gospel. One of the women that were most gracious was Mary Magdalene. She was a woman in the city that was a former prostitute out of whom Jesus had cast seven demons. She had been saved by Jesus' preaching. She had heard that he was in town so she came to show her appreciation to him. Just before this woman approached Jesus some disciples of John the Baptist had come to ask him a question sent from John, "Are you really the Messiah?" John was tepid. Technically he was in hot water. He was shut up in prison, and Jesus hadn't visited him. Having heard no news about what Jesus had been doing caused John to start doubting the purpose and authority of Jesus. Yet, it was John that had said to Jesus, *"I have need to be baptized of thee, and comest you to me?* (Matthew 3:14) Although Jesus hadn't visited John in prison, each time that they had met it was in water. Thirty years before they had met in water (uterus) while waiting for the natural birth. Thirty years later they again met in water (Jordan River) while waiting for the spiritual birth. In each case both were imprisoned in the body waiting to be released in the spirit. John was waiting to decrease in his ministry, while Jesus was waiting to increase and be confirmed in his ministry. (Luke 3:15-22) The only difference between John's incarceration, and Jesus' visitation at that moment was that physical walls separated them, and Jesus was about to knock those walls down. Jesus had told John's disciple's to observe what was happening. Those who were blind could see. The lame was walking without a limp. Lepers were healed. The dead were restored back to life, and the deaf and poor were hearing the "Good News."

There's Enough Woman Left to be Your Lady

Clearly, something wonderful was happening. The disciples carried the exciting news back to John who was satisfied with the answer that he had received. He was now ready to face death.

In Luke chapter seven we read that Jesus was asked of a Pharisee to attend dinner in his home of which Jesus graciously accepted. On this occasion there again was Mary Magdalene the prostitute who had been converted from her wicked course of life by his preaching. She knew that Jesus was eating in the Pharisee's house, and she came to acknowledge her obligations to him. Without a formal invitation she barged into the dinner party at the Pharisee's home. She saw Jesus, and she stood **behind** him weeping. She was overtaken with excitement to find herself so near to her savior whom her soul loved. Her eyes that had been inlets and outlets for sin mirrored torment in her body. Her face flooded with weeping became a fountain of tears. Having no other way to show how much she loved him, she humbled herself, reached down to his feet, and began washing them with her tears. These were no ordinary tears. They were tears of sorrow for what she had done, and tears of joy for what he had released her from. Her tears indicated that she was ready to submit herself to him as an act of reverence. She kissed his feet as if she knew that her type of lifestyle was unworthy of the kisses of his mouth. Her kiss was of adoration as well as affection. She began anointing his feet with expensive oil, which was in preparation for his death, and then she used her hair to dry his feet. Obviously her hair hung loosely and was long enough for her to use as a towel. During Biblical days usually a woman's hair was bound on top of her head in a bun or braid style. Only sinful women of that day let their hair hang down loose. For that, she was scorned by the Pharisee and branded as "that kind of woman." It was as though the Pharisee, a self-righteous man, saw her gift as an effort to buy something from Jesus.

The offense of which the Pharisee took against Jesus was for admitting the respect that this so-called prostitute had for him. He could not understand how Jesus could risk his reputation to admit that he knew a woman like that. He thought that Jesus should have said, *"Do not come near me for I am Holier than thou."* Only arrogant and narrow-minded people think like that. The Pharisee began to wonder whether Jesus was who he said that he was. He is openly scornful of the woman. He saw her as being more voluptuous than penitent. Who did she think she was coming into his home, and disrupting what he hoped would be an opportunity to take Jesus to task, for his counter-cultural actions earlier in the day? The Spirit of God moving in Jesus reproved the Pharisee. Jesus in answering his thoughts said unto him, *"It is true that this woman was a sinner; she knew it, you knew it, and the world knew it, but she is a **pardoned** sinner. You look upon her with disgust, but she is a kinder houseguest that you are. When I walked into your house you did not so much as order me a bowl of water to wash my hands and feet. Wearied and dirty with my walk you did not ask about my feelings or my state of mind. But this woman has done much more: she has washed my feet with tears of affection for me, tears of affliction for sin, and has wiped them with the hairs of her head which is the crowning of her glory. All of this was in token of her great love to me. The washing of my feet with her tears was the fruit of her love."* Jesus' justification for knowing the woman was what she had done for him in the spirit. Some at the dinner may have thought that she was Jesus' woman, but her unofficial act showed Jesus to be the Messiah, the Anointed of God. Jesus knew that her actions were intimate and personal, and he took special notice of her strong affection for him. However, he was neither turned off by her unexpectedly intimate actions nor did her physical touching of his body in such an intimate way turn him on. Jesus received her gift, saw through the type of love that filled her heart, and blessed her in the truth of God's love and His word. Jesus told the Pharisee and his friends, "Her sins, which were many, have been forgiven; hence she has shown great love. But the one to whom little is forgiven, loves little." Then he said to her, "Your sins are forgiven." Notice that he did not say, "I forgive your sins." Jesus knew that the Father forgave sin through the son, therefore she was pardoned, but yet he still did not want to overstep his Father's authority. It was the woman's faith in the Son of God that saved her from sin. Jesus said to the woman, "Thy faith have saved you; go in peace." According to the word of God there is only one way to get into the Lord's one true Church, and that's salvation from sin through Jesus Christ. Every woman has to pull her hair down at some time in her life, and be joyful. Some women had a lot happened in their life, but they don't need to have a somber seriousness all the time. They should have the love of the Lord, and the peace that He brings within their hearts that allow them to be free. A woman quickly discovers the Christian life to be more than attending church. The God who loves enough to save her also wants her to enjoy life. He has given her the gift of life, family, friends, and a whole world full of His beautiful creation to enjoy. Truly the Christian woman can live life to the fullest without regrets when following the Lord's example. A woman shouldn't just talk the Word of God. She must walk the Word of God because if she doesn't walk what she talks she's not going to get to Heaven. She will only get there by God's grace and God's grace alone. Jesus made himself as an example of the love of Mary Magdalene when he labeled himself a servant, and wrapped a towel around himself and washed his disciples' feet. At that point no one in that room doubted whom their leader was. Jesus was the one that they would follow. When leadership is placed upon us, let it be a servant leadership. Having been a servant doesn't nullify or cancel out leadership; it transforms leadership by causing it to stand out. A humble yet aggressive leader gains much admiration. Although we will never get to wash Christ's feet on this present earth, our tears and sorrows from afflictions that we incur fall daily at his feet. He takes pleasure in our wetting his feet with tears of repentance, and drying them with the towel of forgiveness and regeneration. In the Bible Jesus is never called second, third, or fourth Adam. He is always labeled as the Last Adam because He is the only one of a unique kind. There could never be another one like Him. He is the radiance of His glory and the exact representation of His nature. He upholds all things by the word of His power. Although he was the head of God's creation, Genesis Adam failed. His failure brought corruption and depravity on his family and to every descendent down through the ages. Man inherited sin and death from his disobedience. In Genesis Adam we all die, however, in the Last Adam, we have eternal life. Born again believers will never die. Jesus said to Martha, *"I am the resurrection and the life; he who believes in me will live even if he dies, and everyone who lives and believes in me will never die. Believest thou this?"* (John 11:25–26)

The first Adam was tempted and failed the test, and in him we all continue to sin and die. The Last Adam (Jesus) was tempted as the first was, but remained sinless, and lived a perfect life of righteousness. The first Adam was born with authority, longevity, and supremacy. He was given a physical bride as a gift and helpmate, and was commissioned to "be fruitful" and to replenish the earth. The first couple's union was painless. He was anesthetized, placed in a deep sleep, and his rib was removed to create his bride. The first Adam was separated from his bride through age, disease, and death. He had everything provided for him in the Garden of Eden, but sin caused him to lose everything. The Last Adam was born with nothing. He was a poor disgraced fugitive born in a stable. *"For you know the grace of our Lord Jesus Christ, that though He was rich, yet for your sake He became poor, so that you through His poverty might become rich."* (2 Corinthians 8:9) Jesus came to bring fruit (many sons to glory) and to fill heaven with redeemed people known as His Bride. The Last Adam had to purchase His spiritual Bride at the lost of His very life; through the deep sleep of His death on the cross of Calvary. However, the Last Adam will never be separated from His Bride. He has married the church and placed it into His family. He is now the head of the spiritual family of God, and when the church stands to take His hand it will proudly say this is my man.

When the Bible talks about us being a body in Christ it's pointing to the fact of our interdependence. Although there are many parts of the spiritual body of Christ that have different functions, different preferences, and different perspectives, we are still one body. It doesn't matter what the denominational label is that hang over the door or what style of worship is practiced; we are called to work together for the good of the whole body. Jesus the "Vine" or "Tree" wants all of his "Branches" to get along. He was so concerned for the way that church people related to each other, that He made it a primary part of His prayer in the garden, that the disciples would be united as "one" in the gospel. However, poor people are often seen as spiritual failures. Many well to do church members think that the poor don't talk right, think right, live right, or pray right. When the "somebody's" of the New Testament Church heard that Jesus' ministry was going to extend to the boundaries where the poor and "nobody's" lived, and that heaven wouldn't be for just them they were outraged. The "somebody's" were so outraged by Jesus' ministry to take on those outside the boundaries of their social network that they wanted to kill him. They thought that they were somebody, but they forgot that the love of Jesus extends to everybody. To the "somebody's" the "nobody's" were outcast people who weren't ready for a prophetic Messianic messenger sent by God to announce Good News to those who were poor, blind, captive, and oppressed. Women, minorities, and the poor, are vulnerable people who are often shuffled off the main stage of human history and labeled as "nobody's." Jesus in his attempt to bring all the "nobodies" to Heaven, demand through non-violent direct action from the "somebody's" in church a change in the way women, minorities, and the poor are treated. However, until the church flexes all of its spiritual muscles and condemn, selfish, unholy thinking, unconverted members will continue to promote this type agenda that squanders the churches growth and influence. Jesus is not indifferent to anyone. He cares about everyone's pain. He is not just concerned about your church attendance, devotional life, baptismal record, or whether you put money in the plate. Jesus cares about the things that bruise your soul. He weeps with you and he bends low to catch your tears as they fall. The spiritual gifts and the whole word of God must be taught in each church so that the members of that particular church can grow into the fullness of Christ. If not, that portion of the body becomes malnourished, and in its weakened state it becomes open to the many attacks of Satan and his demons. Demons also have knowledge about Jesus, theology, and end-time events. They know that a time is coming for their judgment, and Jesus is in control of it. But are they saved? No they are not. They have a lot of head knowledge but *"Head knowledge alone is insufficient for salvation."* (James 2:19) Salvation is of the heart, not the head. We need the authority and the fruits of the spirit that's given us in scriptures to truly be effective in our ministry. That's the reason there seems to be so much strife and division prevalent in many of our local churches today. Demons must ask permission before they can do anything to a child of God, and then they can only do what Jesus allows them to do. In order for us to gain back a lot of the ground that has been taken from the church by Satan, we must all begin to enter spiritual warfare on first a personal level, and then an outreach basis.

The Pharisee doubted that Jesus was a prophet, but Jesus showed him that he was more than a prophet. Jesus went above the authority of a prophet by declaring that the woman was forgiven of her sins. The dinner guest began to wonder, "How can a mere mortal forgive sin?" He couldn't get it in his mind the authority that Jesus possessed. The woman with the jar of ointment got the message of His power by the healing, cleansing, and deliverance from sin in her life. She realized that the Balm of Gilead was standing in her presence. This woman was grateful of being released from the sentence of sin and death; she had much to be thankful and forgiven for. She could feel the power of God's love and respond to it. First, she experienced something deeply healing her physical, emotional, and spiritual traumas. Then, she passed it along. As she gave, she experienced new levels of peace: first the love; then in response, the gift; and then the peace that passes all understanding. In Mary Magdalene's hunger, need, and desire for God, she had done what she needed to do. She had opened to spread herself into the wind of God's love and soar over her past into a new life. She was ready to give thanks. She took her alabaster jar and caused grace and mercy to be invited into the Pharisee's party. She didn't care what Simon or the world thought of her. She had adopted the cliché "sticks and stone's may break my bones, but words will never hurt me." The woman with the ointment did not come quickly to her encounter with Jesus. It took guts to go against the ways of her people, to give up the life she had known, take her savings and buy the ointment, and then to barge in on the dinner party. But she had the discipline, so when love drew her in she was able to respond. Notice a few things concerning this story and how it relates to us! She approached the Lord just as she was. The gift (jar of ointment) that she brought was a symbol of all that she had and would have that coming year. The alabaster jar that she held contained a sweet smelling savor, high in monetary value. Most importantly to get to its fragrance she had to "break" the seal. Why did she have to break it? First, she broke it because it was a sign of release unto her Lover. It was a voluntary act of submission to the love of God. She was thanking him for breaking her from her sinful past and was humble in gratitude for his love. She had long ago broke her physical seal (hymen) of virginity by way of prostitution, but her spiritual seal (salvation) was still unbroken in Jesus. She knew that Jesus would give his body "broken" as a sign of his love for her on the cross.

Secondly, she broke it so that the scent would drift out to let the world and her Lord know how sincere she was in giving of its content. There was no chance of her giving just part, and keeping some for herself or changing her mind. It had to be total surrender. Many women find the term surrender to be difficult, if not offensive, because they are trying so hard to find a personal sense of their own strength. Added to this is the masculine image of God. Some women believe that if they were to totally surrender to God that they would be surrendering to masculinity. God is neither masculine nor feminine. Nevertheless, women that have grown up in a culture, which repeatedly subjected them to a controlling father or male image that has left its impression feel that the idea of total surrender to God, is unpopular to a woman who's trying to establish her own power.

Thirdly, when she applied the oil on Jesus it became a common bond between her and the Savior. The oil lubricated her soul to help her receive the penetrating power of the Holy Spirit. What passes for gift giving these days is often a duty, or an investment. Some people give because, in some subtle way, they expect to get something in return. But that's not what was in the mind of the woman wiping Jesus' feet with her hair. She was moved by a deeper love, and it gave her the strength to turn something that was lovely, but material into something that was wonderful and relational. Her ointment was an offering to God, shared with someone who had helped her experience God's love. Love is complex. Sometimes it doesn't need to be understood. It needs only to be accepted. Like the Balm Of Gilead her ointment had a soothing, healing effect that gave value to her existence.

What makes a woman valuable? Some would answer physical beauty. The idea that the value of a woman rests in her appearance is deeply ingrained in our society. It starts in childhood. Males are taught to seek pretty girls that turn heads. Women are expected to have perfect figures, clear skin, and gorgeous hair. The style of a woman's hair, skin texture, smell of her body, sparkle of her eyes, the beauty of her smile, the symmetrical curves of her body, the stride in her walk, the wisdom of her talk all declare that "I am woman." The beauty of a woman graces her every fiber. It compliments her man and seduces his strength and weaknesses. If a woman happen to be fortunate enough to be born with the genes that men find attractive: perfect teeth, shaped eyebrows, a trim silhouette of thin hips, large breasts, flat abdomens, and a smooth tan complexion, then she will find that she has her choice of men. The strength of her morals, character, and mental faculties doesn't matter. This global mentality has created a global race of womanhood comprised of self-conscious, self-deprecating, self-criticizing, self-mutilating women who are counting the calories in every bowl of cereal, stick of gum, and drink. They are almost constantly looking in mirrors to see if another facelift, tummy tuck, or breast implant is necessary.

Those type women are spending extra hours at the gym, and away from their families every night. They want to slim down and fit into a smaller dress size in an attempt to stop their husbands from leaving them for a younger, prettier woman who hasn't had four children, and doesn't have the stretch marks to prove it. Some women fight back by hoping, praying, and clinging to idealism that the natural shape of her body, will cause a man somewhere to actually look at her inside before he disregards her for her imperfect shape outside. Then there are those who are career women that have broken spirits, but they develop their brains hoping that men will at least see its value. They may even be lucky enough to find men who genuinely love them for that. Others who stick to their idealism will be left independent old maids, who will mistrust every man. They'll think that all men look on them as best second, and that any man that choose them have "settled" for them on the rebound, because they couldn't get the cuties they were really after. They think that the men will leave as soon as they find prettier women that will have them. Some will try to ignore the facts of the world and live normal lives. Though these women appear perfect and happy on the outside, their inner-selves have all the while been wasting away into denial, guilt, and depression just as their own physical bodies have been wasting away from their treatments of them. They will always see reminders of their perceived failings, and become bitter women. They will never know true love, even if it is offered, because they are afraid it's some cruel trick. If a woman stubbornly refuses to change both outwardly and inwardly, she will never know true love even if he's sleeping next to her in bed every night.

    The church has also undergone many facelifts, but what has been one of the worst features of the church? It has to be the growing enslavement to fashion by both men and women. In every generation groups of people have stated what should be in style and what shouldn't. It's said that women have style men have taste. That's evident in the fashion market. Women buy clothes, household items, and shoes to glamorize and feel good about themselves, and to watch its effects upon others. However, women should not dress in a manner to call attention to them, but jealousy rages like wildfire when a woman spends most of her time adorning herself and someone else gets the compliment. The spiritual life of the church has been distorted and deformed because of social circles that have brought fashions into the church. The modern church teaches the "come as you are" approach to worshipping God. However, without restraints being imposed some members are coming to church half-naked, and that's causing some weak brothers and sisters to be tempted in the flesh. Fornication and adultery is increasing among members and not much is being done to curve it. Is the Bible silent about all of this? The apostles Paul and Peter wrote about how a Christian woman can truly make herself more beautiful. *"I also want women to dress modestly, with decency and propriety, not with braided hair or gold or pearls, or expensive clothes, but with good deeds, appropriate for women who profess to worship God,"* (1 Timothy 2:9-10) It's also said again in scripture, *"Whose adorning, let it not be that outward adorning of plaiting the hair, and of wearing of gold, or of putting on of apparel. Let it be the hidden man of the heart, in that which is not corruptible, even the ornament of a meek and quiet spirit, which is in the sight of God of great price. For after this manner in the old time the holy women also, who trusted in God, adorned themselves, being in subjection unto their own husbands."* (1 Peter 3:3-5)

Exhibitionism is being outlawed by these two words, "decency, and propriety." Paul and Peter's aim was to have a church full of genuinely lovely people in the spirit. That doesn't mean we have no appreciation of style, fabric, colors, and good tailoring, but there is a line that you learn not to cross; for it would mean that you are calling attention to yourself. You have every right as a Christian to wear good clothing, even those colors, and styles that are in today. You have the right to wear cosmetics, and to have your ears pierced. If you are a teenager your parents may not like it, and may insist that you wait until a certain age, but it's not forbidden in the Bible. Parents are disturbed at the price of clothes for their teenager; while pressure on young women to get cosmetic surgery, body piercing, and tattoos are going through the roof, and giving new headaches to parents. There are also the matter of the expenditure of some women on hairstyles, perfume, and jewelry. The apostle Peter is not banning certain hairstyles, jewelry, or expensive clothing. He isn't saying that expensive clothes, braided hair, and jewelry are wrong in themselves. Having such things is not sinful for a Christian, but wrong fashion is incompatible with happiness. Peter's concern here is that he's talking about a contrast between outward and inward adorning, just like the outward lifting of hands in a posture of prayer has been contrasted with the inward need of holiness. Peter is saying that the beauty of a woman comes from her inner self, not in hairstyle, jewels, clothes, cosmetic surgery, body piercing, tattoos and perfumes. They are all applied to the surface of the person, but beauty comes from within. Beauty is that which illuminates a life. Women that depend upon others for admiration are subject to frequent disappointment. Somebody will always criticize their appearance, surpass them in beauty, or will receive more attention. The Bible tells us the kind of clothes godly women are to avoid wearing, and what situations to get out of quick. This is an area of conduct we cannot ignore, but the Bible isn't going to tell a woman exactly what suits her, or where a hemline should be, but it does give some important principles that make it possible for her to figure out the parameters of

Christian acceptability. There should be a restraint in what godly women wear. Women ask God not to lead them into temptation. They also are asked by God not to lead others there. What a woman wears is directly related to who she is, and what she thinks of others and herself. Therefore, what she wears should not embarrass her or tempt others. The principle that women have to remember is that stylish things don't define beauty. If a woman is serious about her relationship with God she can be sure that He wants her hair, clothes, and jewelry to be to his glory, as everything else. She has to make judgments in the light of His word of how much she wants to glorify herself. Of course there are some women that have been caught up in various cults through the ages, who've had men and women teach in their congregation scriptures that denounced wearing anything attractive in clothing. Some ministers have taught or are teaching that if a woman adorn herself stylishly that it's a sure sign that she's being seduced by the Devil, or that she's trying to seduce someone. Some women have been taught that they are neither to wear pants or a dress above the ankles. Some have been told to not wear short sleeve shirts, or wear loud colors such as red. Some have even been taught to not fix their hair, put on makeup, wear lipstick, or use dye in their hair. These are all man made rules designed to keep women under submission. The women that follow those rules think that it guarantees that they are holy women. Holiness is an inward adorning. Clothes cannot stop a woman from sinning or not sinning. Many women have fallen to sin while dressed in plain clothing and proclaiming salvation. People often sin in terms of very elemental characteristics of their make-up. It's very often, merely their sexual glands that cause them problems. Human beings have a disappointing record when it comes to self-control in connection with sexual matters. There are situations in which we will lose complete control of ourselves. These are foolish arousal's that set us off on escapades of lust that are caused by wandering into forbidden areas. It's not what goes in a person that defiles, but it's what comes out of his or her heart and mouth that doesn't conform to Christ's law of modesty. It's hard to enforce modesty upon someone because it has to come from within a person. Modesty is woman's natural defense. It give women the right to withhold themselves from men with less than honorable intentions, and in turn force men to make themselves worthy of the women they desire. Female modesty brings a response from men that entices them to become gentlemen, behave honorably, and develop the manly virtues deserving of a woman's body and soul, especially gentleness, and protectiveness. True modesty wisely takes account of the inescapable differences between men and women in order to protect them both. Women learn early that their power lie in the art of flirtation, charm, manipulation, and subterfuge, but salvation causes them to discover that love comes in many forms, and that her true mate in Christ will love her in any way, shape, or form that she is in. Without modesty a woman exposes her vulnerability, and in fact becomes the weaker sex. Women are then victimized while men become predators. However, mankind has developed a predator and prey relationship with the Earth, and subsequently the women and minorities of the Earth. Women who collectively find that they are often in the role of prey to a predator society of degenerate men; whether it's for sexual or religious discrimination, or exploitation have often found themselves having absence of control over their bodies. They sometimes become the subjects of repressive laws and legislation in which they have no voice.

Immodest dress alters one's approach to the wearer. What will people who are not Christians think about a message, which says they need to repent and believe in Christ, or they will go to hell, from a woman with half her body looking bare? They won't hear the message because of the distractions. The signal from the wearer says: "I am a sex object. I am doing this to arouse men. I am desperate for a man." There comes a time when women have to choose whether they want to be ogled or taken seriously, and if they want to be taken seriously then they need to cover exposed areas that draw attention. When Jeremiah talks about the decadence of his society he says something very striking, *"They did not know how to blush."* (Jeremiah 6:15)

Everyone acknowledges that a definition of true beauty is impossible, but Christians say to be beautiful you must know Jesus Christ, because he is the most beautiful being of all. Everything that divine power can do to make him lovely has been done, "I am the Rose of Sharon, and the Lily of the Valley." The words represent the loveliness and beauty of Jesus Christ. To show external and inward beauty you must expose yourself to those elements. Plain women have been changed into objects of beauty simply by wanting to be beautiful in the Lord. They focus night and day in the spirit on ways of how to dress, fix their hair, walk, and speak in a quiet manner that's pleasing to God. Women must have a noble character, which is fortified by right thinking. *"Charm is deceptive, and beauty is fleeting; but a woman who fears the Lord is to be praised."* (Proverbs 31:30) The word of God is saying that *real* beauty (spirituality) is not fleeting because it's a matter of the inner life, and that beauty is constantly being renewed. Most women have done something to alter themselves. They wear wigs, dyed hair, fake nails, or eyelashes, in an effort to feel good about themselves and to be noticed, but constantly adding on things that are not real doesn't always make a woman feel good about herself. Feeling good about one's self comes from within. All women are not airbrushed, skinny, blonde, and resemble a "Barbie" doll. Most women are real with real bodies. Botox shots, liposuction, and fitness gyms didn't give them those bodies. Why must a woman be "perfect" in body or style to get noticed? The answer is pretty obvious. Being noticed means that she exist, is of worth, and people like her. However, to be noticed all she has to do is to change her attitude, and be positive in thought, words and deed. If the thoughts and ideas that she has inside are beautiful, it will flow down to every inch of her physical being, and no one can resist her. By being a positive force, she will not be "invisible." She will be noticed, and no 42-inch bust or 28-inch waist is necessary. Knowing who you are, what you are about, and what your flaws and abilities are, causes a woman to learn to work within those areas, and keep company with people that are also self-assured. Women become beautiful by being with genuinely beautiful people, and coming under the influence of their graciousness, humility, self-restraint, and the beauty of their holiness. They become wiser by being with wise people, hearing them speak, and especially watching them in difficult situations.

Women are special, and should be celebrated with words and affection. Kindness, love, and beauty have belied the fact that mature women over the age of forty find themselves "dissed" by the world and they feel invisible. Conversely they become coarse, hard, ugly, and worldly by keeping company with worldly people. The best company any woman can keep is with Jesus Christ. In Christ are hidden all the treasures of wisdom and knowledge. He is the one who is prepared to make his dwelling in her. God's word should be her daily influence in every part of her life. Women have to keep reminding themselves of who they are, who saved them, and how much they owe to him. They must profess, worship, and praise God. That's how they overcome the ugliness of the world and achieve true beauty in the spirit. It's hard to estimate the value that society places upon the physical attractiveness of women, but the Bible teaches that the value of a woman is godliness. It's time that women stop trying to live up to someone else ideal image of a woman. What is appropriate adorning for women who worship God? Paul tells us it's, "Good deeds." What lights up a woman and makes her really attractive? It's the light of a life of good deeds and works. That's the high calling of women. The New Testament tells us that we are saved "unto" good deeds. It doesn't say we are saved "by" good deeds. What's the difference between two little prepositions, "unto" and "by"? The difference is heaven and hell. No one has ever been saved *by* his or her good work, but we are saved *unto* God by doing good deeds through Jesus Christ alone. So does that mean that our good works are unimportant? No. The good deeds of a Christian woman are proof that she has been saved by Jesus Christ. She is so grateful to him for her salvation that she shows it by loving other people, turning the other cheek, bearing the burdens of the weak, enduring and hoping all things, visiting the lonely, and doing to others as she would have them do to her. Beautiful good deeds are the clothing that a true Christian woman wears. That's the adorning that attracts males. The Lord Jesus says to all of his women followers, "You are the light of the world. A city on a hill cannot be hid." There's enough woman left in you to be His Lady.

5

What You Want Do For Love

Women are more self examined then men. They can really put themselves in other people's place and see their perspective. They are used to taking care of other people and wondering how those people feel. Yet, women are the most vulnerable to be taken advantage. When it comes down to intimacy women are emotional creatures. The majority of women feel that they must belong to someone or something. These type women need men to love the part of them that no else wants or like. Some men that are good talkers have tapped into this weakness. These are the guys who, after women thought was a great date, said, "I'll call you," and were never heard from again. All women have had this happen to them, or at least to their best friends or sisters. They never know why they don't call, they just don't, and it's hurtful. The next stage is the dumping: the male releases himself from the perceived "clinging" of the female's attempt at emotional involvement. However, women should be clinging to the Lord in everything they do. If they were clinging to the Lord like they're supposed to be, every week when they come into worship service they would be full of praise. Apostasy causes a woman to stop clinging to the Lord. Apostasy is the Lord leading one way, but she turn's another away. She's not willing to walk with Him. Even though she say's that she's going to love the Lord and He means everything to her she still doesn't follow Him. Sometimes she might be walking with him or she might go back, but at other time she's doing what she think she should be doing. She thinks that what she's doing is from the Lord, but what she's doing is not really what the Lord wants her to do. Unfortunately, that's where so many women in the church are right now. They've already gone beyond apathy, they are in apostasy, and it leads to anarchy (no rule). Once there's anarchy, a woman can go into idolatry, jealousy, immorality, and cause internal war within her. She should be glorifying the Lord who is her King, but she doesn't have any absolutes because there is no King in her life. Some women are sleeping with the enemy and are unaware. They can't kick the enemy out of bed, because the enemy is not a person. It's a principality called slothfulness. Women don't have control over it, but the Lord does. Some women have been seduced by slothfulness to sit down and read a novel for three to four hours, or watch a movie. Some look at soap operas, shop all day, or just lie in bed half of the day. Where have they really placed God? Where is the Word of God in their life? Why aren't they reading the Bible and studying God's Word? There is no fear of God in their eyes; for fear of God is found in wisdom, and wisdom is found in the Word of God. It's not only a privilege, but it's a woman's responsibility to open the Bible and not only read it, but dive into it, study it, and find out what it says. She's not just to say, "Okay, Lord, tell me what it says," and start reading it blindly. Also she's not to rely on the little notes at the bottom of the page and what they are telling her. Some women are not living examples holding up a candle, for they have been in situations where there were people that they could witness to, but they didn't want to get involved. They are afraid of the persecution that they would suffer in this world to stand up for the Lord. However, the suffering, persecution, or people making fun of them shouldn't even matter because what lies ahead of them is so much better than what this life could ever offer.

On the other hand men cripple themselves chasing women instead of salvation. Many men may not be sure of what they want to spend their life doing. They wake up years later, well into their middle age, with no skills to support themselves. They resort to all they know to survive by becoming a "player" or a pimp. This is the "new" birth of someone who survives off women without working. Players are little boys who still haven't grown into the role of men. They are still hiding behind trees like Adam did; only theirs are trees of irresponsibility. They spend their lives ducking marriage, child support, visitation, and monogamous love. They hide behind their ability to charm and make love. Many men seek anyplace to lay their head. Some choose to lay their head in making money, playing sports, gambling, in the vial of a needle, the fire of crack cocaine cigarettes, or at the bottom of a wine or beer glass. Women that know what they don't want, but have little left of what they do want, choose these type men. They either choose from desperate desires: men who play on their insecurities, luring them into an ill-considered relationship; or they stay in a neutral position, ready for something, but not quite ready to settle for nothing conditions. They fear loosing control, being inadequate, making the wrong choice or being rejected. They count their risks instead of their blessings.

Pimps come in all shades of color, ethnicity, and professions. They can be standing in the pulpit dressed in double-breasted suits, or standing on street corners wearing oversized denim jeans. These men prey on women who are very young, poor, and not necessarily homeless, but living on the edge of destruction. A pimp love women capable of supporting him, and accepting his faults. He finds young girls or lonely women that will let him have access to their body, mind, credit cards, and bank accounts. They never realize that they have been conned by a good looking, smooth talking, and sweet smelling man who has promised to love all the women that he has fooled, with a relationship of excitement and happiness. "Pimping" is a psychological game that uses manipulation to gain influence over women. Pimps or players attach themselves to women who have spent their childhood with lingering insecurities about their looks, and intelligence while in the caring arms of their mother, and guided by their father's strong moral values. They know that these young women were shielded from the dangers just outside their door. Pimps search around from one woman to another, thinking that if they're lucky, they will find whom they want. When he does find whom he wants initially he will keep his woman off drugs, but soon after he has lured her in he will begin to abuse her emotionally and physically. The woman will develop low self-esteem and at that time she thinks that she deserved the abuse. In an effort to stay employed he convinces naïve women to prove their love to him by selling their body, but love don't mix with pimping because a pimp's main purpose is to dominate a woman and drag her into a degraded state of sexual immorality. Those types of men feel that it's an honor to sell women bodies for sex. A pimp not only sells women bodies, but he also makes good love to women and steals their minds. He makes a woman think that she is important to him. She falls in love and believes that she will be with him forever. She wants the attention and discipline so she starts calling him "Daddy." He eventually offers her support and protection if she would sell her body. Desperate, ashamed, and lonely, she will take the offer of prostitution. Women that sell their body are untamed, elusive, urban tigresses that follow their passion. The world doesn't know how to hold them. They have serious fantasizes that will never come true, and pimps don't buy dreams they sell them. A pimp looks at his women as employees and convinces them that he is handling their business. His "women" risk their lives and the threat of disease to get money, but the pimp doesn't let them keep it. He handles the money and supplies them with food, shelter, clothing, and protection. Pimps in prostitute's lives are not playing a positive role; they're just leeches and seed bearers. They are only in these women lives to act as a buffer against potential danger of hurt from a client, but a pimp will inflict more danger on the woman than she ever dreamed if she doesn't do what he wants her to do. Women who succumb to those types of men are constantly surrounded by death, danger, and living in emergency situations. Many women after having plied their trades have been viciously attacked by their pimps for not making enough money or trying to runaway to a better environment. Satan has cornered the sex market so tight that these vile and repugnant men that has enslaved young girls, women, and in some cases men, will stop at nothing to kill, hurt, or destroy those people who choose to refrain from having their bodies abused. Some young girls that have ran away from home and hooked up with a pimp have been killed just to make a point. Women and teenage girls all over the world that have experienced life on the streets learn only how to react, and not how to act to satisfy themselves. It's a miracle how they continue to live and somehow manage to survive. This mental maze of loneliness and despair is devoid of love and joy. Bored, desensitized masses of American women need to use their female intuition in finding a way out of the emotional wilderness of loneliness. Some women have managed against increasing odds to liberate themselves from self-destruction, but some feel that they are trapped for the rest of their lives. Having been beaten and tortured by husbands, boyfriends, lovers, or parents these young women are not yet ready to trust anyone, especially in a world that they know where no one can be trusted. They are on the right track, but they caught the wrong train. They fail to see that there are two separate worlds with no road back except through Jesus.

Prostitutes start out when they are young and have a lot to offer clients by way of shape and beauty. Breakdown in families, drug addiction of parents, and poverty has caused more and more young girls and boys to fall from the ark of safety called home. Some kids are pushed out the door and told to make it on their own. To make it on their own they sometimes act as "fronts" for drug dealers, and prostitutes. Because kids look innocent, trustworthy and most of the times are not charged when caught, sometimes their own parents use them to do both selling drugs and prostitution of their body. They are victims of parents whose only use for them is making money to satisfy their own sinful cravings. These kids struggle and compete to survive in a world without love, affection, and security. Most are full of the optimism of youth and independence. They turn to the streets to survive. They are happy to escape from abusive families, but they are unaware that the streets can be an unforgiving, treacherous, dehumanizing, place to try to carve an existence. They will never learn from a story being told to them of someone else experience. They must have their own experiences. There are countless numbers of young girls who are miserable, and are starving themselves, bingeing, purging, mutilating their bodies, throwing their hearts away on men that are losers, suppressing their natural desire for romance, and denying their need for family and children. When they can't cope with reality they dope themselves up on Prozac. These kids sleep in ditches, under highway overpass, alleyways, dumpsters, and cardboard boxes to survive. The street is their residential address. It's their entire life. They are prodigal and have no reason to go back home. The word prodigal means *wasteful*, and it can extend to girls as well as boys. The prodigal daughter like the prodigal son of the Bible (Luke 15:11-32) is one who has disconnected from her mother. She doesn't want to remember her mother's words, how she lived her life, and has vowed to be nothing like her mother. These type women experienced anger, guilt, and motherly disapproval in their lives.

    The Bible doesn't say how long the prodigal son had stayed away from home, but with all indications it appeared that the child was home sick. He wanted to go back home to his father's house. Having been stricken with hunger and pain, he knew that home was the place to be. There is no cure for homesickness, except to get back home by any means possible. The prodigal son came home, but he arrived exhausted, and in rags. He had been spiritually ripped apart while in the clutches of the worlds system. In the story of the prodigal son we read nothing of him having a mother, or perhaps she was dead. If she was dead she probably died of a broken heart, brought on by the wanderings of the child. It's sad to see a child whose wayward life brings him or her back home only to find that the person they desire to see most is dead. The mother, who used to sit on the porch a little bent over with glasses on her eyes, her face worn with the years of wisdom and determination, is no longer there to soothe away her child's anger or hurt. She has gone home to her reward. Unlike the prodigal son, some young people today very seldom say, "I will go home (back to church) to my Father." Even though they know that God and the preacher is standing there with arms wide open, waiting for their return. Still, some will not go to church or hear a sermon until they are struck by famine or grief. God has to tear some women spiritually and physically to get their attention. He has to make them naked and ashamed of their lifestyle. He does it by allowing Satan to strip them of their clothes of pride, arrogance, indecency, anger, and sexuality, and buffet them with winds of persecution and afflictions. All around them their life start falling apart little by little until they are ready to submit to God's will. Sometime people can't see their way back home until they have been beaten with their own rod of conviction. There are Wandering Daughter's that are still traveling through sin and looking for happiness. They're not quite ready or willing to come home because their anger and resentments over early childhood wounds inflicted by their mother will not let them. The "Untraveled daughter," whether she's happily married, unhappily married, divorced, or widowed learned from her mother to stand on her own two feet if she's going to survive. This type daughter has had a generally positive relationship with her mother whose mentoring has shown her daughter of not only what she did well when she was young, but equally and sometimes even more powerfully, by what she didn't do. In regard to spiritual health and well-being, many mothers have found religion or a strong faith important in their lives and try to pass that on to their own daughters. Although most daughters were irritated by their mother's constant nagging to attend church, still the mother's faith had an impact on their lives. Many daughters may change religion from that of their childhood, but the spiritual teachings of their mother often comes back into focus. Concerning the road back, these prodigal daughters have one key factor that will allow them to return home: forgiveness. Until prodigal young women come to a right way of thinking, and acknowledge their transgression

There's Enough Woman Left to be Your Lady

before God and man, they're doomed to stay in the uncomfortable position that they're in. In the story of Luke's gospel the prodigal's father was happy to see him, however notice that the father never left home to look for him. Our heavenly Father also doesn't leave his throne to look for a wayward child, but His love and its effect draw us to Him. Like the father of the prodigal son Gods arms are always open to welcome us from our continual wanderings. God is offering way-ward young men and women full amnesty if they would just return home before it's too late, and this is good news, too. It's good news for anyone caught up in thinking God only works through His saints and the good things that they do. God can take anyone's shameful scandals, and turn them into something beautiful and usable. He comes to each of us and says, "Don't be afraid. I understand your failure. I've never expected you to have it all together. Just give me your life as it is, and I will make it into something meaningful." When we get in a right frame of mind to escape from the hog pen of life, and return to God, He will also put a ring on our finger and dress us royally. Getting into the right frame of mind entails our receiving a "tune-up" in the spirit. The house of God is where we will receive "star" treatment. The world has lots of miserable people doing things that they really don't want to do. Many women think that they cannot do anything else except sell their body. Mary Magdalene of the New Testament had thought that way. The woman who'd anointed Jesus' feet probably looked at her diary of clients more than once, as she thought about the night that she had spent with Jesus. Maybe she even framed the pages as a reminder of her past life. This woman at one time had been deathly afraid of Jesus. She thought that he would treat her the same way that all men had. She had been with so many men that she began to feel as if she was nothing. After a wretched life of prostitution all she wanted to do was die. That was until she met Jesus.

He began to put her life back together. Never did she have nor would ever find a lover like Jesus. She knew that she had finally found a real man in Jesus. She knew that her struggles weren't over, but her relationship with God had brought her a new sense of dignity, and worth. She felt clean and hopeful again. She had experienced grace, and forgiveness. She was changed. We should see that as God's love for all mankind. In the words of the parable, she has been forgiven much, and now with tears, hair, and ointment, she seeks to love much. Jesus knows this and he graciously receives her offering of love. When her commitment to him would grow weak, she would have a rough time, but she also knew that she had a small group to help her find strength in the Lord. Mary Magdalene spiritual maturity really comes into focus in the stories of the crucifixion and resurrection. All four gospels agree that she was present at the crucifixion, and all four gospels agree that Jesus appeared first to her after his resurrection. Even when the crucifixion was over, and Jesus was dead and buried, Mary still couldn't leave him. She haunted the graveyard by hanging around it until dawn broke. Then she was able to approach the grave. She was crying, of course, and in a state of deep shock and distress. When she saw that the stone had been moved away from the entrance to the tomb; she expressed no surprise. Neither did she express any surprise when she looked into the tomb and saw not a body, but two young men dressed in white. They said to her, "Woman, why are you weeping?" It must have been obvious why she was weeping and whom she was seeking, but Mary doesn't notice this and answers them directly, "Because they have taken away my Lord and I don't know where they have laid him." She doesn't wait for any response from the young men, but goes out immediately and sees supposedly the "gardener." He repeats the question in exactly the same words as the Angels? "Woman, why are you weeping?

There's Enough Woman Left to be Your Lady

Whom do you seek?" But this time Mary doesn't answer directly. It's almost as though there's a spark of anger in her reply, as if she's tired of playing games. She says, "Look, if you've removed his body just tell me where it's at and I'll go there." Jesus reveals himself when he says, "Mary!" Immediately she knows who it is, and now that she's met the risen Christ, she's a joyful person inside and outside. At the sound of his voice her tears dry up and her depth of sadness is transformed to heights of joy. She reaches out to touch him, but he states, *"Touch me not, for I have not yet ascended unto my Father, but go unto my brethren and tell them that I ascend unto my father, and your Father, and to my God and your God."* (John 20:17) She doesn't concern herself with the possible outcome of the action Jesus has asked her to take. She simply obeys him without further thought. She was so happy to know that Jesus was alive that she runs off and tell his disciples that she's met him and that he's risen. She doesn't care much whether they believe her or not. Their opinion of her no longer matters. Christ loves the Church like Hosea loved his wife, even though she was a prostitute. Hosea watched his wife carry out her professional prostitution through many lovers. He also watched as she was stripped naked on a block and auctioned off as a prostitute for the highest bidder in the slave market. He went into a place and bought her, not because there was anything about her that was clean, sweet, gracious, and lovely, but it was because he loved her. (Hosea 3:1) God also loved prostituted Israel. Therefore, Christ loves His church with a love that can't be killed and it never dies. It's a love that's utterly and completely self-sacrificing. The Spirit-filled husband also loves his wife not for what she can do for him, but what he can do for her. That's how Christ's love worked and works. He loves us not because there's something in us that attract Him. He loves us because He's determined to love us in spite of our unattractiveness. He loves us with a love that seeks not to control, abuse, or humiliate us. His love seeks rather to meet our needs, to understand us, and to provide strength for us. We didn't do anything to earn Christ's love, but it's not a question of whether we're deserving or not. From the time Jesus turned his face towards Jerusalem and the cross events seemed to speed up to overtake him. His love for us plunged him into a situation that could only end in his crucifixion. Because he faced that crucifixion and saw it through to the end without attempting to avoid the pain and suffering, he maintained his own integrity and love, which resulted in a glorious resurrection. Mary Magdalene didn't have to stand at the foot of the cross, watching as the man she loved most in the world was executed, but by standing broken before Jesus to commit her life back unto him she had chose to be crucified with him in her flesh. We must stop being a busy bookkeeper and keeping track of everyone else's sins. In Matthew 7:12 Jesus said, *"Whatever you wish that people would do to you, do so to them; for this is the law and the prophets."* We fail to see our own need for forgiveness, for grace, and for a fresh start. Instead of seeing the prodigal action of others we should see ourselves, in the wandering and lost condition of our selfishness and desires. We should treat each other the way we'd want to be treated. Human beings by nature have an all-consuming desire to be treated well by other people. Nobody likes to be made fun of, ignored, exploited, taken advantage, and treated like a useless person, regardless of what they've has done in the past. A woman's lifestyle makes no difference to God in saving her. Jesus told the chief priest and elders of his time, *"Verily I say unto you, that the publicans and the harlots go into the kingdom of God before you."* (Matthew 21:31) Prostitutes and drug-addicted women are angels who already had wings, but needed Jesus to teach them how to fly. Although Mary Magdalene had been a whorish woman, she was still a **woman.** Upon her repentance and regeneration she found mercy, and became a zealous disciple for Christ.

Have you ever stood broken or dented in the presence of the Lord? Have you ever taken what you have, in whatever state you are, and given it to the Lord? Sometimes when grocery stores open a box they find that some of the cans or cartons has been damaged. Some have lost their labels, have dents, or are crushed so badly that some of the contents had come out. Store managers will tell stock persons not to put those items on the shelves, because no one would buy them. They are often placed in a large basket in the front of the store and on the basket is a large sign that read, "Damaged Goods-half price." or "Damaged Goods-Items reduced." Not many people buy those items because of shame or fear of contamination. Most people ignore them. Often they end up being destroyed, sent back to the manufacturers, or given away to charities. Mary Magdalene may have also felt like damaged goods that had no value, wasn't respected by anyone, and ignored by many when she was looked upon by society. When we read about her in scriptures she is profusely showering tears on Jesus, because he had reacted to her so differently from everybody else. At long last she has found someone who valued her, and the experience brought her to tears. Her community and Bible scholars assumed that this woman was a prostitute and labeled her a sinner, but here we find this woman labeled as a "sinner bringing her very best gift of ointment and pouring it lavishly on Jesus' feet. Did Jesus treat this woman as a prostitute? No, he did not. When Jesus looked at this poor woman, he did not see "damaged goods," but a person of value and worth. He saw a person worth redeeming. Labeling people without justification can ruin or damage a person's reputation. Many divorced or single women with children also look upon themselves as damaged goods.

These women for whatever reasons, either because of things that they've done in life, things that has happened in life to them, or things beyond their control, have made themselves feel like damaged goods. They've felt as if they were crushed, bent out of shape, and of little value to themselves or anyone else, until they met Jesus. Loneliness has also caused some to have sordid relationships with Satan. They condemn themselves as being fat, ugly, unloved, and unwanted. They don't think that they can love someone again or that anyone could love them. Their spirit and sense of worth is zero and broken, but brokenness in the presence of God is His opportunity for healing, deliverance, and total restoration for anyone that's in need of a spiritual blessing. God can give you a new life. All you have to do is give God your old life. I am convinced that God is waiting for all worn, bent, and depleted women to stand, kneel, or lay prostrate on the floor before him in a broken condition that not only includes praying, but also crying in the spirit. Crying is very cathartic. You feel better after a session of crying out to Jesus. In crying you are washing out experiences from the past that has never been resolved. When a woman tells Jesus all about her problems he can fix it. Jail time, alcohol, cigarettes, marijuana, crack cocaine, strange men, prostitution, whoring, fighting, late night emergency phone calls, periods of not knowing where her husband or children are, who he is with, or how she will feed her kids will no longer be a part of her. When problems are turned over to Jesus a woman can go to bed every night and wake up every day with her husband beside her and her babies happy and fed. Jesus is always on the lookout for people with dented hope, but when he looks upon a person he doesn't see damaged goods. He represents a kind of faith and worship that's redemptive and life changing, not one that labels and condemns. He sees nothing wrong with a can that has part of the label gone and several dents. He feels that it's just bent

There's Enough Woman Left to be Your Lady

out of shape, worn, or damaged a little on the outside, but on the inside it's as good as the ones on the shelves. He wants people with all of the bumps and bruises of being a loser. It doesn't matter to him how bent a person is, he knows that it's what's on the inside that counts. You might seem as worthless as damaged goods to others or in your own eyes, but not to Jesus. To him you are valued goods that are of worth. So valued that he has purchased you with his very own life, so that he can recycle you, and put you back in circulation. Any person that was in debt to sin and have been delivered by the grace of God ought to be grateful that God was merciful to them. They had nothing to pay, for silver and gold wouldn't pay their debt, nor would sacrifices and offerings. Connecting with God's love isn't always easy, especially for those who feel that they aren't doing such a bad job of living a righteous life, but your faith can either liberate or incarcerate your spirit. We are called to be a church body, but gathering in a building on Sunday morning is clearly not all that it means. We must support people like Mary Magdalene. She probably had lots of experience with the kind of judgmental, condemnatory, and sick form of religion that Simon the Pharisee represented. Sick religion builds barriers of distrust, pessimism, cynicism, paranoia, and judgment. People practicing religion can be sick, but yet give all the appearances of being well and rational. Simon represented the kind of religion that builds barriers to keep sinners away, and promotes an arrogant attitude of superiority. Jesus Christ has nothing to do with religion. He never practiced a religion. He did not come to bring religion. He didn't start a religion, and He certainly never proclaimed religion. God instituted feasts, Laws and rites amongst the Jewish people, but they missed the point, and turned them into a religion. Through the animal sacrifices, God was pointing the Jews to the fact we all need to trust in the Sacrifice of Christ, the Lamb of God, and only Savior, but they missed it. So blinded were they by religion, that when God came as Christ, and stood in front of them, they didn't even recognize Him. They called Him Beelzebub (Satan), and crucified God's Son. All types of "religion" are false, man-made, and devil inspired to keep people away from the one true God. Jesus came to bring salvation, and to bring us to that one and only God. People still confuse knowing about Jesus, with knowing Him personally. A healthy faith makes you more open, trusting, healing, unifying, and caring. You experience the grace of God and it helps you to understand why people act, feel, or believe as they do. It causes you to examine your life, your sins, and your relationship with God so that you are released from guilt and pain. The woman who had experienced grace was free, but the Pharisee was bound by his own prejudices. God the Father and Jesus has often served their own purpose's and the church's interest by using men and women of low morals. Some of the best men and women in the church are those who have wallowed in the mud of immorality, and have been raked over the hot coals of persecution. Like Mary some women have distinct yet interwoven memoirs of silent pain, abuse, oppression, insanity, whoredom, rape, endurance, survival, triumph, non-faith, and being cheated out of inheritances. Some women have abused their body so long that they began to wonder if there is anyone who cares at all. The answer is yes. God is out there on the streets and he does care, and above all with undying love. Women when you're troubled, despaired, and confused let God's love find you. God's love will find you regardless what you have done in life. Women who follow Jesus look to Him for how to use their bodies, not to the world. A born again man knows that his eyes can guide him into dangerous places, but men who follow Jesus guard their eyes for the good of women, and for the glory of God. Women that have repented of the sins of their youth through grace, must expect to bear shame and reproach of society, but when they hear of their old ways, they should thank God that they are not what they use to be. So, come out of that damaged goods basket. That's not for you anymore. You've been bought with a price. In response, pass along the gift you have received. There's still enough woman left to be His Lady.

6

Jealous Love

Domestic violence against women is a very real issue that cuts across every denominational and demographic group. It plagues women at an alarming rate. It's rural, urban, suburban, physical, mental, ecclesiastical, and international in scope. It acts without restraint of respect for others, and strips away all notion of individuality. Violence violates, break, disregard, ravish, outrage, profane, and desecrate. Rape counselors, battered and homeless women, former addicts pressed into prostitution for survival, and others within the religious community, each have an eye-opening story to tell about the many forms of emotional, religious, economic, legal, physical, and sexual violence against women and children that have been employed by depraved men.

In Genesis 34:1-31 one of the more horrific stories of violence that the Bible has recorded, and that's rarely talked about in worship service or Bible study is the story of the rape of Dinah, Jacobs only daughter. Her story begins with violence and end with violence. This story of a young' girls indiscretion and dishonor is one of moral laxity and chaotic revenge. It shows how violence also leads to more violence. Dinah decided to visit a strange city named Shalem by herself because of its styles, pleasures, and beautifully coiffured women. While visiting other women in the region, a man of wealth and power named Shechem rapes Dinah. Even as he does violence to the body and spirit of this young woman, his act does violence against all women and civilization. After violating Dinah he has a change of heart toward her. Love and tenderness now describe his disposition toward her. Shechem requests that his father make it possible for him to wed his victim. Therein lies the awkwardness. Shechem is in denial that his initial act was one of violence. Once he possesses her as his wife, will violence return to the relationship? Shechem, and his father Hamor, plead for Dinah to be given in marriage at any cost. The aggrieved sons of Jacob set a high cost for their sister's wedding, which was the circumcision of every male in the city of Shechem. Circumcision had been given to Abraham as a sign of the covenant with God. It was the sting of belonging to God and to God's community, but now it serves as a powerful vehicle for them to wreak vengeance on the rapist. While the men of Shechem are still in pain from the physical procedure involved in the circumcision, two brothers of Dinah sneak into the city and kill not only Shechem and Hamor, but also all the other males. Their older brothers follow, plundering and looting the city, taking wives and children as captives. The breaking of hospitality and the rape of Dinah beget the telling of lies. The twisting of religious ritual caused the slaughter of innocent people. In the story of Dinah her voice is not heard. Someone else is always making decisions for her. It's as if she didn't exist. Not only that, no names are given of the men of Shechem

There's Enough Woman Left to be Your Lady

who perished, no faces are attached to the little ones in the city who were carried away, and no characters are connected to the women that are made widows. It's like the rape never happened, and the city never existed. An entire town or nation can suffer or disappear for the sins of its resident. No one likes to be abused, and no one deserves it. Yet, violence such as rape and abuse of women still cycle through our society today. Violence and abuse of women borders on the brink of jealousy, and insanity that recognizes only self-interest, self-protection, and self-justification. Physical violence may be accompanied by sexual violence, sexual harassment, domestic violence, rape, assault, and sexual abuse. Most men haven't taken the Army's motto of "Be all that you can be" towards women, children, girlfriends, or wives. Some men try to muzzle and control them physically, mentally, and emotionally by giving orders. Others imprison their wives by not letting them work, go out with female friends, do grocery shopping, cook, or pay bills. Some men don't even put their wives name on a checking account, and never let them know how much money they earn or how much debt that they have incurred. Some are jealous and possessive, and refuses to let a woman leave or break up with them. Anger and violence are not the same things. Most angry women don't show their anger by striking out violently, unless in self-defense. While a woman may say or do something that angers her partners, she almost never provokes him to strike her in any way. It's a male's choice to be violent. The woman finds that in her relationship with him, no matter how much she may try to improve, change, "grow in the Word," and adapt to his demands, it is never enough. His demands always change and become more unreasonable. She begin to feel inadequate, guilty, and somehow off-balance, because she never knows what is going to set him off next, and no matter how much she prays, he never change. She is convinced that she must be "crazy" and it's her fault that he acts as he does. Even when other relationships at work or church give her positive feedback and encouragement, she loses all her confidence and self-esteem when she returns home. When anything goes wrong in the home or in the marital relationship, the problem is always the woman. The husband remains blind to any fault or cruelty on his part. He thinks, "If she would just be "more submissive" or "be filled with the Spirit" or "obey me like a good Christian wife," everything would be fine. He actually sees himself as sanctimonious for "putting up" with a woman like her. On the other hand, he can become unreasonably jealous if other people, particularly men, pay too much attention to his wife. Thus, the wife no longer feels free to associate with certain friends, groups, or family members because of her need to keep him happy. Even though these activities or people are important to her, she prefers avoiding them so that she can "keep the peace." Most women don't want to end the relationship; they just want to end the violence. Many women are reaching out to emphatic men to help stem the tide of violence perpetuated against them by selfish, abusive, and aggressive men who use physical restraints to gain an advantage over them. It's important to know that the best time for stopping the violence is at the first incident, but for reasons of embarrassment, shame, or fear, victims don't usually volunteer information. This should not be so. Acts of violence will strip a woman of her self-esteem and sanity. It will sometime cause her spirit to turn against God, and leave her wondering if God has forsaken her. Some women have years pockmarked with rapes, abusive relationships, prostitution, children born addicted to drugs, and their own long descent into addiction. Abuse can also be emotional, psychological, social, economical, and sexual. One in every four women will at some time in her life be abused by an intimate partner.

Yet, some display a surprising inner calm. To hear them tell their story or sing a song is to begin to understand how a woman could have turned such a seemingly hopeless life into a source of hope for others. Some might credit their inner strength; some might credit luck, but they know that Jesus is the key and it's that feeling more than anything that has shaped their return to the Lord. Women must confront the demons of their past. In modern times women who had been raped were in much the same situation as that faced by Dinah. Society often looked down upon them as if they had somehow brought on their own rapes by dressing provocatively or being promiscuous. Many women have hid black eyes, beatings, rape, and verbal assault. They were ashamed and angry, but wouldn't go to the police for fear that the police would not take them seriously. Often times when a woman has brought charges of rape, she is put on the defensive more than the man who raped her. Her whole credibility as a woman is questioned. Societies also look down upon women who are battered by men as though being victimized was the fault of the victim. The common characteristic of each of these is that they are acts of dominance and possession of women. Women who stood up and expressed their pain often opened a window into their own experiences in order to make people see and feel the realities of being raped; not just once but twice. The second time by a legal system that did not understand or care. Those accused both males and females have no presumption of innocence, but must prove they are not guilty to committees that have power to ruin their careers and lives. There is also an undercurrent of discontent among men who no longer see their children because of anti-male bias in the Family Court system. These are men who pay taxes to support domestic violence centers, but are turned away from those same doors if they are victims. These men are fed up with seeing their gender portrayed in the media as rapists, wife beaters, or child molesters. All human beings have an equal right to the protection of their bodies and property because we share a common humanity. The laws in courts, and in police matters that protect humanity should look at men and women and see no difference whatsoever, but the law is not gender-blind. In many areas, the law also treats men like second-class citizens. In other areas it discriminates against women. Some women have been abused so long that they will take the law into their own hands. The number of women convicted of non-violent, non-coercive offenses and incarcerated has more than tripled in the last fifteen years. Over seventy five percent of women in prisons are mothers. The majority of women prisoners are survivors of domestic violence or childhood abuse. Many are addicted to drugs or alcohol, or suffer from serious health problems or depression. Women face a broad range of issues in the criminal justice system including mandatory sentencing, sexual harassment, medical and mental health care, transitional service, discharge planning, abuse of women inmates and parolees, and vocational and educational programming. Predominantly, gender power relations have left a legacy whereby women are more likely to be disadvantaged, and taken advantage of relative to men. Women prisoners typically have greater needs than male prisoners do, but they remain the most neglected and overlooked population in the prison system. Women outside prison walls also have less access to resource, benefits, information, and decision-making. They have fewer rights both within the household and in the public sphere. These concerns and the struggle for gender equality have been narrowly perceived to be "women's issue." Prescribed gender roles result in non-identical power relations between men and women. These gender-based inequalities are interlinked with other modifiers such as class, race, geographical location, and physical ability. Gender discrimination literally destroys careers of innocent women. It shows human misery being caused by laws and social behavior. However, a woman is handcuffed and shackled only to herself. Circumstance doesn't make the woman, because she feeds off her inner most desires and that attracts what she is. If she has not accepted Jesus in her heart, her body is the servant of her mind. It responds to the thoughts that she feeds it. Her thoughts can't be kept secret because it solidifies into circumstances of drunkenness, sexuality, thievery, destitution, and disease. It forms into unclean and dishonest habits that lead into persecution or self-injury. When she links her thoughts with a central purpose, which is Jesus, she will be on the road to self-control. Some women have survived situations that most people will never have to go through, because there weren't any safety nets and they made their way in life as they went along. Gender equality can only be achieved, when women and men work together in Christ, but first men must confront the issue of ownership in a relationship. They must learn that women are not personal property that's owned forever, and that hanging on to past traditions stand in the way of new directions. Unless a woman just get up and leave on her own, she will be forever trapped, especially if she has no skills or motivation.

Violence is something that needs renunciation. We must become civilized again. Society needs to learn new ways of conflict resolution that don't include revenge, and find ways to work together. We must return to a society that judge's individuals on their merits, and that weighs issue such as custody or domestic violence on the basis of evidence not gender. Laws against battery and assault have been on the books for many years. All that's needed is to have those laws rigorously enforced. It takes a bit of anger to cease being abused and to demand justice instead. When this demand is made, men will not find themselves alone. The majority of women will stand up as well to defend the rights and the dignity of their fathers, brothers, husbands, sons, and friends. Until this is changed there will be no true equality until Jesus sets up his kingdom on earth. He will become the symbol of the "Enlightened Man."

Jesus himself was a victim of violence. Having been conceived by way of spiritual and human entity, the birth of Jesus was poised for violence. The beginning of violence in Christ's life took place when a teenage virgin named Mary announced to her fiancé Joseph that she was pregnant. She was not pregnant by just anybody, but by the Holy Spirit of God. She knew the divine origin of the conception, but how could she prove that she had gotten pregnant without the aid of a man, and who would believe that an unseen spirit gave her a child? Mary was perplexed, anxious, troubled, sad, down in the dumps, and stressed out. She probably was wondering, "What will the people in town think of me?" "What will Joseph do to me?" She kept calm in the face of opposition because she knew that she was innocent of fornication. Infidelity had never entered her mind.

A violent reaction also took place in Joseph when the Bible say's that; *"He was minded to put her away privily."* (Matthew 1:19) Joseph's perplexity was that of struggling with jealousy and disbelief, in that Mary would be caught in a situation like that. Joseph suspecting that she was with child by whoredom was ashamed to marry her for fear of bringing embarrassment and guilt upon himself. He was also struggling with the idea of whether to divorce her by law, which would have meant for her a sentence of death by stoning. Bringing her to punishment was to make her a *"public"* example, but being a just man Joseph granted Mary clemency.

Violence was also present when this teenage mother was about to give birth in a strange city crowded with visitors, and needed a room, but could find no place to rest nor hospitality. Having found no room in the Inn she struggled to bring forth the savior of the world among wild beast and abject poverty. Christ came in humility. The only witness to His birth was beast, angels, and a star that lit the way to His path, but God works best in mangers. When Jesus came into the world He chose to be born in a most unusual place: a manger. It was no more than a livery stable with sheep, goats, oxen, and other livestock animals. Yet, there was a distinctive fragrance and character about that place. It was filled with odors and dung from animals, but God seems to work best around rotten, foul, smelly unpleasant circumstances and people. In fact, scriptures state, *"Where there are no oxen, the manger is empty, but from the strength of an ox comes an abundant harvest."* (Proverbs 14:4) It's saying that in order for Jesus to be present at the "new" birth in our lives, we must invite those things that bring with them "a mess to clean up." God works best among nasty and messy things in our lives that has often detoured us from his love. From these messes come abundant harvests. When a major spiritual construction project takes place in our lives it appears to be absolute chaos. So much of what we see in our life is torn up and scattered everywhere. It's ugly, inconvenient, and tends to irritate us because it appears we are moving much slower than we would like as we crawl down life's highway. Yet, when we look at that same area of our lives a few months or years later, we see why the construction was necessary. There was meaning to the mess. It actually made life so much better. You may have been through the messiest of times in your personal life, but God revealed His power and strength in your life. It was when those oxen's of hardship walked into your manger that the greatest harvest was manifest. It's only when you have sought to remove the oxen and rid yourself of the odor and the mess that you have fought the ultimate work of God and caused it to cease.

"The crucible for silver and the furnace for gold, but the

Lord tests the heart." (Proverbs 17:3) This proverb describes one of God's strangest mysteries. It's a description of God's formula to refine the human heart in order to bring out its finest qualities. The ecclesiastical leaders who make the greatest mark for the Kingdom have to experience their own crucible and fire. Without it, the dross (waste) can never be removed from the human heart, and the encumbrances weigh us down. God understands the human heart. He understands that for us to become all that He hopes for us there has to be seasons of fire, that sometimes bring meltdowns in our lives. Succeeding in the test qualifies a candidate for greater responsibility. The greater the use of a person in the gospel the greater the crucible that's used to prepare the right foundation. Some of God's greatest crucibles are found where we live every day: the spouse who betrayed your trust, the church member who hurt your feeling, the friend who refuses to pay you money that you loaned, and the Pastor who falls short of your expectations. Each of these is God's test to find out how you will respond. His grace has been provided that you might pass the tests that He brings before you. Should you fail, you need not fear. His grace is sufficient.

God is filled with paradoxes and likes to show Himself in the midst of the messes of our lives. The best crops come from waste that can be used as fertilizer. This is what brings us into the harvest field of salvation. From our "mess ups" in life God gleans a harvest of useful resources for the gospel. The bigger the mess; the bigger the harvest. God is hospitable with his grace. This is what He did with all His highly used servants in the Bible who was full of mess from Abraham all the way down to Jude. By choosing a stable as His place of birth, Jesus was stating to the world that hospitality is crucial to what it means to be a Christian. Hospitality isn't about being friendly. It's about bridging gaps, and building relationships, which is paramount in the pursuit of "birthing" new, converts in the Lord. As born again disciples, we never know when God will ask us to care for a victim of violence. Perhaps it will be obvious as in taking care of someone physically hurt, or it might be subtle as in caring for a person who has become homeless due to the result of his or her life falling apart from an act of violence. Hopelessness is a feeling that comes to children, the elderly, the free, the imprisoned, the rich, the poor, those who are disabled, and those who are not. Hopelessness can either be debilitating to a person's emotional and spiritual self-esteem, or it can be a motivating force to seek help.

Violence also played a part in the death of Jesus. Beaten, spat on, nailed to a cross, and punctured in his side as a sentence for his disruptive behavior of standing up for the least among us, he cries out, *"My God, My God, Why has thou forsaken me?"* The cry of his voice has become the cry of so many voiceless victims across the centuries. What do we do when we come to understand the salvation that God has wrought in a world filled with violence and suffering? We are to believe, sing, and be glad. God's theology is not to remain in the pages of our notebooks, textbooks, and Bibles. It must be sung in songs of praise and adoration.

Where is God to be found in the face of violence? God moves in history not only to balance the books of injustice, but also to balance them on our behalf as He saves us from our sins, and set our feet upon firm ground. At sometime or another in our lives we all ask, "Why has God forsaken me?" Like Mary and Joseph we also go from place to place hoping for a welcome, but we sometimes find doors of Christian brotherhood being shut in our face, and believing that there's still "no room in the Inn."

7

Women Are A Rare Jewel

Satan the great Liar deceived Eve into sinning, and her husband neglected his duties to lovingly protect her. Adam stood idly by while she was deceived. He even sought to send the wrath of God upon her, rather than take responsibility for the condition of his family. God imposed curses for Satan, man, and woman because of each of their sins. For man, his curse is related to his domain of work and provision for his family. For woman, her curse is related to her domain of the home and childbearing. (Genesis 3:16) The Scriptures are clear that Satan the "Liar" deceived Eve, who likely believed she was being helpful, when in fact she was being disobedient and sinful.

Some women sin willfully and intentionally out of open rebellion, while others like Eve are deceived into thinking that they are helping when in fact they are disobeying the clear words of God, and rejecting their feminine role. Women are not aware that they have become the world's greatest women haters, having learned to shun all things feminine. Satan the "Liar" has successfully promulgated a legion of lies including the following: "Women are to be dominated by men. To be equal men and women must have the same strength. The workplace is only for men and it's more important than the home. Every family needs two incomes to have a decent life. Being a housewife is an outdated and degrading career. Women should be financially dependent upon men. Household duties should be done only by the woman." These distorted views of women have been embedded in the minds of bias men for centuries that rely only on their own strength. Men win battles with strength, guns, and bullets; women win battles by love, warmth, and intuition. In anything involving competition men want to know whose side is a person on before they give aid to the wounded. A woman doesn't care about that. All she wants to know is "Where are you hurt?" Women ease themselves into roles and find out later all the sorrow that has taken place in a situation. They will sit up all night praying and tending to those who wounded in mind or have sorrows while a man is busy sleeping.

Women are a lot more perceptive than men give them credit for. A woman's mind is more analytical and searching than that of a man. They examine every situation in life. Most men can only focus on one thing at a time, while the woman's mind works overtime either negatively or positively. This is why women tend to gossip more than men do. A woman's spiritual mind has more contact with God and His spirit in the natural world than men. That's because her mind "woman's intuition," is more perceptive to her surroundings. Women have intuition to see things before they happen. Quite often women keep men from embarking on foolish escapades. This explains why men need women, and exemplifies the foolishness of men not listening. It's no wonder that in scripture, the word "wisdom" is often referred to as a "her" or as "a woman." But women can easily get paranoid. This is because they have so many thoughts racing through their mind, but when a crisis comes most women are better prepared than men are to meet it. Bearing pain is a part of their makeup, but women do more than just give birth. They bring joy, compassion, ideals, hope, and moral support to their family and friends. Women want to be the best for their family, their friends, and themselves. Their hearts break with sorrow at the loss of a family member, or when a friend dies. Yet, they are strong when others think that there is no strength left. They give and all they want back is love, a hug, and a smile. As women age they gain great wisdom. They search for meaning and connection to God in religion, intimacy, poetry, music, art, and meditation. The searching for inner peace makes them more sensitive, caring, and loving people than males. They are engaged in the present, which involves intimate relationships and fulfilling work. Instead of narrowing their horizon, they expand their range of experience and deepen their values. They all know that men are basically driven by testosterone, which has only one destination: sexual desire. Everything nice that a man does has an ulterior motive. Even when he displays humor, thoughtfulness, generosity, understanding, all of those affections are always linked to his most basic need. So when a man brings a woman flowers or says, "I love you" he may really mean what he said, but most of the time he is asking the question, "What am I going to get in return?"

It was only after the fall of Adam that the woman was (cursed) to be submissive to the man. (Genesis 3:16) It was also promised by God that Eve and all her daughters throughout history would struggle with contentment in their role of submission to their husbands. Today our society is battling for control, and dominance of the sexes. In our modern day society this promised conflict is called feminism. This is a gender war that's fought for respect and equality of women. Women are frequently caricatured as manipulative, pains, scheming, and controlling. Men are caricatured as insensitive, non-communicative, stupid brutes with one-track minds. The woman who succeeds in a man's world, although she is not expected to do so is rarely treated as a heroin. She is more often seen as being aggressive and acting like a man. She may well be aggressive, but no more than her male colleagues are. If she try to prove her worth by outdoing male colleagues in tough, male behavior and competition, she's looked upon as being a "dyke." Other women may feel compelled to behave in "feminine" or "maternal" ways to stay in favor with those who would otherwise punish them for stepping so far out of line. Women have a soft, gentle character about them. That's why it's easier for a woman to become a Christian rather than a man, because her heart is more responsive and tender to the pleadings of divine love and the Gospel. Women daily lives are a life of values, love, freedom, choice, satisfaction, sorrow, friendship, and memory. They know that time is too precious to waste on hate, envy, fear, anxiety, or indecision. After all, they've been through the revolution in gender roles, and much progress has been achieved for women on their watch, but they know the challenges have grown more complex. The world of working for a living is easier for their daughters, but living the life part is not.

 A woman is considered the weaker vessel, but without her ship in the forefront man would be on a collision course with eternity. That's why God uses her. Slavery, war, racism, and exploitation of women use to be common and in some places it still exist, but women should not let it cloud their experience or keep them from being a reputable, marketable, wife, mother and person; and not a servant. Yet,

There's Enough Woman Left to be Your Lady

we live in a time when motherhood is not so easy! Moms are expected to be great wives, great lovers, great mothers, great business partners, great influences on society, and available for everyone! Some women believe that they can "have it all," a brilliant career, money, a loving lifelong marriage, healthy children or no children, and happiness too. They believe that whatever awful things may have happened to women in the past, or still happen to "other" women today cannot happen to them, but women are not looked upon as serious contenders and aren't taken seriously. Mistakes made by men are more tolerated while women's slip-ups are exaggerated and made fun of. It hasn't been as hard for them to get to where they are as it has been to stay there. Even more difficult for some women is winding down after a stressful day. They are less tolerant with their family, spouse, and household duties. Most career women house's are always in a mess. Sometimes they feel resentful and jealous of their male counterparts, who are busy building their own careers and making money, while they have chosen to both work and take care of their family responsibilities. Thus, unlike her male counterpart a woman who has reached the top of her profession still has to basically do her job, be mom, and sometimes receive abuse from her spouse. The female chief of police, military general, or judge may not use what she's learned on the job to stop her husband from beating her or mentally abusing her. She's still part of womanhood and whatever she has learned at work won't override what she's learned all her life about being a woman. If she is blinded by love and has a strong willed husband her authority stops at the threshold of the home. Strong willed men sometimes break a "fragile" woman by handling her too rough, and when a woman cannot vent frustrations at home she does it at work by being too hard on employees or on people that has to stand in her presence. Some men forget that they have an heirloom in their possession that must be preserved. Women become broke when they fade into nothingness, and have lost interest in themselves, family, friends, activities, and the general welfare of their children. Sinful men have devalued women, and that's a result of the fall, but that doesn't mean that we must deny all differences between men and women. Both are equal before God, created in his image, but with different role distinctions. Women and men are equal in certain things, but not all things. Even when men and women do exactly the same thing, it means something different. The female employee not her male counter-part is still expected to buy gifts, and obtain food and entertainment for school or an office party, and arrange the boss' schedule. The father who changes his baby's diaper is often seen as a loving father. The mother who changes her baby's diaper is only doing what she's expected to do. "She delivered it so she is supposed to take care of it." That's a wrong way of thinking. Both parents gave the child life. Therefore both parents should equally share in its support in all things. When high-achieving professional women have children, they do so with husbands they can rely on. They work at jobs that have more workplace gender protections and better health care than most women do. They can afford to take time off work to spend with their infants and family. They also have major incentives to return to work and to continue their careers. As mothers, they have the highest labor-force participation rates, and contribute to the economy, all while raising kids who are likely to be as smart and successful as they are. They don't divorce as frequently and they don't have children out of wedlock. What we need are more high achieving women, so that one-day a woman will have the power to reorganize all workplaces to be more women and child-friendly. Women have goals, tenacity, and the capacity to go it alone because they have high self-esteem. Those who went into what were then unconventional jobs for women such as law, medicine, business, and economics encountered a lot of obstacles and stereotypes, including their own. The "Stained Glass Ceiling" is certainly an issue that engenders a great deal of emotion. Many of those beautiful stained glass windows are "stained" with prejudice. Many men today, are questioning the reasons for their own beliefs and want to "clean the dirty windows" of their past narrow-mindedness and change their present way of thinking. But no matter how many glass ceilings are shattered women are not catered to like men who are in the same position. The truth is, women are still far from free. Women are still likely to be pushovers for the slightest bit of maternal warmth that comes their way, but women need only a small amount of encouragement and compassion in order to keep going. Women who have endured any kind of glass ceiling should remember that glass can be shattered if one keeps striking it hard and long enough. When the stained glass ceiling that has kept most women from full service is broken they must pass through it without defensive arguments, or chips on their shoulder, but with truth that responds to the Lord's direction through love. Yes, women are still trying to do everything as they balance competing roles of being "wives" and professional workers, but with lots of encouragement, who knows how far they might go? Whether a woman leads a family, church, or corporation she still can make an impact on the world by choosing to be what God wants her to be. Every woman will not be a movie star, but she can shine from her pedestal in church work and in her own house. This is her stage upon which she receives her Oscar.

Praise God for women. In recent years, women have made some progress in social, political, and spiritual leadership roles. Less than a century ago it was unthinkable for a woman to be a governor, general, or a senator, nor did women have the right to vote in America. Now men say that it's ok for women to own businesses. It's okay for women to be doctors or lawyers. It's okay for women to be university presidents. But it's not okay for women to have positions of leadership in the church? They quote a few texts from Paul's letters governing roles of women in the church, but they don't state that the first convert in Asia was a woman. The first church in Asia met in Lydia's house. Lydia was not an apostle but she was a church leader. Priscilla was also a woman leader with a high profile. Priscilla, with her husband, Aquila, is mentioned seven times in the New Testament. Five of those times, Priscilla is mentioned first. It shows that Priscilla was a higher profile leader than her husband. Priscilla ministered side by side with Paul. She and her husband traveled with him. In Romans 16:3, Paul said, "greet Priscilla and Aquila, my fellow workers in Christ Jesus." This woman was a fellow-worker of Paul's who was worthy of being greeted by name. The gender issue of women roles in the ministry has great pains of exclusion. Some Bible teachers say women cannot lead men. Did you know that the traditional anti-woman-in-leadership position rests largely upon one verb that's used only once in the entire Bible, and that one reference is in verse one of 1 Timothy 2:12? The NIV translates it as: *"I do not permit a woman to teach or to have authority over a man; she must be silent."* There are many today that disqualify women from all of the church's leadership positions largely on the basis of that one verse. The question within the ecclesiastical realm shouldn't be whether women can be leaders, but is the church ready to receive women leaders? The most constant resistance that women have faced is from people who don't believe women belong in church leadership roles at all. A New Testament cultural bias of Paul's saying that a woman cannot teach a man prevents some people from seeing how God used women in the Bible. The traditional anti-woman-in-leadership interpretation of this verse is false because it's inconsistent with God's treatment of women in the rest of the Bible. God has blessed and used numerous women in his kingdom. Miriam, Huldah, Anna, and others were preachers and prophets. Deborah led the whole nation of Israel. She was a religious, civil, and military leader. Throughout history the Bible plainly has allowed women to preach and have authority over men. Paul himself allowed women to teach and respected them in leadership. He allowed Lydia to persuade to him to start the Philippian church at her house. He called Priscilla a fellow worker. He gave greetings to Phoebe the deacon. In Romans 16:1 Paul said: *"I commend to you our sister Phoebe, a servant of the church in Center."* The word "servant" in the New Testament means "Deacon." Deacons were church leaders. Phoebe was likely a deacon in the Cenchrean church. Paul had no need to commend a person who merely cleared tables or cooked meals. He likely commended her for her leadership as a deacon. Paul knew and respected women in leadership. False teaching about the role of women is rampant in the church. Centuries of Biblical curse-oriented prejudices are hard to change. How many godly, capable women have been told that on the basis of God's word they cannot preach, give testimony, teach men, be authors, lead worship, be pastors, serve on church boards, vote in church business meetings, be Sunday School superintendents, or work in any occupations where they supervise men?

The church has been extremely hard on women, but where would the church be without women? Each area in the church is unique, and each has different needs and talents for its women. Look around in church assemblies, and you'll see that they are mostly comprised of women, but many aspects of women lives are affected by spousal violence at home, and ecclesiastical violence from the pulpit. Some women are oppressed in vast areas of the world, and some churches are imposing more restrictions on them by refusing to allow them to preach. Not everyone agrees that women are also called to be servants of God, but there are only two types of Christians: male and female. There should not be two different standards to live by. Both sexes have one Savior, one faith, and one way to God. Women are not the weaker half, nor the stronger half, but the other half of man. Woman was not called to be the second half of a mortgage payment, nor was she created to just "stand" by her man. A woman's function is not just to fix supper, please a man, and have babies. God wants women equipped and used in ministry. Ministry is a team effort and it will take everyone to make an impact on the gospel. Certainly women are second-class citizens in many places, but they have a first class impact. They are the backbone of the church. Every pastor knows the value of women in leadership, without women ministry no church could survive. If women did not show up for service on Sunday mornings there would hardly be anyone there to receive the gospel. The church would be empty. Women voices are rooted in a Church where passion for God and Jesus is heard and seen in the songs, preaching, dancing, and daily at-home meditations. They have struggled with the church and the Bible, but not with the freestyle celebratory worship of the Church. Their struggle has been with the Christian Church's position regarding the treatment of women, and people of color whom dances in the Spirit and speaks in tongues. The demonization of women, the strength of women, and the increasing disparity of class are causing a power struggle within the church. The attacks in the church are coming from within and outside the church. Satan is the driving force behind the suffering that women are experiencing. He attacks because he knows that they belong to the living God. So when they are slandered or falsely accused at their jobs, homes, and in the church there is no good-humored explanation for it. Perhaps they were slandered and falsely accused because they were doing a better job than someone else. The Apostle Peter focus on the danger of attacks from unbelievers against believers and Satanic work that come from within the professing church, *"But false prophets also arose among the people, just as there will also be false teachers among you, who will secretly introduce destructive heresies. Many will follow their sensuality, and because of them the way of truth will be maligned; and in their greed they will exploit you."* (2 Peter 2:1-3) Prayer and a deep sense of calling have motivated women to persist through the toughest of times in religious persecution. In the beginning both man and woman were given the commandment to *"subdue the earth,"* but after Eve was seduced in the Garden of Eden man was given complete authority. Yet, man has allowed the snake of corruption to raise its ugly head and slitter all over God's blessed creation again. Therefore, God is passing the reins of leadership over to Eve to help man rule. Many people have a problem with women leaders. One of the greatest needs among God's people today is to stop debating over dogma, creeds, and doctrine. Believers in Christ need to stop bickering over who is the greatest, or who is right and who is wrong in the church, and did God call women to preach. There are too many other sociological and spiritual matters that need to be addressed. Often men feel intimidated by a female's presence, but gender discrimination is rooted in misunderstanding and fear, which creates feelings of jealousy and intimidation. Denying leadership roles to women is rooted in the attitude, "Well that's the way I was taught." It's so easy to look at everybody in your church and in other churches and say, "Well, we should be doing this, but this was the way we were taught." If you look closely at yourself you will see that the problem with churches and society is apathy, and tolerance of incomplete obedience to the Word of God. Apathy leads to apostasy. What is apostasy? It's when we turn our backs on what we know to be true, which causes the church to begin arguing over petty stuff that can lead to anarchy. When a person is drowning he or she doesn't care whether it's a woman or man who saves them or throw them a life jacket. The same should be for preaching the gospel to those drowning in the sea of sin.

Some church officials view women as nobody's. A burden has been placed upon women to show them worthy of being accepted into leadership positions in the church. Women have bent over backwards trying to fit in, while male pastors have sit around in their palatial offices, or convention meetings playing scriptural politics, and debating whether or not God has called women to preach. But while they are debating God is steadily using women in astronomical numbers to get his word out. God is using women because Revelation Adam (end time man) has failed to keep the charge that his father Genesis Adam (beginning man) was given. Revelation Adam also has placed fault in his Eve for the trouble that plagues the world. However, God is not interested in who gets the snake out of the garden, he just wants to get it out of the lives of people. He wants people to walk without fear of being bitten with the poison of sin. Beyond the physical and emotional consequences for women directly affected, ecclesiastical violence also impacts societies medical, social, and psychological systems. Some male ministers have forgotten that they too had an Exodus experience, but they haven't come completely out of Egypt. Egypt means bondage. When male ministers refuse to acknowledge God's women as messengers of God they are in exile. They must come out of this body of sin and ignorance. It's time for the church and male ministers to make an exodus toward healing hurts of women in the gospel. They should release God's anointed women and let them go preach the gospel. Women are needed to help lift up the cross of the Lord Jesus Christ to this parched, dry, thirsty, and dying world. There's no quota system as to how many people or gender is used to point indiscreet dying men and women to Jesus. Male pastors have to get out of their bent over, bloody issue, dead on their feet stance against women dispensing the word of God. It's time that they took an inventory of their own faith. The church must be careful in dictating whom God has called. The unified shout of women should be "Doctor cure yourself!"

The Lord Jesus Christ is the greatest liberator of women! He demanded that women be treated with dignity in marriage, and not as mere concubines for man's enjoyment. (Matthew 19:3-12) Jesus taught female disciples and entrusted women to carry His message. At Pentecost, the Lord reaffirmed that in the last days, women would preach. There were female teachers, prophets, deacons, and apostles in the New Testament church. Through the apostle Paul, Jesus tells us that women are just as important to the church as men are. *"For as many of you as have been baptized into Christ have put on Christ. There is neither Jew nor Greek, there is neither bond, nor free, there is neither male nor female: for we all one in Christ Jesus."* (Galatians 3:27-28). Since the Apostle Paul said, *"There is neither male nor female in Christ,"* then in 1 Corinthian 14:33-35 the same word for silence would apply to the men at the Corinthian assembly as well. This would make the husband the head of his wife in the home, but not in the church. The Hebrew word for man is *ish*, and for woman it's *ishah*. Ishah literally means, *"she-man."* Because Eve was taken from the womb of man (his side) thus we get the word *"woman."* The English word woman is an abbreviation of the Anglo-Saxon word that means *"the man with the womb."* Women are humans with wombs who complete and complement men. Maleness and femaleness are complementary and completing traits, not hierarchical and competing traits. During the time of Jesus Christ, with the institution of the new covenant, the paradigms for ministry changed. Men and women worked together in the New Testament church to serve Jesus Christ in building the body of the church. Women in the New Testament church were allowed and even encouraged to participate in proclaiming the gospel of the Savior. They were not ordained, but they were not afraid to speak openly to other men and women in the church with knowledge and faith in their own homes, and at the river while doing the wash. Priscilla even filled Apollos in on some of the areas where he was lacking understanding, such as on the subject of the Holy Spirit. Women such as Priscilla, Dorcas, and Lydia were active and visible members of this new church. They had a ministry of loving, compassionate service. With those New Testament pioneers as their spiritual heritage, women today who are stirred by the same Spirit to serve Christ have a need to be encouraged and equipped to do good works. Christian women today are better educated and have more skills. They want to be heard and not just seen. They desire to be involved in their churches in areas where they can use those skills and abilities. It should be clear that (1 Corinthians 14:33-35) is not a universal formula for worship services. It was written to meet a specific type of assembly through which the word of God was prophesied at that time. A woman is part of the royal priesthood of believers. (1 Peter 2:5) As a Christian she is expected to participate in worshipping the Lord through singing, praising and teaching. It should also be clear that Paul was dealing with the needs of the infant church at Corinth during the apostolic age. In fact, there were some contexts in which even women, through the inspiration of the Holy Spirit, prophesied. The evangelist Philip had four virgin daughters who prophesied. (Acts 21:8,9) Women may help in teaching the gospel even if it involves teaching a man. Priscilla helped Aquila teach Apollos the gospel more perfectly. (Acts 18:26) We expect that Priscilla quietly and humbly helped Aquila convince young Apollos of the full gospel. She clearly did not brazenly or presumptuously has authority over him. But she was an important part of a dynamic teaching team. Praise God, that the New Testament has been completed for us today. We no longer rely on men through the inspiration of the Holy Spirit, to prophesy among us. Today, we preach the word that was given to us through the agency of the Holy Spirit and the Spirit uses whom He will. Women seek for meaning and purpose in life through their relationships with the Spirit. Women ministry should be interwoven into the very fabric of the church, and it should be under the leadership of a church pastor that would serve all the members. The endorsement of women's ministry is highest among those who have been powerfully touched by anointed women. Any preacher, or church that silences women attempts a monopoly of God's voice and power, but will be found to silence the Holy Spirit. They will have to give an account.

8

A Stranger in Paradise

In the Garden of Eden both male and female was given power over all things on and in the earth. (Genesis 1:26-28) Yet, man is just a little world that consists of heaven, earth, soul, and body. Over dispensations of time man have developed an attitude of superiority in his position as caretaker of the world. Because of his elevated status man has forgotten that God still owns the earth and that He walks in His garden in the *"cool"* of the day. Man has become immune to the presence of God. He has shut his eyes and hearing to the word of God. Most worldly men and some of those that are in church want to be self-governed and make rules as they go along. Man's desire is to not just be a part of God's plan for creation, but to rule alone over all creation without the input of woman. The church has also built a wall of defense against the world in seeking protection against a decadent society, social conditions, and a culture that's corrupted by sin. Yet, it fails to realize that the greatest danger is from within. Anointed women are in danger from those who profess to be teaching truth and to belong to Christ, but who are feasting on the innocence of the flock, corrupting them, and luring them into all kinds of vile activities. Wolves in sheep's clothing have infiltrated the garden of believers, and are masquerading as angels of light, yet teach hatred governing the roles of women in the church. These emissaries of the devil are working from within trying to undermine the work of God, lead believers astray, and to destroy the testimony of the church. We are often socially and civilly involved in making compromises with those whom we doctrinally disagree. However, some church members think that the pressures from outside are so great, that they need to join in spiritual alliance with those who opposes women working in the church; despite their own differences of opinion. What they really do is invite the devil into the camp so that his work can be done from the inside. This is a far greater danger than attacks from the outside. God takes it personally. Therefore, He's cultivating women in various ways to carry His message. Some are in the blooming stage while others have come full circle. Solomon tells us that, *"He has made everything beautiful in its time and that there is a time for everything, and a season for every activity under Heaven."* (Ecclesiastes 3:1-11) Some women refuse to believe that this is their "season" or God's time to use women in a profound way. Yes, God's time has come for the emancipation of women, but some women are like caves. They have a secret entrance and exit, and are buried deep within a mountain of despair. They can be cold, abandoned, hollow, and drafty chambers, filled with indifference. Many women have been kept down for so long, and hiding in caves of isolation, fear, and loneliness that they often don't want to get up in front of an audience. They would rather serve behind the scenes, but a "behind the scene" woman doesn't have any role, respect, or authority in the church or in society. Some born again women have been asked many times by the Lord to do something, and they have thought, "Who me? I'm not talented enough. I'm not good enough. Why doesn't He ask someone better than me to do this?" It's difficult to convey to women who have relegated themselves to inferior status, or even used misunderstood Bible passages, not to stoop to a subservient position. When stooping under any circumstance it means that a person has been robbed of his or her joy and blessings. These women are getting so lost in the product that they're forgetting about the process and the workings of God. They need to set aside human reasoning and logic and just take a leap of faith. Most of time that women spent in the wilderness of ecclesiastical confusion was a time for soul searching and grieving their ministry. Some thought that it was time to move on, and began to seek another call. They were not at all prepared to hear that the pastoral committee was not interested in their candidacy. Those words were especially difficult to accept when a congregation seemed to be particularly suited to her gifts, but didn't want to call a woman as pastor in any capacity. Perhaps she would have found the rejection easier to bear if another woman had received a call.

God is a loving Father who brings about both the good and the bad, and tenderly guides His children through the difficult places. He wants each of us to know that there is a time when He will restore things done in our lives in order to demonstrate His gracious hand in our lives. *"I will restore to you the years that the locust have eaten, the cankerworm, and the caterpillar, and the palmerworm, my great army that I sent among you."* (Joel 2:25) There are seasons in all our lives that involve times of famine that have a divine purpose. These seasons involve things that by only being in hard places could accomplish, but when those hard places have accomplished their purpose, God begins to restore.

God did this with the nation of Israel after a season of famine and devastation. If God has taken you through a time of leanness, be glad, rejoice in the Lord your God. Know that He is the restorer of that which the locusts have eaten. He will send you abundant showers of autumn and spring rains. Your threshing floors will be filled with grains, and your vats will overflow with new wine and oil. He will repay you for the years the locusts have eaten your testimony and destroyed your spirit. You will have plenty to eat, until you are full, and you will praise the name of the Lord your God, who has worked wonders for you. Wait patiently for Him to bring this about in your life. He will do it.

Every woman has a ministry. Whatever they do to serve other people is a ministry. Opportunities for female ministers are scarce. Antiquated and Draconian beliefs have caused a glass ceiling and walls quite evident to gender to be put up, but actually women are "workhorses" compared to their male counterparts. God put *"called out"* women in the right place at the right time for His purpose. Women have spiritual needs that only other women can help fulfill. Women's ministry is not about pastoring a church, giving sermons or being ordained. It's about helping other women of the church to use their gifts to help spread the word of God. When called by God to preach His word women should not compete in authority with men, yet they should treat them as men, and make them feel like men when they are in a woman's presence. The word "authority" in Greek means, "to beget, project, and stand forth with power and dignity." Authority in the Lord provides the guidance that enables other believers to mature and find answers. However, the greatest aberration most clergywomen ever have to face is actually walking in their God given authority, or the "supervising" that has been given to them. They hesitate to take it. Only God enables and selects leaders whom he will, and then equips them to rule according to His will.

There's Enough Woman Left to be Your Lady

A woman's goal shouldn't be to convince others that she's gifted or called, and she can't decide to "call" herself or fight for recognition. She must know that she is called, and just be the person that God has called. She must remember that it's the anointing of God and not people attitudes that she's called to represent. She isn't set apart just to challenge the system, or to debate minority rights. As a woman, mother, wife, and preacher it's very important that when the spirit of God is working in her that she understands the end result and not the reason why she was chosen. Obviously God has a blessing in store for her. Anointed women control the flow of the Lord's blessings by what they're willing to receive and allow into their lives. A woman has to be willing to be used by God. But if she never ask the Lord for his blessings, they are withheld. Christian women can become "bound" by trying to prove that they are God's "man" for the situation. They need to accept the fact that it is okay to be God's "woman" for the situation. A woman should not try to be anything other than a woman. A woman who walks close to the Lord will be secure in the knowledge of who she is, what rights are hers, and she will have great freedom and peace within her heart and mind. She will know the joy of being a total woman in God's plan. Jesus' death tore the secrecy of the veil in the priesthood, and made born again saints a priesthood of all believers. All members of the body of Christ have been endowed with spiritual gifts, and He empowers us to use them. Jesus did not hold anyone back, but offered the opportunity of kingdom work to women as well as men. Women represent a vast pool of gifts and energy, and if the church is to grow and do all it can to advance the kingdom of God, it must follow Christ's example. It's vital to the health and growth of a church that male leadership provide every member the chance to recognize, develop, and use his or her spiritual gifts. God has given gifts to women and he expects them to use those gifts. When coming out of their cave women need to learn to trust each other spiritually, and stop being so jealous of the way God uses another woman. With a bit of trust, they can practice open confession, instead of keeping their sins and weaknesses locked up inside. Overtime women spend way too many years competing with each other over numerous and superfluous things. They should concentrate on compromise, and faithfully start each day together with prayer. Women in the church grow through personal nurturing received by other women's groups, Bible studies, and prayer group. They are limited only by their creativity and energy. God's anointed women are facilitators, but they should learn how to pray, nurture, trust, encourage, and open up to each other to become better friends. Other women will begin to see their gifts and vision and think of ways that they can help each other on their spiritual journey. Women's ministry can enable women to recognize their gifts and provide an atmosphere in which to exercise them. The leadership skills that they have been practicing at church, home, or at work will have a chance to emerge or shine more brightly through the opportunities that arise in women's ministry. Holding on to Jesus in spite of the church's view toward women, and the tortured interpretations of scripture used to mortally wound women faith. Some women have become a casualty, and have paid the ultimate sacrifice in the war against women. What plagues a woman most is never knowing: "If I'm right?" "If I'm doing the right things," or "Am I making the right choices." Not that there is a single, straightforward "right," but women and minorities think that there is a lot of "wrong," by so much of what they see in society. The savage inequalities between classes, races, genders, and sexual orientations seems more wrong than right. Women still have to fight unimaginably hard for each small gain. However, women must learn how to sidestep some blows and endure the unavoidable ones, by keeping their eyes open, maintaining clarity and naming each blow accurately for what it is. They must remember that they have not caused their own pain, and it's psychologically crucial that they don't blame themselves, and not to automatically take things personally. The truth is that many so-called personal things are quite impersonal. When faced with the bitter pain of personal attack believers should entrust their case to the Lord. But before they shrug their shoulders and walk away they need to ask some important questions. Is the criticism justified? Do I need to hear what's being said? Is there a sin I am involved in? Is there a problem I have not admitted? Am I misunderstanding what's being said? Is the other person saying something out of concern and love that I am taking as an attack? Did they mean something different than what was meant? Two different people can say, "You look nice today" and people will respond in two different ways. Some may be flattered by the first person's remark, and others may assume that the second person meant, "You look nice today... for a change." They are reading more into the comments than what was meant. This is overreacting and that's a deformity. It shows that a person is bent out of shape in attitude, but anything that's deformed and bent can be transformed, and straightened into a thing of beauty if it so desire. All it takes is a small seed of belief.

Women are a resource for pastors, but all pastors don't know or appreciate the worth of God's anointed vessel. However, women should not assume that men are the enemy. It's spiritual wickedness in high places that's trying to hold them back. The Devil knows that women are a force to reckon with when it comes down to preaching and serving the Lord. Therefore, he tries to silence them as often as he can by using a high official in the church to not recognize women ministry. Women's ministry involves extraordinary impassioned women seeking a deeper level of intimacy in Christ. Their desire is to obtain complete satisfaction with

Christ as they discover their identity in Him. They have found it at the feet of Jesus. Gathering to fellowship gives women the opportunity to share their lives, burdens, and aspirations with one another. Strong bonds of love and compassion are formed. Sometimes amongst laughter and sometimes amongst tears their hearts become knit together in prayer. If you are a Christian woman that feels suppressed, don't feel that way anymore! You shouldn't automatically assume that God doesn't want you serving in Church. God is the one who called, anointed, and gave you gifts for your ministry. Woman, you have tremendous value! It doesn't matter if you are not physically pretty or if you have many spiritual gifts or few. What does matters is that you love God, and that you use all the gifts God has given you for his glory, and that you allow the spirit of Jesus Christ to give you a godly character. Get the chip off your shoulder, and be filled with fruits of the Spirit. Don't let your culture or society keep you from your calling. Even though Jesus knew that a prophet wasn't recognized in his own hometown, he continued to declare the Gospel there. You might not be accepted either, but keeping on preaching with fervor and remember what your predecessor in the Gospel said, *"...But His Word was in mine heart as a burning fire shut up in my bones, and I was weary with forbearing, and I could not stay (quiet)."* (Jeremiah 20:9)

Man's world is empty without woman. The whole sum of Christian living is where women are one hundred percent involved as men. Selecting four or five women out of a congregation of a thousand during the worship hour, and giving them some public function to fulfill, would do nothing at all to express the fact that the Christian life is full time, and women as well as men are devoted to it. If man could shed his ego and woman put away her fears the church could have a devastating effect on the world. Paving a road less traveled by women has not been an easy task. For women it has been a life long journey. Trying to find their way, following the Light, and refusing to believe Jesus didn't love them is the foundation of their preaching. Women are desperate people on the margins of society, who are struggling to make sense of their lives. They find God in the struggle for equality, parity, and justice. Their struggle is the long, strong, deep, resonant bass that all men preach, sing, and pray about. *"Through many dangers toils and snares"*...is foundational to their worship, and the locus of their passion. Faith based sermons help to build self-worth and self-value in the lives of people who have often been stripped of all that's righteous. Women bear obstacles and trials on the road to success in a male-dominated profession, but there's no need to disempower male members of the church, and men should not become so angry in that they that view women as the enemy. We simply cannot forget about such things as masculinity and femininity in the name of equality, but we should concentrate on what it means to be human beings. There are differences between male and female that go beyond the biological part of humanity. The church should expect to have a large group of angry women in the near future; who will wonder why seminaries gave them easy entrance, but failed to prepare them for the struggle of being recognized as preachers. They will be disillusioned by church officials who refuse to recognize their ministry, and angry with denominational Pastors and Bishops who refuse to fight for their placement. They will also feel betrayed by women peers. Therefore, women will have to learn how to struggle by struggling to get somewhere. Women may have to get themselves together to talk about their strategic problems in order to involve more women, and often without the aid of men to help fight their battle. However, it is not their outward power, and it's not what they do, but it's who they are as a group that is the force. A woman condition shapes and motivates her. When women are unified it shows an active part of solidarity. They are very attentive to things that try to divide them, or create negative differences. They stress cooperation within their ranks, and at all cost they try to avoid conflict. Yes, women are experiencing Babylonian exile right in the church. But God will lead them out of captivity towards their own land, and then there will be a new day in "Babylon." God will thoroughly sweep, garnish, houseclean, and purge the church of oppression of women and sexism. The relationship of ecclesiastical struggles within the church will cease. The old order of doing God's business has to be destroyed in order to bring about change. By the rivers of "Babylon" the Willow shall stop its weeping, and women will hang up their harps of sorry and neglect. They will not say like the Israelites, "How can I sing the Lord's song in a strange Land," for they will no longer have to sing sad songs such as, *"I'm Pressing On."* They will not have any more burdens to share or bear. Women will see the sunrise and redeemers will walk the earth. They shall not go out with fear and trembling, but with great joy and triumph. Their journey home over the mountains shall be sweet and pleasant. The hills, mountains, and all of its inhabitants shall not hold their peace, even the trees of the plains shall burst forth in acclamations and applause, and shall sway with wild abandonment as they bid women welcome when they come into their own land. God will raise friends to women where there had been enemies. *"Woman"* shall have a name whereby she will be known, praised, and respected. God shall give her bones rest from the sickness and labor under which she has been chastised, and will make a great change in men character toward women. He shall raise up foundations of God-fearing men and women, who will work side by side for the promotion of women in the gospel, that will continue for many generations to come. There is a new beginning for men and women to be full, equal, and respectful partners in society and the church; the way it was always meant to be. Women redemption shall be for the promise that relates to the time of the end of the gospel age. If born again men can't see the hand of God in women struggle for recognition in the gospel, or believe that God will make it all right for women; then they cannot see God at all. When bias and jealous men fully understand the possibilities of women's ministry, it will be like finding a buried treasure. That treasure will turn out to be in the beauty of God's feminine design and what they are able to accomplish with His gift. As men speak out in favor of women leaders in the church, I think that they will be amazed to see how many other people will get up and stand beside them.

Godly women desire's are to be in a New Testament congregation where godly men rule through the word of God. Women are seeking a deep longing for spiritual connection, and respect from dominant leaders within the church. At prayer meetings each man should be sitting on the edge of his seat waiting for an opportunity to pray, and women in particular want it to be so. It shows a lack of spiritual leadership when women look to one another and say, "Why don't the men pray?" However, when there are pauses and silences in prayer, it's as much an invitation for women to pray as it is for their silent husbands and spiritual brothers. When Christian women pray men seem to be blessed in some special way by hearing them intercede. Even though sometime women's voices may be too soft to be heard, they still introduce affection and devoted earnestness into the prayer meeting, which is a God-given grace. Praying women will take any task and turn it into a trophy victory for the glory of God. Although God created woman last she's first in the hearts of all mankind. Women have truly become "Mother of all living." The church of Christ would surely fold if it were not for the work and support of women. It seems as if God has ordained women for a special type of work in missions and charities." Women can counsel and get money from some of the worst of people. That's because they have an extra supply of faith. When God says to her in time of crisis or need, "You go into that bank or credit union and get the money." She doesn't ask why or how, she just goes by faith, and trusts in the Lord to give her a blessing. All the saints of God should say, "I'm going to have whatever I want if it's God's will." Women are the strong bearing the burdens of the weak. So women please pray!

Men should pray in particular to be men of prayer and faithfulness to the gospel, because they have careers, and are out of the home all day. Men are more aggressive and are vulnerable to certain temptations. They want to climb the corporate ladder, and do well in their vocations, which puts them into more places of temptation than women. Generally speaking women are not as enticed by the excitements and temptations of the world as the men that they are married to. They are more conscious of their children and their homes; they treasure more highly the values of domestic peace, reliability, faithfulness, and trust. For many Christian women their homes and children are their careers. They have committed themselves to their homes and families, and they exemplify Christians loving their neighbors as themselves. Yet God says, *"Nevertheless, I have this against you: You tolerate that woman Jezebel, who calls herself a prophetess. By her teaching she misleads my servants into sexual immorality and the eating of food sacrificed to idols."* Revelation 2:20

One of the most major, ruling, and destructive spirits opposing the Kingdom of God, and influencing the church today is the spirit of Jezebel. It has dominion over many aspects of society including the marketplace and the entertainment industry. It predominantly lives in females, but is not always gender specific. The spirit of Jezebel is best seen

There's Enough Woman Left to be Your Lady

in the story of Naboth's garden in First Kings 21. In this story King Ahab desires to purchase some land next to the king's palace. Naboth refuses to sell. When Jezebel hears of this, she embarrasses Ahab, telling him he should be ashamed because he is the king and has every right to the land. She promptly plots against Naboth to get the land for the king. This leads to Naboth's murder. Ahab does not know of this plot by his wife, but when the king shows up to claim the land, the prophet Elijah shows up too and pronounces judgment on Ahab and his wife. In this passage we see that God held Ahab ultimately responsible for the death of Naboth.

The Jezebel spirit is born of jealousy, witchcraft, and rebellion that seek to manipulate, or intimidate with the intent to dominate women. It's one of the most common spirits in operation today, and is a powerful enemy of the body of Christ. She operates freely on sincere believers whose hearts are for God individually, and has also attained positions of power within the Church. It functions as a "controlling" spirit, and prophesies "nice" things in order to control. Jezebel is in full operation in controlling spirits in the church, the family, and the land. This spirit establishes its stronghold primarily in women; however, many men have been victimized by it as well. Jezebel's many avenues of control reach deep into the religious, economical, and political systems. Her manipulations and witchcraft's are many, and she is a seducer of God's women working in the ministry. She masquerades as a prophetess, but she's after the prophets because they expose her. The spirit of Jezebel seeks to destroy true worship, family, morality, and God-ordained leadership. It misleads and corrupts the Church, and seeks to neutralize the lives of prophets, pastors, and other leadership. Submission to her spirit can cause people to believe a lie and come under deception. If a church allows her gossip, slander, and anger to simply be overlooked and rationalized it can bring sadness and torment, put members in a sickbed, or divide the church. Some members will excuse the divisions by telling themselves that God is purging the church. God's people need to know and recognize the Jezebel spirit of which there are two main personality types. The high-profile type is generally outspoken and highly visible. She's often seen as the "woman who wears the pants in the family." The low-profile type is generally soft-spoken, giving the illusion of being solicitous, motherly, protective, and even very submissive. The low-profile type is the most dangerous because she's difficult to discern. She relies heavily on manipulation for her power, but she does it in an extremely subtle way. Jezebel hates men and distrusts women. She cannot have a true godly relationship with men, because her underlying desire is to strip them of all their perceived power and then destroy them. Jezebels are desirous of moving up the ladder wherever they are. Jezebel type women are often natural leaders whose ultimate goal is always control. Therefore, they can be found serving "at the feet" of prominent leaders, and despising them at the same time, even in the church. Jezebel's true desire is to wrest the power from the person being served. If that person is prophetic in nature, the actual mission is to destroy his credibility, or undermine his authority. The deception or seduction of Jezebel is often so successful that the leader does not recognize who is at his right hand. Often subtle and deceptive, Jezebel type women are proud, independent, and rebellious. They end up friendless with other women unless they find friends that are powerful and are useful to them to gain power. Other than that lasting friendships are rare. A Jezebel type woman is extremely authoritarian "bossy" by nature. She is easily offended if her authority is questioned, and will often respond in anger at even the slightest offense. Perfectionism is a common characteristic and she despises others around her who fails to meet her expectation and demand for complete submission. This is an excuse for disrespect toward others, especially those in authority, but to her no one "measure up" so she doesn't have to show respect. If someone does try she despises that person, or casts him or her aside when she has what she wants. Nothing pleases this spirit. Anyone attempting to relate to a person with this spirit is literally in a no-win situation. Jezebel's loud, stubborn, adulteress, and manipulative spirit is in the government, church, and family. She seduces and ultimately wants to destroy men's souls. One of the main reasons that Jezebel is so active is because Ahabs (spineless men) have permitted it. Jezebels cause fear, flight, and discouragement, but they cannot live and operate unchallenged without the Ahabs who allow them to be effective. Ahab type men fail to operate as godly, loving leaders. Rather, they give in to pressure from the Jezebels, often due to their own insecurities and sexual needs. When there is rebellion in the bedroom, there are problems in the rest of the house. Because the family priesthood has been destroyed, the husband is bound by his own inability to effectively stand in his rightful position as head of his family. Men should not use this knowledge as a license to lord over or control women, but understand that this spirit opposes God's design of the two equal but distinct roles for men and women.

The greatest help in winning this battle and getting deliverance is for a family to get the Ahab and Jezebel spirit out of the home. If you are in any way controlling family and friends, or if someone else is controlling you, chances are the Jezebel spirit needs to be dealt with. If you find yourself confronting this spirit, ask the Lord to give you discernment and wisdom. For the woman who is influenced by the Jezebel spirit the answer to defeating it is true repentance, humility, and brokenness before God. Being broken is the first principle of Divine life. The "Jezebeled" woman must firmly stand against the sexual exploitation of this spirit by fasting, praying, and calling upon the blood of Jesus to come out from under bondage. The devil loves chaos, he doesn't care how it's caused in your life, but you've got to smite the rock. Yield to God and cry, "Yes Lord, smite this thorny heart. Let your Word break me to pieces and make me as clay in the potter's hands." Bleeding causes healing! You must fight for your garden or barley field. Defend it. Don't stand on the outside looking in. It's yours by right. It's your inheritance. Stand in the middle of it. Fight for your family, your husband, and your land. Don't allow the enemy to destroy what belongs to you! There is an Elijah ministry coming forth in the earth. It's an army that will come against the Ahab and Jezebel spirit in the church. God promises to deliver His people from Jezebel, and bring her to nothing. He is going to judge and burn her with His fire of vengeance! The Spirit of the Lord is rising up to destroy this lethal spirit and release the people of God for His Kingdom plan and purposes. God chose a holy woman to bring man's only hope (Jesus) into the world. He is the reason for the hope that's in other women and in the gospel. Women should be encouraged for service in the Kingdom of God. They are useful and valuable, yet they own less than one percent of the World's property even though they work sixty percent of all the hours worked. Of the available world income, women receive only ten percent. It may be a man's world, but in God's kingdom women are not second-class citizens. God is presently calling women to the full redemption for which they were created and which He purchased for them on Calvary. He wants a woman to walk in the fullness of the original, pre-Fall relationship that she had with Him as well as with Adam. When the Lord Jesus redeems a family, most of the time he first saves a wife and then her husband. He restores this Adam and Eve pre-fall relationship in their home every single time. Everything that's bullish, authoritarian, and domineering in the man the Lord Jesus begins to remove, and everything that's rebellious and coquettish in the woman he also removes. For people who want to neglect women, minorities, the poor, silence their voice, and deny their existence; may God give us the voice to speak to them in the name of love, and to offer them peace. So that when the world has beaten them down, destroyed their spirit, and crucified their life they can also seek the love of Jesus. Men everywhere need to lift up holy hands in prayer for women. Holy hands down through time has been a universal symbol of surrender. In reality, holy hands are merely a symbol of a surrendered and holy heart before God. However, holy hands raised in worship to God are meaningless unless our hearts are holy as well. A holy man, who can pray, but refuses to pray, deprives his home and church congregation of God's intercessions. Be encouraged anointed women. God has a high calling for your life! There's enough woman left to be His Lady.

9

Just A Touch from the Master's Hand

Expecting more patients Jesus settled down in his office on the seashores and mountains. From there he healed bodies both physically and spiritually, and wrote prescriptions for sin. There were great multitudes that stopped by his open-air office seeking a cure. He had admitted all sorts of people into his practice; the poor as well as the rich were welcomed, and there was always room for new patients. Jesus' practice never involved using chemicals, shots, or pills. Such was the power and anointing of Jesus that all he had to do was either speak or look upon a sick person, and they would be healed. The key to being healed was to seek him, believe in him, submit to him, and then lay at his feet, to be ruled by him at his pleasure. Most people that came to Jesus were concerned only about their bodily ailments. Few were concerned about their soul's spiritual diseases, but

Jesus also worked on their spiritual ailment. People that were healed glorified God. God always must be acknowledged with our praises and thankfulness, for sin has turned the world into a hospital of spiritually blind, dumb, and maimed people whose only cure is to get a good dose of the Holy Ghost. Jesus knew that demonic forces mentally challenged some of his patients. The mentally ill are people that have accumulated vast amount of hurt in their lives. Their hurt has been around a long time. Some have been abused, denied love, came from broken homes, and dabbled in drugs or alcohol. They lack identity, emotional security, and a tremendous sense of guilt, but Jesus came with authority to unloose the shackles of mental bondage, and to undo the chains of spiritual defeat. The mentally ill that Jesus encountered was definitely upset whenever he came into contact with them, but long-term separation can lead to feelings of hatred. A man who lived in caves and was demonically influenced to separate himself from others expressly showed it. This is validated by such questions as "What have you to do with us, O Son of God?" Have you come to torment us?" (Luke 8:27-35) This man had devils in him for a long time that were strong and had kept him away from people. The demons isolated him to keep him from receiving news from the outside world; news that possibly could have given him some hope. Isolation equals guilt. It's an attempt to cut off the part of the personality that we don't want to admit as being part of ourselves. That's why most women seek to remove themselves from the public when something bad has happened in their lives. They want to hide their face from the truth. Many women have compartmentalized and shut up their life. They use drugs, alcohol, tranquilizers, sex, and inappropriate language to mask their fear. They live in constant fear of being discovered for who and what they are.

Alcoholism and Women

Alcohol abuse is a serious problem that leads to a variety of serious health and psychiatric problems. Chronic alcohol problems involve social problems that manifest directly from alcoholism: marital conflict, domestic violence, child abuse, panhandling, thievery, destruction of the family, and community cohesion. Those at risk for developing alcohol addiction are individuals who experience a lot of stress in their lives, have difficulty coping, have easy access to alcohol, and are encouraged to drink by their social environment. Alcoholism is especially likely when individuals grow up with one or more alcoholic parents. While the rates of alcoholism are relatively low amongst women, they do face the challenge of coping with the alcoholism of their male spouses. Most male alcoholics tend to be violent and in denial of their problem. Alcoholics blame and manipulate others to maintain their lifestyle and avoid consequences of their drinking. Their family may also be affected by "codependency" which is the tendency of family members to protect the alcoholic and take on alcoholic-like characteristics, such as denial, blaming, and rationalizing dysfunctional behaviors. Black women must be extremely aware of some of the sources of depression unique to them, which contribute to their turning to alcohol as a coping mechanism. Stress, depression, racism, sexual exploitation, increasingly poor relationships between Black women and men, alienation from traditional African American values such as spirituality, and being taken seriously are often factors that are cited. Because an alcoholic woman often compromises her principles and morals due to her compulsive behavior, she can feel spiritually, and patriotically empty. African American men and women typically don't feel powerful in U.S. society. Their "powerlessness" may lack the empowering effect it has for others, no matter what position that they hold in an occupational field. For Black women "surrendering" to the idea of being an alcoholic may be a more appropriate attitude toward power. When drunk she can exhibit all of the cursing, ranting, and raging that she wants to vent toward others, yet lack the nerve when sober, and then blame her lack of control on drinking. Later she experiences feelings of guilt and shame due to her inability to keep promises to herself (and others) not to drink. In addition, because she has used alcohol to escape negative emotions, she may have failed to learn how to be responsible and may be emotionally immature. Given the obstacles every African American woman must face, adequate coping skills are critical for prevention of alcohol problems. The first thing that stands out is her relationship with God, but Jesus came to earth to show and tell humankind that God was willing to forgive everyone of all manner of sin, and take them all under his wings if they were willing to return back unto him. Treating the alcoholic woman requires an understanding of the inner nature of her problem including breaking through denial and building a vision of a healthier lifestyle, and to devise strategies to meet the challenges of healing her. Healing begins when she admits that her drinking is out of control, and recognizes the destructive consequences that drinking brings on herself and on others. The road to recovery for African American women often leads not only to physical healing, but also the ability to abstain from drinking, and to discover a sense of spirituality coupled with increased self-awareness and self-esteem. Life is a pattern. People can learn to live it or learn to be stereotyped within it. We make great complaints about our hardships, but how little we talk of our blessings. It's wonderful to look back and see the dangers that we have escaped, but our happiness is not dependent upon outward circumstances, for all of our earthly conditions are transitory.

    Jesus was also a doctor that made house calls and stopped on the side of road's to assist patients. Luke 8:43 tells us that Jesus was on one of his missionary journeys, when he came across a pale woman that had an issue of blood that constantly flowed from her for twelve long years. She was suffering from uterine bleeding and she was weak. Somehow, her menstrual valve was stuck in "open" position. Neither she nor her doctors could turn it off. Her gynecologist had failed to diagnose her problem. D&C (dilation and curettage) were unknown, but in her day, nothing was really effective. For twelve years she had dragged herself around half dead and fully terrified. The diseased woman in the gospels is an unnamed woman who was labeled as a "certain woman." She was on the opposite end of the spectrum of social prominence. In fact she's an outcast in that community. Yet, she represents all women of the world. The grace of God is not verbally mentioned in the text; but it's written all over it. Grace had chosen "a certain woman" to hear about Jesus, and caused the Lord Jesus to pass her way. God never bypasses the appointed means of grace, and no one is ever saved apart from the hearing of Christ's gospel. The woman was healed when she met Jesus who was on his way to Jairus' (a rich ruler's) house to raise his daughter from the dead. It's one thing for Jairus to go and ask Jesus to help for his daughter; he could do that freely and openly. But this woman's condition is hard to talk about because no one knew how to stop the bleeding. Menstrual bleeding that doesn't stop for twelve years would also be a problem in our society, even with today's medical skills. A hysterectomy is the only treatment that helps many women. However, we need to multiply the pain and frustration many times before we understand this woman's predicament in that society. Not only were there physical problems associated with loss of blood, but there was also a devastating social stigma attached to her problem in that culture. The problem of this poor woman was complicated by the lack of understanding of the problem even by doctors of her day, and it was made worse by Levitical law. This religious law rendered her continuously unclean and shut her off from the worship of God and the fellowship of her friends. Jewish ceremonial law declared that a woman, during her monthly period was "unclean." She was not to be touched. Even if a husband would touch his wife during that time, he would have to go through a ceremonial cleansing. The law of the Old Testament (Law of Separation) also declared women such as this woman to be declared ceremonially unclean for seven days after having a male child, and fourteen days for a female. During those days a woman was to be separated immediately from her husband and friends after the birth of a child. Anyone that attended her was also declared unclean. If she had a male baby it was to be circumcised after the eighth day, because it was thought that it had participated in its mother's pollution during the days of her separation. After the son was circumcised the mother was to continue on in the purifying of her blood for thirty-three days for a total sum of forty days if it was a boy. During the thirty three-day cycles she was separated from the sanctuary and forbidden to eat of the Passover. If she were a priest's wife she would not be allowed to eat anything that was holy unto the Lord. After the forty days of purification was over she was to bring a burnt offering (a Lamb) or if she was poor she was offer a pigeon. The offering of either the Lamb or pigeon would free her from the law of sin and shame. The number thirty-three is representative of Jesus who symbolically and figuratively was the Passover Lamb that cleansed the blood of Israel for thirty-three years, while Israel refused to eat of His body and drink of His blood. He was also thirty-three years old when he was placed on the cross and separated from the sanctuary (presence) of his father. The number forty is another number of importance that involves testing, trial, and probation. The number forty shows completeness and purity. The significance in the number forty is shown in the fact that it rained forty days and nights during the flood. Moses was in the mountain for forty days while receiving the Ten Commandments. Jesus was tempted in the wilderness forty days and nights. After forty days of purifying Israel Jesus was offered as a Lamb. He also stayed on earth with His disciples' forty days after the resurrection.

Although Jarius' daughter had died, the woman with the issue had resigned herself not to die if she could find a cure. Evidently she was a woman of much faith and determination. She knew that this disease was causing her life to slip away and eventually she would meet the grave. This woman began to seek the likeliest means that she could think of and that was a doctor of medicine. What else could she do? Doctors are people set apart to deal with human suffering and diseases. She was a weary soul seeking to find salvation from her suffering. She was tired of having an irregular issue of blood flowing out of her. In other words she was sick and tired of being sick and tired. There was another trauma in her way. She had endured frequent pain, and had a vivid sense of her own unworthiness. She saw her medical condition as an embarrassment, and she didn't want people to know what was going on in her life. Can you just imagine how this woman must have felt? Not only did she have this medical problem, but also if others knew about it she would be shunned. Her disease caused her according to Jewish ceremonial laws to be unclean, and unable to mix in crowds. She had no right in the crowd, since her touch defiled all that came in contact with her, but she was so weak that she knew she could not force her way to him in the crowd. The issued woman can't be blamed for looking to men who claimed to understand the science of medicine. Perhaps she thought that she was predestined to be in her condition. Someone had told her about a man named Jesus who was moving through the city and that he was healing sick people. She listened attentively and started believing what she had heard. This daughter of Abraham knew that Jesus was the Lamb slain from the foundation of the world, who came to fulfill the Law and that his blood was pure. She also knew that like the number of days in purification he was also thirty-three years old, and that He was offering himself as a sin offering for the world. The shame of her disease had prevented her from asking him to heal her in public, but her faith to believe that he could heal her was strong. She said, "I will get in the crowd, and if I can but touch the hem of his garment I shall be made whole. He is so full of power he can heal me." This poor woman believed that the smallest contact with Jesus would heal her. She had the kind of faith that desired to possess healing abundantly. She had looked upon Jesus as someone being powerful as well as Holy. She adored as well as trusted him. She was seeking her liberty at the mercy seat of Jesus. The woman thought that Jesus was loaded with electrical power. She seemed to believe that Jesus was so full of sacred force that she would be healed if she could just touch him. Yet, she had to summon the courage to touch him. She knew of his purity, but feared that he would be angry if she touched him. She had heard of the fullness of Christ's power to heal and save. Therefore, this diseased wretched woman did not utter, "If I can but touch" with her lips, but she believed in her heart that she was going to cleansed of her disease. However, the issued woman wanted to privately touch the hem of His garment. She didn't want anyone to know that she had a personal encounter with Jesus. Some people say that their faith is "kind of a private thing." It doesn't work that way. Faith in Christ is never intended to be a strictly personal thing. A "Just between me and Jesus" religion doesn't work. You must share your testimony of how Jesus delivered you from affliction. Jesus never intends for us to just have our own little private thing going on with him.

On the "side" road Jesus had met two desperate people, and the contrast is striking. Jairus was seen as a prominent religious leader, the issued woman crawling to him was seen as a social outcast. Jesus on the other hand was seen as a fanatical religious leader. A large crowd had gathered to see these two celebrities. You can imagine why that as Jesus approaches, the crowd parts to let him pass, because they all know Jairus has money and influence, and Jesus had spiritual power. The woman on the other hand had spent all of her money and had neither influence nor power. The residue of her life desperately needed balancing. The woman probably was concerned about how she was going to get to Jesus in such a weak and feeble state. Although there was a gang of unruly people between the woman with the issue, and Jesus, she decided that she had to press (crawl) her way through the crowd to get to him. When she could not go straight through the crowd she went around them. Knowing of her unworthiness to be seen face to face with Jesus, modesty led her to go behind him and grab his coat. She didn't want to be in front of people, because she didn't want to be known. She didn't even want Jesus to know what she was doing. She said nothing as she crawled towards Jesus. Perhaps this was the quietest moment ever in her life. She did not cry out like the blind man who was groping in darkness. She did nothing except stay quiet. In total silence she stole upon him and touched the hem of his garment. Immediately her blood dried up. She felt in her body that she was healed of her disease. Jesus feels it too. Though the press of the crowd against him was jostling and bumping him constantly, their touch doesn't have any effect. But when the woman touches him, Jesus is suddenly aware of it: *"Who touched me? Somebody has touched me,"* Jesus said. *"I know that power has gone out from me."* (Luke 8:46) The Greek word translated "power" (NIV) or "virtue" (KJV) is Greek dunamis, from which we get our English words "dynamo" and "dynamic," and it means "power, might, strength, or force." Deep within him Jesus had felt an explosion of her faith and love. Her touch of faith had reached him through his clothes, and he rejoiced by sending healing virtue from himself. He perceived that virtue was gone out of him, when he stopped walking and asked the question, *"Who touched me?"* He did not recognize that the virtue had gone out him by any pain that he felt, rather it was pleasure that caused him feel an unusual joy flow through in and out of him. He asked the question "who touched me" to prevent any misunderstanding of how the miracle was performed. In fact when Jesus healed this believing woman He did it in the commons (street) in the midst of a crowd. There was not a penny to be spent because open air is free to all people. The gifts of Jesus are also free as air. When first reading about this woman it appears that she had a leaning towards magic. "If I can just touch the hem of His garment I can instantly be healed." Her theology wasn't exactly right. What would touching Jesus' garment do for her? Did it have some magical healing power of itself or perhaps she misunderstood. However, the woman understood very well the significance of the hem. The hem was a symbol of authority. When David cut off the hem of Saul's garment, he was taking his symbol of authority. (1 Samuel 24) The King's (hem) symbol of authority gave whoever had it in their possession the power to proclaim anything they wanted as theirs in the name of the King. That's how the issued woman got her blessing by believing and touching his authority to heal. After he healed the issued woman Jesus didn't seek public recognition for restoring her to health. He just wanted her to know that her healing was the result of her relationship with him, and specifically her faith in Him. That's what healed her, not a magic piece of clothing. He was clarifying what had happened so that it wouldn't fall into the realm of magic and superstition. *"Your faith has healed you,"* he acknowledges. He was letting her know that His outward clothing material didn't impart healing, but that it was his inward clothing of righteousness that healed her. It was in God's working through Jesus, and her faith in God that brought about healing. Jesus wanted her to tell the world by the public affirmation of her faith where her healing came from.

The lady who was hemorrhaging was motivated to leave her surroundings, make her way through the crowd, and secretly tap the power of Jesus for her own healing, but she wanted the gift of healing without any responsibility. Unable to worship with her Jewish family and friends may have caused her embarrassment or shyness; so she secretly came to steal the gift. But as sincere as her desire for anonymity was, her idea was wrong. She wanted to slip away without being noticed and without having to enter into a relationship with Jesus or his disciples. Jesus was alarmed that someone wanted his gift without entering into a relationship with him. He demanded to know who touched him, and when she told him that she did; Jesus engaged her in a conversation. He would not allow her to just be a passing stranger who touched his garment. He wanted to know all about her. He drew her out, treated her like a person of worth, and entered a relationship with her. It's evident that the disciples also entered into a relationship with her because Mark's gospel knew enough about her to report the details of her life history. This woman had a pushy don't-take-no-for-an-answer faith. That's the persistent type faith that Jesus seeks in us. What she realized was that the power that dwells in him overflows even down to his garment, and while he wore them they were charged with the virtue that she needed. She knew that connected to him she would receive a blessing, but apart from him she would continue in her misery. She also knew that the power was not in the clothes, but rather because they were His clothes, the garments became a medium of exchange for communication between Him and her. Jesus was so full of power to heal that the secret virtue of healing saturated his clothes. It was like he was carrying a plague. Therefore, if the issued woman's touch were made in faith, then it would not have mattered where she touched him; she was going to catch the plague of deliverance. Within herself she felt a marvelous cure that had come to her by the touch of Jesus and she could not praise him enough. She instantly fell down before him and told him all the truth. She told him about all the money that she had spent and all the prescriptions that she had filled, which was a long list, but the idea to reach out and touch his garment was a short list that involved a simple matter of having faith. She took a leap of faith. Note the dispensation of years in her case. Ironically this woman had been miserably dying for twelve years, when all she had to do was come to the man that had the keys to the twelve gates of the kingdom. The number twelve scriptually speaks of governmental perfection and rule. A dispensation is a period of time during which God deals in a particular way with man in respect to sin and man's responsibility. The word dispensation means administration. In God's administration service, power, and deliverance are manifested in a perfect system of government. The sun and the moon were made to rule the day and govern the night by passing through the twelve signs (months) of the zodiac, time thirty days, which completes 360 degrees. Both night and day have 12 hours. Jesus also chose twelve apostles that will sit on twelve thrones to judge the twelve tribes of Israel. When he was twelve years of age Jesus stated, "I must be about my Fathers business."

It seems that women face greater natural challenges in life. Ever since the fall of Eve in the Garden of Eden women has faced issues of one kind or another. Because of the issue of disobedience women have inherited the pain of birth, and the uncomfortable periodical cycle of flowing blood as their punishment for sin. The issue of blood that flow from women at its appointed time purify their bodies and dispose of their eggs in the process. A woman is usually born with a large number of ovarian follicles close to half a million in both ovaries. Only a small percentage of eggs (about 400) ever mature because a female produces only one egg per month during her reproductive years. Eggs are present at birth, but they age as the woman ages. Each follicle contains a potential egg, which can be fertilized by male sperm. Once a month the follicle undergoes complete maturation. The developing egg contains 23 chromosomes of the mother. The follicles spread out from the ovary and burst releasing the egg. This is referred to as ovulation (loosing) the egg. The woman who reached out to touch the hem of Jesus' garment had lost one egg per month for twelve years totaling 144 (12X12) eggs. She had lost the same number that God says will be *"sealed"* evangelists who had a testimony before the return of Christ. (Revelation 7:4) The one hundred forty four thousand evangelists will represent restoration to the tribes of Israel, and New Jerusalem (city of God) will also be restored to 144 cubits in height. However women cannot bring <u>old</u> issues into <u>New Jerusalem.</u> Looking back we realize that everything about the issued woman symbolized death. The blood that flowed from her was dead blood; no life at all flowed in it. The eggs that she had lost were dead, and eventually unless she received a cure she would also be dead. But, there was one thing that she had not quite given over to death and that was her faith. She realized that she had to face life to overcome death. Jesus was that life-giving fountain that she had hooked up to. The woman with the issue who had endured much in seeking a cure was restored in the "New Jerusalem" (peace and quiet) of her health. She was sealed in God's glory, and she also testified to world about the restorative and reproductive powers of Jesus Christ. She discovered that Jesus had the key that could open any door or gate of sickness and death. When she had ***heard*** of Jesus her faith was really restored in finding a healing. The woman with the issue could have begun to hate everyone around her, declared life unfair, isolated herself, and died, but she didn't. She was a determined woman who believed that regardless of who wouldn't make it; she would. Regardless of whatever obstacles she would find in her way: storms, broken bones, sweltering heat, displaced families, non-believers in Jesus; she was determined that she would survive. She had moved by faith towards the Lawgiver, and there she found mercy. When a woman makes up her mind that she's tired of being sick, depressed, tired, and under bondage to the Devil, she also will crawl around spiritual hindrances of deliverance. She will crawl to Jesus just as she is, and beg to be healed, and forgiven of her sins. When she has been blessed and delivered there will be no more afflictions. For twelve long years this poor woman endured not only the disease, but also doctors. She tolerated the use of them until she had spent all of her money and substance on them, and received no benefit from any of them. She had become bankrupt of alternatives. Her money was wasting away as well as her life. When she came to her last monetary cent, she also came to her God given sense of wisdom. She realized that man was limited in his abilities, but that man's extremities were God's possibilities. Her purse was lighter and she became weaker, but her faith never wavered. At the bottom of every purse or wallet people will discover wisdom. Jesus is ready to be spent. Defeatism will turn to victory because the believer knows that it can be done, for without God's grace even the best of medicine will not work. The woman that bled for twelve years had a hemorrhaging issue, but everybody has issues flowing from them: We have cantankerous, evil, and negative attitudes. Some of us are uncooperative, debt ridden, addicted to smoking, alcohol, illegal and legal drugs. Some of us have issues pouring forth concerning men, women, sex, gambling, married men,

There's Enough Woman Left to be Your Lady

married women, food, loneliness, anxiety, and indifference. Have you been bleeding to death over issues that can't seem to stop flowing from you? Have you given your all and ended up no better, but worse in relationships, jobs, family, and marriage? Have you given and spent your all in a relationship, and the love of your life messed over on you, played you, cheated on you, abused you-physically and emotionally? Brother you may have given your all to a partner, and changed your life for her. You gave up your "running" days for her. You gave her access to your cash, credit card, and car, and then she split on you and left you worse than you were. Sister you may have deprived yourself for the sake of your kids, and now they will not call or come to see you. You gave your all on the job, you arrived to work early and stayed late, yet you still got passed over for the job promotion. You have faithfully stood by your partner for years, and helped him to succeed; now he wants to leave you for a younger woman. When you have given your all, and it gets worse instead of better, and you are fed up by frustration and drowning in despair, what do you do with your situation? You fight your way out even if you have to crawl to hook up with Jesus. Your issue doesn't have to get the best of you. If you are fed up with whatever your issue is; you and Jesus can handle it. Fight your way to Jesus, even if you have to crawl on hands and knees. There is hope for you. No matter how long you have been suffering there is hope. It was twelve long years since the woman with the issue had felt like a *living* woman. She had been in constant pain and death, but now she felt her strength come back. She did not go to Matthew, Mark, Peter, or John to beg them for an introduction to Jesus. She went on her own and tried for herself the virtue of his touch. You can also receive a blessing when you come to the well of salvation, but you must come with an empty bucket. You must empty yourself of pride, envy, deceit, arrogance, hatred, malice, and then let God overrun your cup like he did with David. When all of the virtue has gone out of you, then you will find the virtue that flow out of Him. If you feel that the world has grown cold just reach out and touch the hem of His garment. He will be there to lift you up. You don't have to wait until the Pastor or church members can get with you to pray. That's all well and good, but you just need to go into your own secret closet and tell Jesus all about your problems. In Exodus 34:14, it reads, *"For thou shalt worship no other god: for the Lord, whose name is Jealous, is a jealous God."* All of us may have worshipped a prize car, boat, house, or possibly deified some sports figure, fashion, or a preacher's personality. But anything that becomes the focus of our time, affections, and money is well on its way to becoming an idol, which divert the eyes of mankind from its Creator. Today many people worship their pastor or head leader of the church as opposed to God. Some people don't realize what they are doing, but it just becomes a habit. For example, some women of the church may go on errands for the pastor, or cook the pastor's family a dinner before cooking for their own families. Some women eagerly stay in church all day or do mission work without cleaning up their own house. Some give money or gifts to their Pastor before they are willing to pay their tithes and offering. This gives the Devil an opportunity to cause division in the household, whereby the husband may accuse her of having an affair with the pastor or of being his fool. It's good to do things for a pastor, but a woman shouldn't worship him or her. She should not want the pastor or minister of the church to get so high and mighty that he or she forgets about God and where He's brought him or her. Women of God have to remember where their blessings come from. Their blessings don't come from the pastor or whoever is the leader of their church. They come from God. The easiest thing that the issued woman could do was to reach out and touch Jesus. When she touched Jesus while hiding in the crowd she put her bloody issue on him, and immediately her problem dried up. She came empty handed and undeserving and received a blessing. It was a non-relational non-communicative final experience. Everything inside of her wanted and needed him. She had the energy that he needed and he had the blood (life) that she needed. Blood identifies with the soul for without blood and oxygen there is no soul. Her health and strength were gone, but she felt his healing virtue in her soul. She had hooked up to the **Dialysis** of life and got a blood transfusion that not only purified her blood, but also thinned it out so that it may not clog again. Jesus dried up her fountain for He is the fountain of life. It's no wonder that the Hymnologist wrote, *"What can wash away my sin? What can make me whole again? Nothing but the blood of Jesus. Oh precious is the flow that can make me white as snow."* Jesus' healing touch of earthly mercy presented within her life a moving melody of *"Lord lift me up where I belong."* The issued woman's part in the healing was very small. All she did was crawl and extend her arm through the crowd. She had refused to settle for another day of sickness and resolved to make a move. Healing begins when we take a step no matter how short to reach out and do something. God's help is near and always available, but it's only given to those who seek it. Compared to God's part, our part is miniscule, but necessary. We don't have to do much, but we do have to do something! The immediate cure of the issued woman was not so much of how long she had suffered, but rather how that she was cured. The cure of this woman was remarkable in that it was a cure done by the wayside. Jesus often leaves the "main" road to search for people with bloody issues on the "side" road of sin. He seeks "issued" people because he came to seek and to save those that are lost.

Women that have regular periods know when their period are going to flow, and they prepare themselves for the onslaught, but when something is irregular you cannot prepare for it. The every day cycle of life is sometimes irregular. The cares of life pours down on some people in a never ending cycle, rendering them weak and draining the life out of them. The menstrual process can be very painful or annoying to some women. Some women easily endure the discomfort while others dread the very thought of having to go through the process every month. When the womb and menstruation are seen merely as necessary uncomfortable sanitary stations, a woman's self-esteem is very low. Deep down in the bottom of her heart she doesn't love herself if she doesn't wholeheartedly love her body and its functions. She's either not aware or has forgotten the value of menstruation in her life. A woman doesn't love her body if she catches herself saying, "I hate having this mess." Many women don't want to go deeper into menstruation because they are scared of what they will discover about themselves. It suits them better to numb and suppress their feelings with painkillers, to spray with vaginal deodorants to disguise the smell of blood, and to absorb their blood with tampons so they never have to actually see it. In fact some women believe that it's easier to be a successful woman in a man's world if she hardly acknowledge that she menstruate at all.

The issue of bleeding in today's time doesn't seem to be anything to cause great embarrassment, and it's similar to the complaint of many of the female patients of today who have the same complaint and describes it simply with the words, "I have a female problem." Yet, the woman with issue had a consistent ongoing problem for twelve years. It not only wasted her strength, but it threatened to bring her quickly to the grave. It may have been the last bleeding to cleanse her uterus to prepare her for menopause. Women going through menopause can be linked to symptoms that include: hot flashes, night sweats, mood swings, fatigue, depression, poor libido, vaginal dryness, drying of the skin, insomnia, breast tenderness, and anxiety. It's important to understand that menopause is not a disease! It's a natural process and normal change that happens to every woman's body. Actually it should be called "mental pause," for it gives a woman time to relax, refresh, restore her vitality, and reflect on her future. In our world today there are many women that are like the issued woman. They have been bleeding for years with an illness or issue that has brought shame in their life. Nobody will reach out to touch them or talk to them. For years they have sought the world over for happiness, but have found only emptiness. Their hearts are punctured with sadness. They walk around carrying heavy burdens of relational baggage of hurt, and can't stand to be around the person that hurt them. They have tried to hide in the crowds, but they know their guilt. In this gap between who they are and who they becomes an "other" person emerges. The "other" person defines their humanity or inhumanity. This secret self is often the key to how some women live, explains what choices they make, and what drives them out into the world or away from engaging in it. The "other" person can destroy relationships, do damage, make repairs, build, ruin, or cement friendships, separate fathers and daughters, or bring mothers and sons together. Understanding that people have "others" secreted away keeps us from trusting anyone, but by uncovering what individualizes us, we move toward an understanding of those we know and, ultimately, ourselves. However, sweet or bitter, the "other" secretive side of a woman fascinates us because that "other" person is ready to either ruin, illuminate, or enrich the public's perception of her.

    Women keep secrets for many reasons. A woman has to work very hard to keep her reputation looking good, so that nobody will find out what her secret is. Secrets are kept in an attempt to erase the past. The deep, dark, musty, places of secrets are often cloaked in shame, guilt, and confusion. Secrets imprison, breed suspicion, and at times they can paralyze a woman with fear of being discovered. Most women want to be acceptable to others and must look good at all costs. Some women fear that their reputation would become tarnished if they were shown to be who they really are. Therefore, they conceal things out of fear, shame, rejection, exposure, and abandonment of friends, family, or perhaps even being ridiculed by enemies. Some women have issues involving past mistakes of raising children, infidelity, unbridled passions, theft, drunkenness, and lying spirits. Some have tried drugs, men, sex, and even dabbled at religion, witchcraft, or some other cult in an effort to stop the bleeding in their lives, but the more they try the more they fear. Some have bitterness, and anger from long ago and don't know why they are so angry. They feel guilty and unworthy. The wall that she hides behind with her secret protects her from letting others in, from getting close, and from being real, but it keeps her from being free. Some women have bloody issues involving secrets in their lives that never seem to stop flowing from them. Some are still bleeding from bad divorces, unrequited love, drug addiction, fornication, adultery, jealousy of a sibling or friend, or from bad choices that they made many years before. Some have dated married men for years in the hope that he will leave his wife for her. He used his kids as an excuse for why he will not leave his wife. Some women are so naïve, needy, and gullible that they obsess about a man who has politely, and correctly, told them to back off. They will still pursue him and believe anything that he tells them. They refuse to recognize that their lover's words don't match his actions. The situation that she puts herself in is largely a fantasy. She has become addicted to the excitement of the secret affair, and has filled the empty space in her life with a make-believe romance. It's all right to think anything. What is not all right is to act on thoughts that would be self-destructive. When the affair becomes known, the pain and the shame involved are never worth the excitement. A woman that's used to being with a married man enjoys the attention. She even starts to become the woman the man wants her to be. She wants to please him because she wants the fantasy. When she sees yet another failed relationship, instead of backing up she continues jumping in and out of adulterous love affairs. She's searching for the personal fulfillment that she believed she could only find when she was in a committed relationship with a man. She has to learn that she doesn't need a man, but she does need to spend time with herself, healing herself, and learning to love herself. In the final analysis by making a man grovel at her feet a woman has to decide whether she wants to be labeled as desperate and cheap, flirtatious, or empowered with ownership. She should prefer to harness her feminine energy to nurture a truly spiritual man who rises up in his entire splendor when he is with her, and shares with her the best of himself. When she is whole and complete in herself a woman will discover that a man is not someone that she needs to mould into her own design, and he's definitely not someone she has to submit to illegally. Instead she will see a man as someone she can laugh with, love, and enjoy for who he is without losing her respect as an intelligent and successful woman. Women should be wary of men that keep a relationship secret. When a man doesn't take his woman to social events, company parties, around his friends, or his family he either doesn't care. He is just using her for the moment, or he's still putting notches in his headboard. A woman on the rebound from a failed relationship or marriage presents a problem. She is in need of affection and healing, and will be grateful for a man's presence and solace. Still, her feelings for a man will be flickering and tenuous, her moods changeable, her attachment to him shaky. She will alternately cling to him and push him away at the same time. She will sweeten his existence and bring him misery. Entanglements with married men should be avoided for very common sense reasons. Not only might the relationship be poisoning a family or perhaps hurting children in the process, but the woman run the risk of encountering an angry, and possibly armed wife.

Abortion is another secret that many women keep to themselves. Instead of it being a wonderful right to celebrate, abortion hurts women mentally and opens the doorway to pain, death, and suffering in their life. Their secret isolates, restricts, chokes, and prevents them from intimacy and submission with another person. Some women have depression, anxiety, panic attacks, are devoid of emotions, feel suicidal, and some feel as if they have committed murder by having an abortion. Emotions run deep within them from happiness to sadness, all the way down to feeling nothing. Sometimes women re-experience the abortion in flashbacks. On the date that the baby would have been born, or on the date of the abortion, women feel kind of mixed up and crazy from guilt and anger surrounding the abortion and the inability to come to peace with themselves and others involved in the abortion decision. It may cause her to want to become pregnant again.

It is time for this injustice to end. The church and the nation should be tired of the death of children and the destruction of their mothers. They should listen to the pain of women who have had abortions and give them an opportunity for mercy, forgiveness, and reconciliation with their God and their church through the shed blood of Jesus Christ. One day many unrepentant women will stand before God to give an answer for innocent blood, and if they haven't been forgiven by the blood of Jesus do you know what God may ask? "Where's the baby? The blood is crying out to me from the ground. Where is the baby?" All the pastors of America should join in prayer for an end to abortion, and the beginning of spiritual healing for women. Women that constantly bleed with issues are bloated with cramps and attitudes, but that shows that their ovulation is normal. Vitamin C (Christ) helps reduce excessive bleeding, increase iron absorption, and give tissue strength. The only way that women will stop the overflow of issues is by having a spiritual hysterectomy. A woman must move into forgiveness and resolution by embarking on a spiritual journey with God to cut out all of the filth in her. Like her uterus, the prison walls of guilt will still be there; but it's there that she has to face her need for God, forgiveness, rest, and peace in the safety of Jesus Christ. It takes a lot of emotional energy to hold up that wall. These are not unbreakable walls, nor unbendable steel. Where a woman can't break through prison walls of self-incrimination, Jesus will do it on her behalf. The Son of God has the power and authority to forgive, reconcile her to God, and to bring restoration in her life. Secrets are a prison full of fear, but there's nothing like the pain of fearfulness to let you know that you are headed in the wrong direction. In the Bible, Jesus says, "You will know the truth, and the truth will set you free." Women can emerge from the prison of isolationism, and also have the peace and balance that they are looking for through Jesus Christ.

Women are like cars. They have to be properly maintained. A man that cares about his woman keeps a check on the operational maintenance of his relationship with her. Most men know that if car tires are under-inflated it uses more gasoline. They know that if the tires are not rotated and balanced ever so often they will display uneven wear, and if the weights are not evenly distributed it will cause the tire to shake the whole car and give a bumpy ride. Therefore, a man who cares about his woman keep her esteem inflated at the right height with praise. He keeps her engine running with prayer, her windows washed with understanding, and her chassis lubricated with the oil of the spirit. He tries to avoid putting unnecessary miles of wear and tear on her. This is called conditioning and preventive maintenance. This keeps a woman moving forward in life. Women with personal growth issues dread moving forward, they are always looking backwards. They are confused due to early conditioning and lack the confidence to move about in certain situations, places, and among people. They mistrust trustworthy people and withdraw from all contact with society. Looking backwards doesn't bring healing, but looking forward to touching the hem of Jesus' garment daily brings blessings and richness to all that reaches out to him. Some women like to ride the rapid rail scenic route when God is only giving a light rail tour. Women must learn to choose a new direction, especially when life seems to be unfulfilling and draining their emotions. The aerodynamics of life sometimes demands that women strip down and become sleek enough to soar on the magnetic wings of God's glory and salvation. To be saved means to be converted; conversion means to turn three hundred and sixty degrees from your old position in life. The desire to turn from the way in which one is traveling is the first step toward conversion. You must have a desire to turn from sin and begin traveling in the opposite direction, but before you can turn, you must realize that you are going in the wrong direction. Then you must confess that realization to God before He will save you from sin. There is no need to say that you are not as bad as some people are, or that you have not done this, that, or the other. What a blessing the issued woman gained by coming out of her hiding place, and just as she silently stole upon Jesus, you can also be saved in silence. At this moment while reading this book you can believe and live. Just speak to him from your heart, and tell him your desires for your life. Nobody will know that you are touching the Lord. You don't need a handful of Jesus, but rather just a touch will do. When all other doors are shut, touch Jesus and salvation is yours at once. All believers in Christ have that same assurance if you trust Him. We all must show the same spirit as the issued woman who fell at the feet of Jesus. We must fall on our knees and "Tell Him all the truth." Today, it seems that everybody only values what he or she will get from Jesus or from church. There's a great market for religious experiences in our world; but there is little enthusiasm for what earlier generations of Christians called "Holiness." Some people want all the benefits of church and salvation without commitment or responsibility. They don't want to become a real part of the body of Christ. Many people want to have enough Christianity to make them feel good about God, but not enough to make them commit to living the Christian life when times get tough. We have become a consumer society and we have brought that consumer mentality into the church in the form of religion. People want to be consumers of faith, but they don't want to pay the price of having a right relationship with Christ. The Kingdom of God is the kingdom of right relationships. Therefore, there can be no pretense or hypocrisy in true worship. Like the world the church is caught up in loud, sensational, instantaneous service. There are many Christians who want fast worship services to go. They want to grab their faith like a burger that's put in a paper sack to go. They don't want to hang around and get involved in something as greasy and messy as a church. They have no time to set down and enjoy God's word. Some sit in their seats puffed up, criticizing the sermons or choir, and counting the time it takes to end service. Physical attitudes affect our Spiritual lives. We have become a generation with the mentality that if it hurts then drop it. When we become quitters in physical life, we begin to find this same attitude in our spiritual life with God. We begin to drift, rationalize, and find reasons why we need to get out of this thing called Christianity. In order for the church to survive, it must meet the needs of the people who attend. People will go to a church that meets their spiritual needs. Yet, churches that keep doing everything the same old way that it has always been done without being flexible, and refuse to provide for the real needs of its members in the challenges of our fast-paced society; they will see a drastic decline in membership. There are many excuses not to come into or to leave Jesus and the Kingdom of God. Some excuses involve people, disappointments, and some are circumstances. When born again believers have bad blood among themselves and seek to keep issues flowing, they defile not only themselves, but the place where they worship as well. The Pastor and unrepentant church members can cause a church to suffer reproach, and feel the backlash from public opinion. Pastors and leaders of the church are given responsibilities to operate the church and set a godly example, but the church doesn't belong to the pastors and the leaders, it belongs to Jesus Christ. Churches today put more attention on members in the world with high paying positions, than they do with born again members with less income. The higher a person's position is in society the more attention the church will focus attention on him or her, but crowds will also turn on a person. When the person that has position and clout is used for all that they are worth, they are discarded for newer and younger members. The admiration and attention of the crowd cannot get a person closer to Jesus or into heaven. Moral hypocrisy haunts the church. Religious hypocrites will never receive from God what a sincere God-fearing person would. Hypocrites are trying to gain a reputation for spirituality by playing the role of God-lovers. They are unholy fakes trying to fool people, but they can't fool God. Good Christians are those that stay focused on pleasing God. The key to staying positive or focused lies in the fact of never looking backward. Backward thinking denotes where a person heart lies. Moses gave a written warning to us about looking back in the account of the destruction of Sodom and Gomorrah. (Genesis 19:24-26) From the example of Sodom the wicked are warned to turn from wickedness, and by the example of Lot's wife the righteous are warned not to turn from their righteousness. Lot's wife looked back because she wanted to take a last look at the lifestyle and society that she had come to love. She looked back on the good times she and Lot had. She looked back on her neighbor's whom she had left behind. She probably also thought about all of the fine furniture and servants that she had left behind and was sorry to leave it. Lot's wife disobeyed the express command of God. She had shown unbelief in the word of God, and she questioned whether Sodom would be destroyed. The Bible says, *"Love not the world neither the things that are in it."* True Christians have given up the world and flesh, and now look heavenward. In Heaven there will be seen a general assembly of the first born, a congregation of the righteous of all saints, and nothing but saints. The wicked will not be in that congregation. Hypocrites in this world under the disguise of righteousness may put themselves into the congregation of the righteous and may remain undetected for years, but the day is coming where God will separate the sheep and the goats, the tares and the wheat, but the ungodly will perish. Looking busy, shouting, and calling on God's name will not gain entrance into heaven, but being sincere does. If we have confessed to leaving the elements of the world we should not have a desire to be drawn back into perdition. Lot's wife was punished for her disbelief by being struck dead in her place without falling down. Although she was exposed to the air, which quickly decays a body, she stood erect and fixed as a pillar. The salt deposit had preserved her body. She was preserved as a monument to show to the world what can happen when we disobey God, and look back on being in the world. Her fate to become a pillar of salt can be used to season the whole world in humility. It's time for God's people to be like a tree planted by the rivers of water. It's time to take a stand! Standing shows something. It says that I am not moved by what's going on around me. It's when you have done all to stand, and are still standing that the devil will come and laugh in your face. He will say, "So you are a faith person. You have told everybody you believed God for this or that situation. You went around telling people you were healed, look at you now. You told people God led you to do that, and look at the mess you are in now." Just because you get into a mess it doesn't mean you missed God, you're out of the will of God, or that God has somehow abandoned you. The devil is a liar! We have to call those things that were not as though they were. Abraham believed that if God promised to do something He was able to perform that which he had promised. If God has promised you something, you are probably on the brink of your miracle. The devil knows that as well and that's why you are going through what you are going through. The church is like Noah's ark: The stench inside would be unbearable if it weren't for the storm outside, but its member's shouldn't loose heart, quit, and give up. If we are to be a Holistically healed people we need to keep our eyes fixed on Jesus Christ. Perhaps, you that are reading this book are getting tired of the Christian race. Maybe your beginning to think that it's a bit demanding, you're weary and wanting to do something else for a while. Weariness is a word that many of us have experienced. We are tired, bone tired, and exhausted, but there is a harvest in due time, if we remain steadfast, unmovable, always abounding in the work of the Lord. In running this race our greatest shame is not in falling, but in never rising every time we fall. It's not difficult to get a person interested in the

There's Enough Woman Left to be Your Lady

message of the gospel when they are knocked down; but it's difficult to sustain their interest when they are rising back up. The fact is whatever you're focusing on right now is the biggest thing in your life. Be encouraged to not focus on what you are going through, but focus on where you are going. Get your eyes off the problems and get them on the promises of God. When your enthusiasm is drained, and the fun ceases, you will have to hang on to the arm of Jesus. Hang in there even when the excitement fades, and some around you are dropping under the load. In the Christian life, only you can decide whether you will slow down, finish, or stop during the race. What an enemy, teacher, or preacher might say may help or hinder you, but in the final analysis *you* have to decide whether you will win this race. You will have to stop, take a long hard look at your life in Christ, and make a decision on whether you will continue on, and grow closer to the Lord, or if you will just go on hold, or maybe even find an excuse to drop out. Older spirit filled Christians knows that we may have to take a few tumbles as we reach for the gold, and that we are in for some losses the longer we serve him. When the road gets weary, the disappointments heavy, and the feeling of emptiness a reality, you will already know what the newer Christians are beginning to realize. You've been where they are, and survived. The battle's almost over, but the crown still has to be won. You may not be in first place, but finish the race. The race is not given to the swift nor to the strong, but unto he that endures to the end. There is the promise of an eventual reaping, harvesting, and a reward, if we don't grow weary. In every race it's only one victor who's declared winner, and receive the crown, but in Christ, everyone who crosses the finish line wins. The motivation is of course the glorious crown of life. You may not be the greatest champion of the faith, but keep the faith with all your heart. You have a course to run. There is a life to be lived, but it's longer than just a few laps around the field. It's a course that starts with your commitment to follow Christ and ends when you race past the finish line. It may not be an easy run. It goes further than just the first few disappointments that you encounter. It may have more hurdles and potholes than you would expect, but you chose the Lord, and he has chosen your path. You are moving in the direction of salvation. Therefore you cannot faint in faith in your walk with God. *"Abraham staggered not at the promise of God through unbelief, but was strong in faith, giving glory to God."* (Romans 4:20)

The healing of Jairus' daughter presents a different side of Jesus. This is a powerful story of a relationship broken by a painful past. A relationship in which the person had been determined sick was now dead. Jairus had come to Jesus saying that his daughter was lying near the point of death. He asked Jesus to come and heal her. As Jesus moves toward Jairus' house, the streets are utterly jammed. Capernaum's streets were not designed to handle these kinds of crowds. Jesus is able to push forward only with difficulty and progress is slow. Jairus at his side is ever mindful that his daughter's life is slipping away every moment that's wasted, but before they reached the house other messengers had met them saying, "Thy daughter is dead; why trouble you the Master any further?" They were in essence saying, "Death exceeds his power. There's nothing that even he can do now." They had set limits on the power of Jesus. Unknowing to Jairus he was about to have his faith tried. To prepare Jarius for the shock of his daughter's death, Jesus gave him a special miracle. Jesus said to him, *"Fear not, only believe, and she shall be made whole."* When Jesus arrived at Jarius' house people were going through a fake motion of mourning. When he said, *"She is not dead, she is only sleeping"* they laughed him to scorn. The mourners did not believe that Jesus had the ability to raise the daughter, for they had walked behind many funerals crying yet, never having seen anyone raised from the dead. If they had really believed that Jesus had the power to raise her, they would not have sent a message to Jarius nor laughed at Jesus. Jesus said to the deceased, *"Talitha Cumi"* signifying *"Damsel arise."* (Mark 5:41) He gave the young lady an alternative. She could have stayed in a premature death, and had the mourners continue the fake crying that they were paid to do, and then carry her to a burial sight, or she could choose to get up. Jesus did a great work in this young girl's life, because his ministry lifted her up, and did not allow her to be lowered in the ground. Jarius' daughter death had broken the relational bonds between father and daughter. Her rising from the dead is a powerful story of a relationship broken by a painful past that was restored to a glorious future. Jesus confronted death, raised the daughter, delivered her back to her father, and restored their relationship. In that one moment when she heard Jesus' voice there is exultation of new life, hope, and the promise of what was broken again being restored. God speaks to our soul in many ways to restore broken relationships. Moses heard the Lord's voice from a burning bush. Joseph dreamed dreams. Paul saw a vision, but rarely do we hear voices, see visions, or dream dreams. Jesus reconciles and brings back to normal, broken, stagnated, and hostile relationships. He's in the restoration business. He can restore relationships between father and daughter, mother and son, boss and employee, husband and wife, churches and communities, and Pastor and member. A woman's relationship with God is seemingly severed by her mistakes and the sins of her past, which constantly echoes in her mind that it's not over. It seems that she's doomed to live in that darkness, but the voice of God is heard in her ears to proclaim," *"I forgive your past and I remember it no more; come and join with me in a new relationship; a relationship of freedom, life, and love."* Jesus is telling women all over the world, "Daughter arise out of your coffin of despair. Come forth and let your glory along with the *Shekina Glory* of God shine as the sun. Let the world bask in the warmth and brightness of your spirit." We all have those moments in our lives when the darker side of our humanity (the sin that lies within us) causes us to make decisions and choices that exhibit behaviors that we regret long afterward. However, we mature and grow from those moments. We move on to other more fruitful parts of our lives, and in some instances we may feel as if we have turned loose all of those past moments. We feel that we've gotten over them and they no longer bother us, but always the winds of circumstance, the winds of guilt and shame, the winds of anger and bitterness, begin to blow. Soon the lines connected to those moments; lines that we thought we had severed draw tight, and before we know it we are again looking at the corpses of our past rising up as if they still have life. It's if they still have some influence over us; some ability to control us, move us, shape us, or even scare us. Some of those corpses may be things that we have done, or things that others have done to us. We may find rising up in our lives an empty relationship with a parent, a love from them we desired, but never received and it haunts us. We may stare at the abuse we received from a close friend, or one who wasn't close to us at all and remember the way it made us feel about ourselves. We may also see rising up before us an abortion had years ago; cheating or misrepresenting a business deal for tax or personal gain; willfully bringing emotional injury to another person or behavior which wounded our spouse or our children. We may even see rising before us an experience which angered us at God, and therefore separated us from Him. Regardless, whatever may be on the end of your line, the reality is that we learn to live without thinking about our past evils or the evils done to us, but then suddenly and sometimes with increasing frequency it comes back again. We thought that it was long dead and gone, and that we had conquered it and were over it. Now it's rising up as if it's still has life and power to tell us what we should think of our world and ourselves. Whatever you may find in the recesses of your mind today you must cut the dangling cords left in your life. God gives us good news about the experiences of our past and his attitude towards them. In Jeremiah chapter thirty-one the nation of Israel was bound by the failures of her past and her repeated sins. Israel is in a state of dispersion. Her homeland of Jerusalem and its temple of worship had not only been taken away, but also destroyed. God later announces that Babylon would be taking Israel into captivity. The conquering nation of Babylon took her people and scattered them throughout all the known regions of the world. They were separated from family, fellowship, and worship. The brokenness of Israel at this time is almost undesirable, but Israel must deal with the fact that she had brought this on herself. It had been her sins and failure before the Lord that led to her demise. *"For twenty three years the word of the Lord has come to me and I have spoken it to you again and again, but you have not listened. And though the Lord has sent all his servants, the prophets to you again and again, you have not listened or paid any attention. The prophets said, "Turn from your evil. Do not follow other gods." But you did not listen to me and you have brought harm to yourselves."* (Jeremiah 25:3-7) Over and over and over again, God had tried to get the attention of Israel to show his love and compassion for her, but she was never able to keep the commands. She was always enticed by the evil desires that lurked within her, and as a result of her disobedience, God allowed King Nebuchadnezzar of Babylon to come in and take over Israel.

Can you imagine the game of "if only" that Israel must have played as she languished in captivity? "If only we had been obedient. If only we had realized. If only we had taken God seriously, then we would not be experiencing such pain." Surely the people tried to go on with their lives by building new relationships, and starting new families. They had endured captivity for multiple generations, but just when they thought they had overcome what was past, or perhaps felt as if the burden was lifting the wind of guilt would blow to show her the disobedience of her past. God later repents and speaks the most exciting words, but at the same time some very unexpected words. For God announces something new that has never happened before. He throws out the first covenant that he made with Abraham, and he says there is going to be a new covenant (agreement). *"I will make a new covenant with the house of Israel that's not like the old covenant, because they (Israel) broke my covenant."* Can you imagine the response and the sense of excitement from Israel when they heard these words? There is almost an audible sigh of relief that you can hear from Israel as God proclaims that her current state is not permanent, and that the sins of her past will not forever doom her present, nor her future. God brings the most precious of commodities to Israel and to all of us, and that's hope. God is going to rearrange things and in effect help Israel to cut the cords of her past sins. The good news that God proclaimed to Israel is the good news that He proclaims for us today. He lets us know that we can experience freedom from our lifeless past. We are not bound or trapped by the pain we have given or the pain that has been inflicted on us. There is hope for our future through the promises of our God. What's the Good News of this new covenant that God announces? First, this new covenant is continued evidence of God's great and abiding love for us, because the new covenant is completely and totally God initiated. He says, "I will do this or I will do that." Clearly, God is the author. This is not something God has to do. Israel was suffering because of the choices she made to sin. Very little has changed. We are just as Israel was in the time of her captivity. We also reap the consequences that result from our sin and experience the repeated pain that comes from past mistakes. That pain only serves to compound or exacerbate the difficulties of our present circumstance. In fact given the sins of people, the holiness of God's character, and the fact that he has repeatedly warned people about sin, God would be justified in walking away, but He doesn't. Again, as He has so often done in scripture He initiates wholeness, healing, restoration, and demonstrates His unconditional love for us. In this future time "new" covenant that we know is to be fulfilled by Christ His people will respond to Him out of love, not constraint. They will worship Him not in fear, but in adoration and humble thanksgiving for the blessings of His goodness, mercy, and love for it will spring forth from the heart. It will be a response of love to God who has rescued us from ourselves. Our relationship with God will not be based on a rigid following of rules, though rules will exist. Instead our relationship with God will be based on what's in the heart. God's people will not carry a written, external law as was received by Moses, but the law of God will be internal written on the hearts of those who receive him therein. The scripture says, *"I will be their God, and they will be my people and they will all know me, from the greatest to the least."* For the first time, God is talking about individual humans being able to know Him and relate to Him as God beyond a tribe or nation. The implication from this text is that it won't just be for Israel as a nation, but this new covenant will be for "all people" and that means individuals from everywhere on earth. In that coming day a personal, individual, relationship with God will exist to humanity as never before, and as a result of this revelation, people will have a strong knowledge of God and an understanding of His will. In this new covenant, the scripture says

God will also, *"forgive past sins of Israel and remember their sins no more."* In essence God says, *"All of the disobedience, all of the poor choices, all of the bad decisions, it doesn't matter. We're going to start over. Not only am I going to forgive your sins, but I am also going to forget them. I am going to wipe them from my memory bank and consider them no more."* In that one statement, you can hear the sounds of a Holy knife being drawn. A holy, sacred instrument enters into the heart of the nation Israel and into the lives of all people who would believe on His name. You can hear the sounds of the cords of uncircumcised hearts being cut, the aorta being released, and the sheer, unadulterated freedom of new life entering in. What we have thought all of our lives that has broken us, and trapped us has now been released and restored. At His initiative, He forgives and forgets past sins. We should respond today with heartfelt cries of thanksgiving, and love to a God who has forgiven and forgotten our past. What a blessed and holy gift we receive in the Holy Amnesia of God. For He is able to do something that we have been trying to do all of our lives, and that's to forget the dead and lifeless things of our past, and move forward to a new life of freedom in Christ.

Christ restored a relationship in his own family when on the cross he said to his mother, *"Woman behold thy son."* (John 19:26) Referring to the disciple John who was to take his place as Mary's son after his death, Jesus was saying to her, "Here is your new son." He was preparing her for his death by letting her know that everything in life must die, and be transformed, but life goes on. His focus was on transformation, not stagnation. As the creator of every good and perfect gift, Jesus was telling her that death transforms us from one dimension to another, and that it would not be put on hold until He had tasted of its sting. The world say, "don't trust in God, he doesn't exist." But, the cross of Jesus transforms a believer from death unto life. Jesus sees all of our troubles and he is ready to heal and restore broken fellowship in our lives. Like Jairus' family we must put the mockers out and not give in to their disbelief. The church should be like Jesus. Preachers and congregations should tell women that are down and out, that they can rise above circumstances that have knocked them down and have flattened them. They should tell those who are dead in spirit that they can rise up to be productive, happy, fruitful, and enjoy life again. Women can rise to a new day and a new way of living through Jesus, or they can choose to stay in a pitiful condition of death by submission to sin, locked into a stiff mortified way of life, and never able to move among the living. To survive persecution religious women must avoid a mindless openness to everything thrown their way. Women, after all, are the unsung heroines of many a liberation struggle that rid them of oppression. Unfortunately, many of their exploits, accomplishments, and sacrifices have gone unrecognized because of past or present events in their lives. Most women believe that the right of all people to self-determination cannot be realized while women continue to be marginalized and prevented from becoming full participants in their respective societies. As a centerpiece of this problem is the increasing lack of control women have over themselves, and their long-term security. Security, militarism, the globalization of the economy, the further marginalization of women, disrespect and increasing intolerance of them, are problems facing all women and future generations as they struggle for a better world. The human rights of women, like the human rights of poor people, and their inherent rights to self-determination are not issues exclusively within the domestic jurisdiction of courts and states, but rather it's wrapped up in the Theocratic rule of God.

God has chosen a Day of Atonement and fasting for himself. The fast he has chosen consists of reformation in our lives. He wants to undo the damage that we have entangled ourselves in. He wants to loose the bands that have forcibly detained us for so long. He wants to undo the heavy burden laid upon us, under which we may be about to drown. He wants to let the oppressed go free, and break every yoke that binds us. God wants to take away the yoke so that those who have been oppressed may never again be re-enslaved. God also calls forth a religious fast in our lives, a day that afflicts souls. It's a day where we must emit genuine sorrow for sin, and seek restoration from God. It must be an acceptable day unto the Lord. Looking sad with a hung down head and putting on grave clothes is not real affliction. To mortify the body and spread sackcloth and ashes under it, while the spirit of Christ lies dormant, is hypocrisy at its worst. To obtain His mercy we must be ready to study, and to show ourselves approved unto Him. The born again woman of God in today's time will also have abundant blessings if she just claim the symbol of her authority by reaching out to touch the hem of His garment. Women can claim their authority by confronting Jesus and calling him to action. There are many biblical models of women who spoke using their own voices in conflict. These women insisted upon God's healing grace through Jesus and confronted His authority in order to do so. The claiming of authority will in turn lead to assertive management and healing of conflict, and then, a woman will no longer be hidden. She becomes a proclaimer of the good news that Jesus is an awesome God. People have a thousand and one ideas about how to get to heaven, but according to God's infallible Word there is only *one* way, *one* door, *one* name, and *one* truth. At the name of Jesus every knee shall bow and every tongue shall confess that He is Lord. Your feet are clay, and Christ is the only one who will not let you down. He is capable of leading you across difficult waters, and providing the ultimate direction. The crossing of the Jordan

River is never a picture of the Christian dying and going to heaven. It's a reminder to you to crossover death and live. Healing power can come to people just by Jesus speaking a word of healing. Anyone that comes into contact with Jesus by the touch of faith will partake of his healing power that will heal his or her heart, soul, mind, and spirit. The greatest overflowing of blessings today is contacted through prayer and faith. The unruly passion for the opposite sex, that mass of spiritual hypocrisy, the insatiable taste for money, and power, all can be dried up in you if you just reach out to touch Him. Jesus came to challenge and deliver captives of sickness and death with an ultimatum to the Devil, "Let my people go." Death, disease, and disaster all fled at his presence and word. Never before has instances of divine power been seen such as Jesus displayed. It doesn't matter who you are, what uncleanness you may have, or what your character may be, if you just reach out and touch Jesus while contact is being established you shall be healed. Any sort of contact with Jesus will answer your purpose. Jesus' patriotism was that of flesh and blood. He was born for the Holy obligation of building a bridge-connecting mankind to Heaven. He took up residence among the poor and disenfranchised. Mark 12:37 tell us that, "the common people" heard Jesus gladly, but the elite spurned and rejected the humble carpenter. Jesus' knees were calloused from bending over, and praying for people that he loved, and for his enemies. His biography leads from the pavement (street) to the parchment (Bible). Men and women have been healed of all kinds of spiritual and moral diseases by coming into contact with Jesus, who gives His grace to those who have neither money nor anything valuable to offer him. Some people are so physically, spiritually, and morally sick and eager to get well that they dream of buying salvation and health from doctors, lawyers, preachers, and teachers whose advice is shallow. Others look for new medical discoveries for certain cures, and therefore place their trust in medical science. There is no medicine discovered now or in the future that can stop the heart that's in fear of the judgment of God. No earthly surgery can take away a tumorous load of sin from the conscience. No preacher, priest, prophet, or philosopher can clean a heart that's leprous. Only Jesus can heal leprosy of the mind, raise those in trespasses of sin, and comfort those in the crack house of despair. Saints of God claim deliverance from sickness, sin, and material things as theirs by stating, "In the name of Jesus I claim the victory." People soon discover that they have lost valuable time and money relying on other sources for advice, and that they should have gone directly to God in prayer. Doctors today rely on antibiotics as cure all for everything in the body. Yet, the most expensive drug that cost no money at all, and can cure any disease now, in the future, distance future, or for that matter forever, was not found under a microscope, but it was in a ***nail*** that had pierced the hands of Jesus. He is a disease free man that has the antibodies for all disease. That means that absolutely nothing can ever come into your life without having passed through His nail-scarred hand. It means that your prayers really do count because you are praying to the one who has complete control over all things. When people come to Jesus they nail their denominations to the cross, and receive an inoculation against sin by getting a good dose of the Holy Ghost. We don't have to read chapters in the Bible everyday, or witness to a certain number people, or use a special prayer to be heard by God. All we have to do just reach out and grab hold of the hem of his garment. It's His job to do the rest. Jesus often made himself accessible to anyone. In everyone life there is something that should make us want to touch him. When we do, we make the connecting link between Him and ourselves. All things that touch us touch him. We are like electrical currents in the gospel. As electrical currents have a positive and negative charge, so it's with fellowship and prayer. When we touch and agree while praying for deliverance there is a current of sorrow flowing from our heart to Jesus and a current of forgiveness flowing from the heart of Jesus toward us. Perhaps you are thinking that you have done too much to be forgiven, that you have gone on too long in sin, and that there are too many things between you and God. These are issues of hindrance. These are things that are blocking your walk with Christ. They may be issues that have piled up for years, but instead of trying to walk through them, you need to sidestep and go around them, using faith and prayer as your guide. People who have issues that they cannot stop from flowing need to reach out and touch Jesus; no matter how nervous or trembling that they are. A telephone line will shake with the wind, but it will still send full current through the phone. A trembling faith can also carry full salvation from Jesus to you. Though you may be trembling like the woman that Jesus healed, as long as there is contact between you and the power of Jesus, His power will travel along your trembling finger and bring healing to your heart and soul. When you are in fellowship with the Spirit your life will totally change. The moment the Spirit of God comes in your life your spiritual struggles will be minimized. You will no longer have to wrestle and do battle with the adversary alone. You can throw away your battle plan because God's plans are more successful. In searching for hidden souls we must strip away the careful constructions and mythology we each create out of pride, delusion, or even hope; for when a woman comes to the end of herself, she comes to the beginning of Christ. One touch of Jesus will cure her problems. When life is at its darkest, there's still an impulse that points her forward to the conviction that there's yet more to be done. She knows that Jesus is the historylogical now and the eschatological not yet.

10

What To Do When You Have Blown It

Often times when Jesus traveled his entourage consisted of women who had come to be healed or just to meet his presence. Women may have followed Jesus because they are usually more tender hearted toward the gospel then men. Women are strong believers and worshipers of Jesus Christ. They could not have accomplished things otherwise. The indomitable spirits of women who believe in the righteousness of a cause bring the power of the Holy Spirit to full fruition. When it looks like they are hopelessly defeated women emerge victorious through prayer. On one occasion during his travel's Jesus had met a woman that was a Gentile of Syrophoenician origin who lived in the Roman district of Syria. She came to him as we all do, out of her deepest needs and fear, to avoid the possible loss of her daughter to an illness that was demonic. Fearing that her daughter had but a short while to live, she cried at the fullness of her lungs capacity, *"Have mercy on me, O Lord, thou son of David; my daughter is grievously vexed with a Devil!"* She had a great and pressing need that was conscious, dangerous, and burdensome. She had cried to Jesus as a person earnestly seeking a cure not for herself, but her daughter. She couldn't stand to see the misery that an evil spirit had caused in her child. She had heard about Jesus, but she was not content with second hand information, so she sought to try its value for herself. She approached him and bowed down at his feet. She begged him to cast the demon out of her daughter. Here is the strangeness of this story about Jesus. He seems not to be seeing her at all when he says to her, *"Let the children be fed first, for it's not fair to take the children's food and throw it to the dogs."* Believers don't expect such harshness and insensitivity from Jesus. In Jesus we have come to expect that no one is invisible, especially those who live at the very margins of society. Yet, he was speaking to this woman as if she was invisible to him. It was as if she had no anguish, no flesh and bones, no tears, and no dying daughter. The mother of this sick child had pitifully come and thrown herself at Jesus' feet. Her child's case was urgent, and Jesus answered her in no tone at all. It was if he was deaf and passed right by her. Yet, she was not put off by his behavior. The woman calling on Jesus perhaps thought, "She may have a devil, but she is still my daughter, and I am going to shout until I get his attention." She loudly petitioned him to *"Have mercy on me."* She doesn't care what kind of mercy he gives just as long as he extends mercy to her child. She wouldn't accept the condition of her invisibility, but he answered her not a word.

There are times when the legs give way to the floor, the eyes have grown dim, and the heart yields to life's stop sign. This is known as the hour of God's silence. This is the time that he takes to listen rather than speak. This is the hour for prayer. By his silence Jesus had tried her faith. He wanted to see just how far this woman would go in her love for her daughter, and her faith in him. To add insult to injury his disciples tried to have the woman thrown out of the house by asking him to send her away. Her noise annoyed them, but she had never cried after them. She made noise only for her Savior. Her faith could not be silenced by the irrational fears of the disciples. Sometime we as disciples become important in our own eyes. We think that people are pushing and crowding to hear us, when in actuality it's only Jesus and the gospel that attracted them to the church. **"I am not sent but to the lost sheep of the house of Israel."** Jesus said. What the woman may not have realized was that she had to market herself. She had to sell her personality to Jesus and to persuade him to her way of thinking. She was not of the house of Israel. She was a Gentile, a stranger to the Commonwealth of Israel. Christ had not come to save or be committed to do anything for her or the Gentile race. Salvation was of the Jews. Jesus' personal ministry was to be the glory of his people Israel. When the woman continued hollering for mercy, Jesus insisted that she was not worthy to have such honors given to her. *"It is not meet to take the children's bread and cast it to dogs,"* he said. (Matthew 15:26) Jesus here seems to allow that Gentiles, whom he had created, should not share in the favors bestowed upon Jewish people. He implied that ordinances of the church and church privileges are for the (Jewish) children of God. This is their bread, and must not be prostituted to people who are unworthy or unsaved. Common charity is distributed to all, but spiritual things are only to be appropriated to the household of faith. How can anyone expect to eat bread in another's house without being part of the family? When a person is not part of a family he or she has to sell their personality to the family to gain its trust. The family is fully satisfied and trusts a person when it gives him or her "honorary" family status. When anybody is allowed to eat at the family table the bread reserved for true family members is wasted. The church world calls it taking that which is holy and giving it to the dogs. The woman knew that the Jews looked upon Gentiles with great contempt. Gentiles were called and thought of as being *dogs,* in contrast with the house of Israel, who were so dignified and privileged. The woman was met with indignation, reproach, and much discouragement. She may have said to herself, "What a fool I have made of myself. Here I am in distress. My daughter is near death, and I know that he has the power to heal, yet, he taunts me and abuse me, and to top it all off he calls me a dog. I should have stayed home." The reference to her as being a *dog* could have drove her to anger or despair, if she did not have strong faith. This woman was cut off from any hope at all. Such actions would have caused others to curse, argue, or misplace their trust in Jesus. This may have been a blemish on Jesus' reputation as well as her opinion about him. She may have wondered why he was called, "The Good Shepherd" when all she had been treated with was roughness. "I am not a dog; I am a woman, a virtuous honest woman. Although I am in misery I am not sure it's not suitable to call me a dog, yet the dogs eat the crumbs that fall from the Master's table. I cannot say that you are my father, because I don't stand in relation to you. Therefore, I can't claim the privilege of being a child, but you are my Master, and master's feed their dogs even though they may be stray's. Then again, I am a dog under the table of grace. I may have been a dog in my way of life while I was out in the street, and far apart from you, but now you have come and preached at my borders. I was a sinner that was permitted to hear the full gospel fall from your lips of mercy. I have seen sick people get up off of their beds of affliction, I have watched you call decrepit bodies from tombs, therefore Lord let me have the crumbs that fall off your table of Grace." Her humility and necessity of a healing for her daughter had made her happy for crumbs. Jesus had referred to this woman as a dog, but he knows and understands that people who have been living a rough life often tend to lose their sense of humanity, and the beast within them comes out. Often we see people performing acts that we think only the lowest animal would do. We may not outwardly call them dogs, but we get uncomfortable when see: drug addicts, crack heads, drunks, gangs, hoodlums, pedophiles, rapists, transvestites, drag queens, homeless people picking out of garbage cans. We become even more offended when we see people urinating in view of the public, young boys dressed like convicts with their pants falling down and harassing young girls, and young prostitutes jumping from one car to the next. We secretly have our own names for all of those types. Jesus was not being mean when he called her a dog. He was letting the woman know that the saints of his church get first priority. A woman isn't really enjoying the fullness of salvation if she's settling for "crumbs of life" when she can have the bread of life. It's like a man who has both a mistress and a wife. He knows that his priority is with his family and wife, and it's where he spends most of his time. His lover is only getting the "crumbs" or left over time as his mistress and she only sees him at a scheduled time. Even when he's with his lover he still may accidentally address her by his wife's name because he is married and committed to her. Jesus is also telling this woman that his bride, the church, gets top priority and that she was on the bottom of his list, because he is married to the believer. Yet, this woman was so thankful just to be in his presence that she may have thought, "Master if you shut me out of one door I will go to the other: if you shut me out at both doors I will climb through the window. If the window is shut I will lie on the doormat: and if you kick me in the street, I will lie here until you come out, then I will follow you. If I be a dog then I will follow at the heels of mercy."

"I will," are two of the most powerful and challenging words in any language. Whether spoken quietly, loudly, or silently, those three words have propelled lots of people to success. Many brave men and women who have been attacked by enemies, wild animals, disowned by families, have survived terrible storms, cold, heat, hunger, and thirst, under what seemed to be impossible conditions because they said, "I will survive." As we travel toward God we will face many obstacles, but you must have the "I will survive" attitude. When the challenges of life are faced, and ordeals are placed in front of you; you must be determined with all your heart to get through to the end to survive, and if necessary to do it alone. This is what we need in our heart when it comes to Christianity. Not just starting the race, but moving forward one step at a time toward the finish line. Regardless of what Satan may send we shouldn't be deterred from reaching our goal. The woman was fearful that she would not be blessed, but fear impregnates faith. Faith at full term delivers blessings. She realized that as a non-Jewish person she could not demand anything from God's table that had been reserved for his chosen family. She was hoping that the Jewish race would find fault, play, and grow tired of their bread (blessings), so that some of the blessing may fall on the floor to a Gentile such as her. She was thankful for anything that Jesus could do for her child. She realized that she deserved nothing. But her faith encouraged her to expect crumbs from her master's table. If she was a dog, she was his *dog*. She had come to worship him. The thought of her little daughter at home, and of the misery that the demons had subjected her caused the woman to press against the savior's feet. She quietly said, *"Lord help me."* By quietly saying *"Lord help me"* she had improved in her prayers. God doesn't need us shouting at him. It's like we are demanding him to do something for us at that very moment, even though we know that we are not worthy of His blessings. When answers to our prayers have been put off, God is teaching us to pray more earnest and sincere prayers, but most of all to *worship* him. We are visible to Jesus because he loves us even when we cannot conform to any patterns or belong to any privileged class. Worship is the act of paying divine honor to God. Reverence to God is when we lie prostrate (flat to the earth) or bow ourselves to render sacred gifts, honors, and sacrifices to God. Worship is showing God that He alone is worthy to receive honor and glory. When believers truly worship Him God gets the glory and responds to the believer's prayers. That's when born again believers receive their blessings from him. The words "born again" means *"born from above."* It's that part of life and soul which is capable of relating with God. Being born again is not an identification tag: a religious feeling, church affirmation, or doctrinal distinction, but it's a reality. We must be born again spiritually, and it may be viewed as a form of resurrection. (John 3:1) The idea of being born again didn't start with Jesus. God the Father had ideas of redeeming Israel. In the Old Testament He declares *" I will put my law in their inward parts (minds) and write it in their hearts. I will be their God and they will be my people."* In (Ezekiel 11:19) He states, *"I will give them one heart and I will put a new spirit within you; and I will take the stony heart out of their flesh, and will give them a heart of flesh."* (Jeremiah 31:33) God is telling the world that His love is to be inscribed on tablets (hearts) of flesh. This wasn't the usual method of writing. In the Old Testament stone tablets were usually used to inscribe words, but the work was expensive, labor-intensive, and tablets could be lost or broken. God's message is so important that it has to be put into our hearts. It's to be written so that its message can be passed on. *"For the vision is yet for the appointed time; but at the end it shall speak, and not lie: Though it tarry, wait for it; because it will surely come, it will not tarry."* (Habakkuk 2:3)

Many people are troubled about coming to Christ. To some coming to Jesus is a struggle. Some have a half-and-half gospel, part law part grace. They cannot see that salvation must come by grace and faith, and not by the works of the Law. It's out of a spiritual burden, and desperation that they are forced to come to Jesus. Faith obeys God's precept and will not go on without His command. Peter's faith did not try to walk upon water until Jesus gave the word of permission by bidding Peter to come to him. *"Bid me come"* denotes a fear of not moving until there is an assurance from the Lord that it's safe to venture. Faith goes further because if a person begins to sink and he or she prays, "Lord save me" Jesus will be there with outstretched hands. How can you sink beneath them? When you are in trouble and don't know where to turn, you should turn immediately to prayer. Prayer mixed with faith causes us to pour our hearts out to the Lord. The easiest thing for anyone to do, but yet, it's the hardest thing to do is to believe and live. In reality and out of desperation, this woman had cried out, "Lord help me." The first time that she cried out she was equating Jesus with earthly power by calling him, *"Thou son of David."* Although, it was true that Jesus came through David's lineage he did not need to be reminded of that fact. When believers pray in church at the altar, or for a weaker saint they should leave off all of the Pharisaical way of praying, which is using great sounding words, and saying things to try to get the crowd stirred up to excitement. When praying Jesus doesn't need to be reminded that he is the God of Abraham, Isaac, and Jacob or that he created the sun, moon, and the stars. He knows that he delivered the three Hebrew boys from the fiery furnace, and that he drove Pharaoh into the sea. He is not an old man sitting on a throne with Alzheimer's. All he wants a believer to say in a sincere prayer is, "Lord help me." The woman's shouting would never have drawn Jesus' attention. That's why people should be careful hollering and shouting in church under their own glory rather than under the anointing of God. God doesn't want to hear how loud you can scream or see how good you can dance. He wants to see how well you humble yourself and live right. Jesus knew what he had done by not answering the woman, even though he did not immediately give her the answer she expected. Instead of blaming Jesus for being sarcastic the woman placed the blame where it belonged, upon herself. She suspected that in her first encounter with Jesus that she had not been humble, earnest, or reverent enough with her prayers. Therefore, she received back from Jesus what she had dished out. Jesus condemned the sin of hypocrisy more than any other sin; especially the open, arrogant, and flagrant kind practiced by people of his day. Her crying had annoyed the disciples, but Jesus loves to be sincerely cried after. No matter how loud we cry, every prayer is not always immediately answered. Sometimes God doesn't answer prayers just to improve or prove a person's faith. Jesus had treated her vile to test her; he knew what was in her heart, and the strength of her faith, but he wanted her to see how much she wanted deliverance for her daughter. He knew that she was able by his grace, to break through such discouragement. Jesus later commended her faith and cured her daughter who was at home. The healing virtue of Christ had traveled through time and distance. Jesus affected a cure for the woman's daughter, because of the mother's faith. This woman was in a crisis that had her desperately seeking a solution to her problem. She knew that when she came into the presence of Jesus that she would cause a disturbance. In today's time some people that are down and out, still come into the House of God creating a disturbance by calling loudly on the name of Jesus to remove their sin. They may cause a disturbance in Jesus' house by wearing outlandish hairstyles, body piercing rings, flip-flop shoes, nasty jeans, shorts, tee shirts, mini skirts, or "halter" tops. It may take them longer to find scripture in the Bible, and they may not know the words to a song. They may even place notes in the collection plate asking for help when they have no money, or just pass the plate along. They may speak out of turn during worship and say prayers that make no sense to us, but that is why they are called "heathens" because they do not know the principles of the church, but they do know what they desire from Jesus. They know that Jesus has no prejudice in his compassion, and that he is available to serve the helpless in the face of social, religious, physical, psychological, and financial pressures surrounding them. Some saints of God today roll their eyes and talk about others when they come to church because they're not one of them, but a desperate person in need of Jesus' help don't pay them any attention. The woman seeking a cure for her daughter knew that her child was out of control so she sought help outside of her culture, race, and possibly her religion. You see this woman realized that in order to save her child she had to re-arrange her schedule, and re-organize her priorities. Whether she wanted to or not, she had to take a day off from work and seek out Jesus. She had to go some extra distance to get some help from God. When a believer's will conform to the will of Christ they can ask anything of him and receive it, but some women are locked into an emotional "time zone." Their faces are etched with pain. They worry about romance, finance, and wayward children. When children are sick and the doctors have done all that they can do, it becomes troubling to parents to feel the misery of their children, which are also pieces of themselves. Emotional shock, anger, and distrust results when a doctor has told a parent that its child have come down with a debilitating or terminal disease, and he or she doesn't know how to treat it. Many of us want help from the Lord but we are not willing to go out of our way to get that help. We are not willing to make time or take time for Jesus. This woman knew that she needed some help with her parenting skills, so she had to leave work early to make an appointment with the Lord. Perhaps she canceled her only night out with the girls, or lost a few dollars by not working on her job, but that was ok because she was desperately seeking Jesus. In today's society, there are many like this woman still seeking Jesus. More people are seeking after the true God than before because there is a great spiritual thirst in the land. Women are willing to go anywhere and do anything to get a blessing from Jesus. They are no longer motivated by money, the beauty of buildings, doctrine, or denomination. They just want to be in the presence of Christ, and see the manifestation of Jesus in their lives. They are looking for answers and not entertainment. Women want to know how to deal with their adulterous or fornicating habits, addictions, attitudes, and jealousies. They want to know how to mend their broken homes and raise a difficult child that something or someone had possession of. The woman of the text is not alone in her plight. Many of us have children in the same condition. Something or someone has taken possession of their minds and their lives. They now have an ugly, arrogant, unrecognizable, personality. Some of our children have become possessed by those great American spirits of selfishness, pride, materialism, and rebellion. Some are possessed with their looks and appearance. They cannot survive without the latest hairstyle, beeper, cell phone, clothes by Fubu, and having their nails done every week. Can you imagine this woman's daily struggle with her child? She has with a demon possessed child who has bouts of temper-tantrums and acts of rage. Doors and windows in her house may be damaged from the stress of slamming and kicking. The mother could also have scars from physically battling her daughter to keep her from sneaking out of the house to be with some boy or group of kids that she knows. It would seem that no matter what she tried; nothing could save her daughter from this cycle of self-destruction. This woman had reached the end of her rope. So, she came to Jesus thereby causing a major disturbance. This woman knew nothing of protocol and procedures involving Jewish customs and rituals. She just knew that this man Jesus was representing the God that turned Canaan and Israel upside down, and that he had a reputation for fixing problems. Like the woman of the Bible, we need Jesus' help. We are powerless. When our back is up against the wall we turn to the church asking for prayer only after its confirmed that a child is pregnant, dead, in the hospital, or when he or she is found with a gun, joints, crack, or foils of white powder. There's no sound that can match the wailing, crying, and moaning of a mother whose child has died while using drugs or was involved in an accident, or drive by shooting. When a family crisis arise the preacher is usually the last person on the list who gets called in, and that's only after the police have a child in lock-up. A Preacher doesn't come to beat a child up, but to raise them up. He or she gets on them, but they also welcome them back with love and embrace them. When the preacher cannot do anything that's when parents prostate themselves at Jesus' feet.

    You that are reading this book; your life may have been punctuated with one loss after another. You may have lost a job, relationship, been divorced, or had someone close to you that caused you to go into a major depressive episode. Your situation may have caused you leave your community and moved thousands of miles away from where the tragedy occurred. For years you may not have been able to work and battled with suicidal thoughts. Your children may have been

There's Enough Woman Left to be Your Lady

the only reason you didn't take your own life. The strong-woman act you had put together crumbled in when you suffered one loss too many. You were emotionally unresponsive, battled with depression and rage and was not the least bit interested in allowing yourself to ever love anything or anyone again. You blamed your God, country, military, parents, or even the church for the difficulties in your life. Overtime your anger hardened into resentment. You realized that you could no longer carry this emotional load on your own, but instead of seeing it as a curse, you learned to meditate on God's word, and used exercise and living in the present moment as a barometer. You may have discovered that when you began meditating, it was very difficult to sit still for just a few minutes, but the longer you're able to sit still, the more peace you found and it did so much to nurture and sustain you. It's God's way to get your awareness into your body and out of your head. When parents suffer pain and loss they sometimes wonder why God let it happen. Sometimes it cause a parents imagination to work overtime wondering, "Why me?" or "How much time do my child have?" Instead of negative thoughts pure thoughts should run in the mind of the affected person. The brighter the thoughts the deeper the roots of faith and belief will grow. Faith will find the ways and means to overcome all obstacles in a diseased person's life. If you are going through circumstances that you don't understand, cry out unto the Lord. There's enough woman left to be His lady.

11

I Have A Problem

There's a story in the Gospels (John 8:3-11) that have a shady history of a woman taken in the act of adultery, which at that time was a capital offense. There was no question about her guilt, because the Scribes and Pharisees that had brought her in testified that she was caught in "the very act" of adultery, but where is the man? The law said plainly: *"If a man is found lying with the wife of another man, both of them shall die."* (Deuteronomy 22:22) The manner of execution was not described, except that it's in the case of a man who committed adultery with a woman, who was engaged to another man. Therefore, we can assume that she was married. In that instance the law said, *"You shall bring them both out to the gate of that city, and you shall stone them to death."* (Deuteronomy 22:23-24) The woman's accusers were prepared to stone her to death. Jesus, who is often shown in the Gospels as resisting the rigid application of law, and speaking powerfully about the necessity of forgiveness, is confronted with the ultimate test of his interpretation of law and grace with this case. The Pharisees demanded, "Now the Law of Moses commanded us to stone such women; what then do <u>you</u> say?" They were ready to misquote Deuteronomy 22:22. They had stressed stoning only the woman in the recorded quotes of their conversation with Jesus, but the Law demanded that both parties be stoned. It was only to be applied under the condition of persistence after previous warning, and after the actual witness of the act of adultery by two competent witnesses. If the charge was proven the couple was to be publicly stoned to death. How many people would be so stupid as to expose their sexual activities openly to the public, knowing that death was the ultimate penalty? Jesus responded to their question in a manner that epitomizes the woman, but the Pharisees and scribes continued to press their point. They wanted grounds on which to accuse Jesus. They were not after the poor woman as much as they were after Jesus. He was the one they were really after. This was a well-rehearsed plot by religious leaders to skillfully lay a trap to "test" Jesus with the idea of proving Him false, and to upset Jesus' popularity. Those self-righteous, self-appointed judge and jury were filled hatred toward Him and what He taught. They were out to hang Jesus. As these religious leaders persisted in questioning him, Jesus stooped and wrote in the sand. The Bible doesn't say what he had written, but I am inclined to believe that he was writing each man sins in the dirt, and as they saw what was being written they were convicted in their hearts. Or it could have been that he was letting them know that they were former customers of the woman. Men will never own up to cheating, because it makes them look cheap and disrespectful. It takes a lot of threatening and pleading from a woman for a man to admit that he has strayed, but even then he may tell a lie. Jesus specifically invited anyone among them who was sinless, to throw the first stone, "Go ahead, you are right, the Law says stone her. She is guilty. Now which of you are sinless? He that's without sin cast the first stone." By this statement they could not possibly say Jesus rejected the law. The Pharisees and Scribes who had hauled the woman in abandoned her one by one. They were suddenly preoccupied with their own sins. Afterwards He stood up and said to her, "Woman, where are thy accusers? Did no one condemn you? Neither do I condemn you." He was in context saying, "Since no one has found you guilty and sentenced you to death, neither do I sentence you to death." Why did he say that? The truth is that he had found her guilty. That's why he told her to go her way and sin no more. The reason Jesus released the woman with no more than an admonition not to sin any more was that he knew the Law was being applied in a discriminatory manner. The scriptures state that she was, "Caught in the very act of adultery." It took two sinners to commit this sin. Where was the man? Why didn't they bring her partner? The law explicitly stated, "That both the man and the woman should be put to death." Who is trying to get even with the woman? Who had set a deliberate trap for her? Was it her husband, or a former lover? Perhaps the husband had set her up for divorce or to have her stoned. This condemned woman needed forgiveness and grace, which Jesus offered. The woman did not make any excuses. She was guilty. She knew it, and the world knew it. She stood condemned. If she had not been a woman, perhaps she would not have been in danger of losing her life. It may be a very good reason to suspect that has been at least part of Jesus' motivation to forgive all manner of her sins. What we have in Jesus is a window of divinity, displaying the very Holiness of God revealed in human flesh. Jesus was demonstrating the grace and forgiveness of God. What's the nature of Christ's Gospel? It's the gospel to forgive all manner of sin that has lead to the repentance of the perpetrator. This woman didn't have to be convinced of the fact that she needed grace, but she also knew that she didn't deserve it. She knew that the wages of sin was death, and that the soul that sinned would surely die. She was a spiritual midget in the need of the riches of God's marvelous grace. Jesus did not tell the woman to clean up her act, and then He would forgive her. He just said, "Neither do I condemn you. Go your way. Sin no more." God is not willing that any should perish. If capital punishment had been meted out to all the biblical characters that deserved it under the law, there would have been no Moses, David, Paul, Psalms, Ten Commandments, and Torah handed down from Mt. Sinai. Perhaps there wouldn't have been any epistles to the early Christian churches. Paul asked, *"Who shall deliver me from this body of death?" He answered his own rhetorical question, "Thanks be to God through our Lord Jesus Christ."* (Romans 7:24-25) Paul never tired of contrasting the person he had been with the person he had become, by the grace of God. By God's grace neither Paul, Moses, nor David received what law said they deserved. History is richer for it, and we are blessed of it. Jesus didn't say be obedient and then I will save you, for God doesn't wait on works of righteousness before saving a person. There is salvation for all that will put their faith in Christ. A very wicked sinner can be saved today, at this very moment if he or she give their problems to Jesus. Jesus doesn't care about what happened in your life last night, last month, last year, or whenever. What He does care about is that you will come to Him and receive the free gift of eternal life right now. Many women can give testimonies to the fact that, "Grace is greater than all of their sins." Like Moses, David, and Paul, they have been redeemed by the grace of God. Therefore, they must go about proclaiming the Gospel of God's gracious redemption. This woman isn't the only one who has had a problem. As Christians we are married to God in the spirit, but we all have moral and spiritual problems involving faithfulness to God. An eternal, life long, monogamous marriage is as exciting as you make it. We should not assume that every relationship called a marriage by society equals the Biblical definition of a marriage. The Bible says, *"What God has joined together let no man take asunder."* Some couples that have a marriage license issued by the civil authority are not married in the eyes of God because one or both of the partners didn't believe in God. Therefore, they were not joined together by him. For example if a drunken man marries a woman that he just met, and the next day he sobers, and regrets his action, and they are divorced, was that marriage sanctioned by God? What complicates matters is that in today's society worldly habits are the shaky foundation upon which many marriages are built. What do you do if your husband has activities that center on lying or violent behavior, doing drugs, partying with you, and womanizing with others? What if you decide that you want live for God and he doesn't want to cease these activities? Will you leave? Will this cause a divorce in your marriage? If you decide to go through these challenges you must face the adversary head on. One small breath of true love can spark a flame that last forever, but one of the hardest things that a woman face when she become converted and her husband doesn't is the fear of losing him if she becomes a new person in the Lord. Friction and fear often occur when one spouse is trying to live a Christ-like life while the other is still in sin, disinterested in church, or even hostile and taunting. Often when faced with this type of crisis women think, "What if I change my life, follow Christ and then my husband doesn't want me anymore? What if I change so much that he thinks I'm boring or rejects me completely. I can't bear to lose him!" If you give in to these fears and thoughts, you may give up or retreat away from God completely. If you're afraid you'll lose your husband if you change and follow what God is telling you to do, be honest and direct with him! Say, "Look, God is making certain changes in my life right now and I don't feel comfortable with you and your activities anymore. I'm afraid that we've built our marriage on the wrong type activities and if I don't do these things anymore with you, you'll leave me." Fear of losing your spouse is just Satan's way of halting your progression, but if God is really what you want what have you really got to lose. Until you realize that you want God in your life and want to do His will, you'll struggle with this issue. Free yourself and let God deal with that person. You simply must decide ahead of time that you will rely on God during moments of temptation. You have to let the Holy Spirit speak what you will say when your husband or someone else tries to convince you that it's ok to continue doing something that you know is wrong. It will flow naturally from you when faced with the challenge. This will either force your husband to ask himself, "Am I ready to lose her?" Or he may not even care. Either way you will know, and then you can stop sidestepping and avoiding the real issue in your marriage. However, you must realize that when you give up any activity or habit that's negative, you must replace it with something positive. That positivism may even be envisioning the person you want to become and the life you want to live. Prayer and Bible study is indispensable fillers for the void. As critical as it is to fill the void in your personal life, it's just as critical to fill the void in your physical and spiritual marriage. Many marriages need to go back to the altar where the vow was made. At the altar you fill the void by first recognizing that you have a problem, and then discussing it with God until you come to some point of resolution. Sometimes it can be short lived and other times it can take months to get to the bottom of it, but you must remain optimistic. It's possible to live day to day until God settles the matter. If you are heading down the path the Lord directed, and you're going with a single eye focused on His glory, you will meet with opposition. It most likely is the adversary's attempts to keep you from going forward. It's important to distinguish the difference between Satan's attempts to keep you from doing what God wants, and God telling you that you're on the wrong path, or pursuing Him with the wrong motives. Even when you decide to follow Jesus Christ, life doesn't suddenly get easy. All your challenges and temptations will still be present and may even be heightened because Satan knows that you have to take a firm stand. When you have the courage to stand on God's side of the line He will neither leave you nor forsake you. That's why it's so important to study God's Word to know what His policies are, and also why it's so important to seek a solid answer from Him when making important decisions. If your marriage is built on improper activities, then replace them with activities that build your relationship with God and your spouse without destructive consequences. There's still enough woman left to be His Lady.

12

A Love Like Yours Don't Come Knocking Everyday

Life is so satisfying and fulfilling when you are wedded to the spirit of the Lord. You get the feeling that you are loved, which causes you to give love, and receive greater love from God. You become committed to love, which means giving and forgiving every day, and choosing to love, no matter what the circumstances. It means doing your own personal work even if you know it might mean big time changes for you; and being willing to spend the time and energy to make your spiritual marriage work. It also mean putting Jesus first when you really want to put your own interests first, and being willing to compromise, until you and God are both satisfied. No degree of love can stand the test of time without strong commitment. Commitment seems like such a "duty" word that takes the joy and fun out of life, but that isn't how you should look upon it. Commitment is the concrete foundation for marriage. Commitment is from the heart. It has to be there even when you don't "like" your spouse or God at times, and when life gets rough or overwhelming. Overall people want to love and be loved, and have someone to build and share life together with. The initiative rests with women. A woman can make a romantic evening unforgettable or a nightmare from hell. Women come in all sizes, colors, and shapes. They are smart, honest, loyal, and forgiving. They know that knowledge is power, but they still know how to use their softer side to make a point. They live in homes, apartments, hotels, boats, and cabins. They drive, walk, run, fly, or e-mail you to show how much they care about you. Women are like hummingbirds seeking nectar in every sunny field and rarely setting on one flower. They hover over relations until they find the right scent. Some flit from the first ray of sweet romance and often drift when things get serious or dark in their lives. The heart of a woman is what makes her world spin! The only way a woman can bring a real man into her life is through honor, decency, true romance, and a commitment to everlasting love. Romance is about caring, thoughtfulness, sensitivity, and creating love. Romance is a strong intoxicant that we have all drank from. It's so strong that you can fall in love with the mere idea of being in love. Some people get such a high from romance, that they actually believe it will solve all of their problems. "If I just had a man it would be all right!" If I had "a woman I'd be a better man!" Romance helps a woman to feel cared for, even if she is resistant. Men can move mountains of resistance from women if they only use the right approach. Every woman has her own "hot buttons" and men should pay special attention to those. Some men are natural at creating the kind of romance that women want, but a lot of men think romance is simply preparation for sex. While most men are less in a hurry to commit, they are almost always anxious to hurry sex. Men find it easy to give their body, but backup when asked to give their heart in a relationship. A virtuous woman can bring the heart and emotion together. She will not sleep with a man outside of matrimony. She refuse to sacrifice herself on the altar of love. In order to be emotionally and physically available for sex and reproduction, a woman needs to feel that a man is kind, wants marriage, is a good provider, and that he cares. In general, women seem to be in more of a hurry about seeking marriage and commitment in a relationship than men are, but most women still seem to keep God in their knowledge. Women have good reason for wanting to speed the up process of romance. They know that if they are sitting on the sidelines waiting for a man to take the initiative, it can seem like forever, and if they don't hurry relationships, they may remain single forever. Unfortunately, rushing relationships too often leads to breakup and heartache. It's easy for women to get impatient and seek a deep and abiding love in the arms of a stranger. When it doesn't work she will come to the conclusion that all men are romantic idiots. Romance is wonderful if it leads in God's direction, but sometime a person's feeling can be so focused on another person that his or her attention is pulled away from God. When that happens it's called spiritual seduction. Romance has a past, present, and future, and it can cripple any or all of those time frames in a life. It can do some crazy things to a person's head. It can cause impulsive decisions to be made with no regard to the future. Romance can send calm people into a rage; cause some to take their own lives, or to take the life of another person. Sometimes it's so strong and poisonous that it can overshadow the working of the Holy Spirit. When a woman rush off in love in a moment when her defenses are low or illusions high; she may wake up days or years later and find herself sorry for what she's gotten into. Romance is a feeling, and we imagine those feelings to be proof of a long lasting love. However, romance is like the ignition system on an engine; if the engine has locked up or the timing isn't just right, love won't start. Christians are not immune to the ups and downs of romance. So many Christians are hurting from a broken romance, a lack of romance, or a romance with the wrong person. However, Christians must live according to the word of God and not the flesh. To live a spiritual lifestyle is to be set apart from a person practicing sin. How can a spirit led person enjoy a relationship with a person led by the flesh? An unbeliever's conscious is ruled by lust of the flesh. Lust is making decisions that the brain ought to make. If a person's mind is set on flesh they are mostly conscious of another person's body and not commitment. The person whom they desire spiritual walk with God means little to them. The deepest form of romantic love, which commits people to each other for their well being no matter what the cost is Agape. The goal is to grow in divine love through prayer, worship, and intimacy. Jesus said, *"Behold I stand at the door, and knock: if any man hear my voice, and open the door, I will come in to him, and will sup with him, and he with me."* (Revelations 3:20) A love like Jesus' doesn't come knocking everyday. When his love knocks you better answer the door of your heart. All forms of love in Christ are greatly enhanced in a relationship through a shared spirituality. Praying and worshiping together as a couple or family builds deep and lasting beliefs and values. It can open the floodgates for God's grace in the areas such as forgiveness, acceptance, reconciliation, faith, hope, and peace. It's also the core for building family celebrations and traditions. A marriage keeps growing because couples work at making it grow. They are committed for the long haul. When conflicts rise they work them out honestly and quickly. They trust that their love for God will grow stronger each day, and that His love will provide shelter and a safe haven each day. As in all marriages or relationships there are good and bad times, and sometimes your marriage or relationship with God might also hit rock bottom. Everyone experience's spiritual divorce from God when they have failed in His sight to remain pure and committed to the Gospel. Everyday in some capacity we all commit indiscrete acts of spiritual infidelity, and adultery with Satan. You divorce yourself from God when you give the Devil an opportunity to test your love for Him. When you don't pray, get angry, curse, gossip, and take too long to forgive, or rundown your Christian and sinful brothers and sisters you have split from God. Sensuality of prayer, praise, and even worship will disappear and you will wound God deeply by your mask of silence. You will move farther and farther apart from Him until you are almost broke. When you have neglected your spiritual life for years at a time, God brings so much meaning to your life by sharing all of your interests and passions. That's when you have to take long walks alone or together with God; and search for mutual intimacy and feelings. The road will still be bumpy. However, you will have moved away from rejection and intolerance, toward greater acceptance and understanding of God's special qualities. You will learn to be more honest in sharing your anger with Him. You will again fall deeply in love with Him. Without Christ the experience of a woman falling in love is invariably temporary no matter whom she's with. This is not to say that she cease loving the person with whom she fell in love. But it's to say that the feeling of heart stopping, swooning, and ecstatic lovingness that characterizes her experience of falling in love almost always passes. The flowering bloom of romance fades and the honeymoon always end. Women don't love a partner *all* the time. If they say that they do, that's a lie. Women at some point in a relationship don't love as much as they should because of things that affect them in a relationship. But, of course, ceasing to be "in love" need not mean ceasing to love. If partners want to express their innermost desires in love and not be strangers. They must let the magic of their love flow. The closer a woman gets to her man the more she realizes that his love has captured her heart. He has turned the keys to the door of her heart and unlocked her inner emotions. When a woman is properly maintained in love her skin is soft as a rose petal, and her mind is at ease. Just the touch of her hand can send her man reeling. She is his summer in the winter of his life. Her love is kind, gentile like the rain, and warm as sunshine. She kisses with lip locked tightness, and have eyes that glow. She can cause a man to call her five or six times a day. His hands can't help reaching out for her in the night. In darkness and fear she will make him strong. When he closes his eyes he sees her in the silhouette of love. A symphony plays in his heart like ten thousand violins in the air. It lets people know that they are no good without each other. Love involves family, church, play, and quiet time together, or just planning a special evening with just "the two of you." Women also like to do things without having planned it. Sometime all a woman wants is to be held and reassured that she is loved. Men should also take time to just do things spontaneously. Couples should take small "journeys" on the ship of love. Instead of dreaming of far off exotic places that are out of their reach couples should enjoy moments of local relaxation while engaged in stimulating conversation. They should take walks in the park or on the beach, and have a picnic basket along with a blanket to sit on the grass or sand. Anything that sets a mood for romantic gestures such as: Playing favorite love songs. Picking her up and carrying her to the bedroom. Drawing him hot bath water, or just looking him or her in the eyes and saying, "I love you" can be one of the most romantic things couples can do. Men must do things to keep a smile on a woman's face. When a man kisses a woman she must feel the tremor of it because she needs to know that she is needed. She may not say anything, but he must make sure that her voice is heard. If a man wants to be his woman's leading man he should let his love flow. If he doesn't like his part, then he should remove himself off the stage of her heart.

Love is also disagreements, tough times, and feeling overwhelmed. This is called having "issues." Some women have issues that they are not yet ready to confront. When that happens a woman need her own "down time." Some face the issue of losing their looks and sex appeal due to birth of a baby, age, mastectomy, or a hysterectomy. All of the plastic surgery in the world will not help a woman cope until she realizes that her beauty lies within her. She has to be eager to think, act, love, laugh, surprise, and dream beyond herself. Some women have issues of loneliness, because their men don't have time for them. Therefore, they search the Internet looking for the perfect love, and may have committed fornication or adultery at a time that they were weak and needed support. There are lots of things missing in a marriage that cause a woman to stop loving her man and stray. However, some has brought upon themselves the persecution and suffering that their vice has produced. They may have lost family, money, and home, but suffering purifies the soul. It burns and purges out the iniquity and impurity of her inner self. She becomes knowledgeable in the law of God and applies them to oppressors who seek to keep her in selfish thoughts and bestial sexual indulgences. If you are a born again woman Jesus have a variety of expectations, value, strengths, dreams, and spiritual goals for you also. He will bring out your best, and compromise and compliment you. Women that have chosen to share a life together with Jesus must eagerly look forward to spend eternity with their ultimate friend and lover. God wants you to keep your eyes wide open. He doesn't want you to let

Satan trick you into believing that you can change yourself or that your faults aren't significant. If you love Jesus and want the relationship to evolve and grow you've got to learn to cling to Him. Jesus won't take someone to the altar to alter him or her. The person must willingly come to the altar and be open to change. If a person wants to be successful in a long-term romantic relationship, he or she can't leave the choice of a mate up to astrology, chance, or to other prophets of love who all come from their own perspective of what they want in a relationship. It's easy for a woman to love a man that's good looking or fun to be around, but she doesn't like men who make her feel uncomfortable. She would rather stay away from men who aren't as healthy, beautiful, or smart as she is. Women represent continuity. When a woman changes suddenly a man feels vulnerable. A man need to know that a woman's attitude against him will not change, but only a woman's actions truly reflect her feelings toward a man. All of this is contingent on the prospect of putting himself out there in the dating scene, and risking rejection from a woman at an invitation to dinner, amusement, or a night at the movies together. Rejection is man's most despised emotion, but it's the woman's way of telling him, "Get lost." Yet, rejection is just a word. You can't actually touch it or hold it. If you feel rejected, it is an extension of how you choose to feel about the situation. Men never ask themselves: "Why is it that certain guys never seem to get rejected by women? Could I be repeating mistakes from woman to woman that I am not aware of?" Men, who constantly experience the pangs of rejection, fall in love faster and propose marriage on the first date more than men with high self-esteem. Born again men with high self esteem in successful relationships move with reality. They don't fight and invent things that are not in a relationship; but why aren't more Christian men asking single Christian women out so that they aren't left vulnerable to the advances of non-Christian men? How seldom nearly all-single Christian sisters seem to get asked out. It's if they were experiencing a bad case of halitosis. When so many vibrant, intelligent, God-fearing, reasonably attractive single women spend nearly all of their Friday and Saturday nights for years hanging out with other Christian women and not always by choice; you've got to wonder what's wrong? There are obvious reasons single Christian men go out on dates less often than their non-Christian counterparts. For example, when unsaved people go on a date the big question seems to be whether or not they'll end up in bed together; believers (at least those past a certain age) go on a date wondering if at some point they'll wind up getting married. While the bed thing should be taken seriously and considered sacred, sadly it often isn't, but for the most part, people understand there's a potential "until death do us part" promise hanging in their face. Meeting and dating women may be hazardous to a man's health, and in particular his emotional well-being. Risks include making a fool of himself, subjecting himself to humiliation and ridicule, being exploited, and, of course, heartbreak. Women frequently choose jerks over the nice guys, but the woman who has the character traits that a male want in a mate will want a guy who's tough and strong, and who's also genuinely sensitive and soulful on the inside. Even sweet gentlewomen bear within them the same sickness, capacity for corruption, depravity, and the same depths of rage as men when they feel that they have been used. They will put a man down, play "games," lay blame, and whine. Nearly as nerve wracking to deal with is the woman who is not quite sure that she loves her man, but will play up to him when he starts to distance himself, yet pull away when he wants closeness. This damages a man's emotions. Likewise, single Christian sisters have done their fair share of damage to single Christian men by sometimes not responding well to the few dates they've been asked to go on. Some occasionally don't allow Christian brothers to "be a man" on those dates because they are "looking for the perfect man." Those type Christian women often have unrealistic and unreasonable desires concerning love and deep relationships. They see everything as being sinful. They were saved by New Testament grace, but are trying to live in Old Testament Law. Some are so heavenly minded that they become of no earthly good. Many women want perfect relationships without struggle or failure. They expect the people in their lives to know the script, do the right thing, meet all their needs, and never let them down, but they are not ready to compromise. Some men believe that women today can be so independent and forceful that it can be quite intimidating. Women have taken over some of the roles men have traditionally played, leaving them without much of a place in relationship. Women today own homes, adopt children, have great jobs, travel all over the world, and have financial independence which have left men without a "job." There are men that are turned off by women, who take the initiative to ask for a date, or pay the receipt for an evening out, as if that's weakening them. They believe when a woman is too independent that it's putting them off. Men like to feel needed, and have a specific need to be filled in a relationship. It's understandable that people are cautious, especially if they've been burned in the past, or they're still healing from a painful divorce or breakup. However, that's no reason to shy away from potential new relationships. Some women wouldn't be married to their current husbands if they hadn't made the first move themselves. Yet, single Christian women shouldn't just be sitting around waiting for Mr. Right according their expectations. If you are a single Christian you should of course read the Bible, pray, go on trips, meet in cell groups, or do positive things to fill voids of emptiness and loneliness. God can be a great date for

There's Enough Woman Left to be Your Lady

---

your health and communication! You should plan a date with God where you both can do something together, and talk while you're doing it. You should be committed to fitness "power" walking and talking with God several times daily each week in the spirit. The higher a woman reach for salvation the more pure and virtuous she becomes and she realizes that nobody's perfect, but she and Jesus are perfect for each other. Jesus knows her vulnerabilities, flaws, differences, and pet peeves. Because of his unconditional love, she is able to face fears, try new things, and laugh at her mistakes. The most important communicating tool that she should use is the "no distractions" rule. Prior to involvement and making a commitment to God in the spirit, she shouldn't let ignorance, desperation, lust, low self-esteem, or immaturity blind her to warning signs coming from the flesh. The issue with most women is that they spend time dreaming of a storybook *"And they lived happily ever after,"* ending to relationships. Believing in Fairy Tales is wishful thinking. Women are all about fantasies. They sit around fantasize and dream. If a man caters to a woman's fantasies she will project whatever she wants to do onto him. That's how women attract men. Most women have a behavior pattern that when they meet a new man that is able to talk, shows emotions, and feel their pain then they are ready to rush off into the future to plan a life with this man. They are attracted to men that represent an ideal life, and create an idealized fantasy that becomes very real where they will have a family or whatever and live happily ever after. Some women barely have time to get over a divorce before they got involved in another hopeless relationship. They blindly try to fit the man into the mold they have created of a good father to their children and a husband who is intelligent and good-looking. Women are attracted to a certain type of man that has looks as well as confidence. It has to do with the energy that he gives off. This is why women often fall for the bad guys. Most "bad guys" don't worry about failure. They have confident behavior. These factors set off a signal in women to date confident men because of the way they make them feel emotionally. What women want from men is confidence; not arrogance, dominance, useless bravado, or macho heroics. Confidence simply says: "I can deal with all of your faults... somehow... well at least I'll do my best." Confidence with every kind of woman in general regardless of whether they are beautiful, plain, smart, dumb, nice, mean, old, young, is a social skill; which can, and decisively will be learned if a man wants the greatest intimate relationship of his life. Although a woman likes to believe a man is willing to deal with a lot of things, what really counts is that he is able to deal with her. A healthy, mature, spiritual woman resists impassioned commitment to a man who is afraid of her sexuality, her intelligence, or her emotions. Women are complex creatures. They scream for equality, yet complain that men are not gentlemen. They want financial independence, yet still expect the man to pay in restaurants. They complain about having to work twice as hard to attain recognition, and to climb the career ladder, yet still want the freedom to stay at home and raise a family. They want independence, yet give their men grief when the men want to go off and do their own thing. It's no wonder that men are confused. There are many times when men are in a no-win situation with a woman. Take the thoughtfulness aspect, for example. If a man telephones her to let her know that he will be home late from work, she will assume that he's having an affair. If he doesn't phone to let her know, she will assume that he's having an affair. Yet, women can talk for hours on the phone to a girlfriend whom they'll be seeing later the same day, but the male better not say anything about that! There are so many peculiar little rituals that women perform that completely evade men's comprehension. If he makes an effort to get home on time and consequently miss out on overtime or a promotion she will label him as being "foolish." When a woman makes it obvious that a man has made her angry; the answer to his, "What's the matter my love?" will always be an ice cold, "Nothing." However, understanding the strange ways of females, means that men must know when to open their mouth, and when at all costs to keep it closed.

Women are more intrigued by what they hear and see. A male must have a good conversation to really mentally intrigue a woman; no matter how he looks. A man mentally resorts back to primitive cave man games when he doesn't really have any communication skills involving women. It's as if he was living in a cave and saw a woman walking down the pathway, and he runs and hit her in the head with a stick, and then drags her in his cave by her hair and say that she belongs to him. There are some men walking around with that mentality. They aren't really focusing on their verbal skills. Some men physically try to attract a woman by grabbing her arms, hands, hair, and talking dumb. There's no creativity to it and a female will feel like she's lowering her standards to cooperate with a man who obviously has no verbal skills, or who is clearly not interested in her mind just her body. She thinks that he just wants a female, and women can see through that. A male's job is to just become the best man that he can be. Then he will magnetize a quality woman into his life. When a woman has no peace of mind happiness can sometimes be an illusion filled with sadness and confusion. In searching for the ideal man, many women whose spirits run free spend their lives going from one disappointing lover to another. Some have spent a lifetime with the wrong man; men who would not or could not make a commitment, were unavailable in some way, didn't want children, marriage, or to give up drinking and drugs. Women become angry at those types of men. Since a woman make the greater biological investment in offspring, her thinking is more concerned about her mate reneging on his commitment, and therefore she's more attentive to signs that her mate might be attaching himself emotionally to other women. Most women journey through swampy black water that involves wrong turns, going backwards, and exhibiting jealousy. A woman can become so attached to her own jealousy that it becomes a part of a relationship. Jealousy is often the catalyst in arguments that lead to abuse. It mostly stems from the idea of having power and control. Women want to feel as if they have chosen the man, and unless a woman chooses the man, whatever he says or whatever he does isn't really going to get her. Men that constantly get rejected by women have egos that are very fragile, but when a man approach a woman he can't be stepping up to her with his ego on his shoulder. He will get his feelings hurt. The most handsome men and the finest women will get their feelings hurt if they approach someone wrong. Sometimes it has nothing to do with them. Men must display courtesy to women on a woman's level. When the average guy walks up to a female at a function, and the first thing that comes out of his mouth is, "Hey, what's your name?" "You got a man?" "Can I have your number?" That's very impersonal because she knows that it's not about her. She thinks that he just wants a woman and that he doesn't care about her. Beside that, all women have heard those same tired lines. So a man can't come across acting juvenile like that. He has to come across like he's genuinely trying to get to know her as a person first, and then give her the option to give him some body language and cooperation. That's her way of letting him know that she's feeling him also. Most females might just talk to a man and, may not show any interest in him. She's just going along with the conversation. She's not feeling the man and he's not picking up those signals, but when women get dressed up and are in a social spot they want a man to respond to them, but he's got to make her earn his attention and really feel her out. However, if a man is at a mall and he approach's a sophisticated woman who is dressed in a nice conservative looking suit and has a Ph.D., automatically her defenses are going up because she don't know where he's coming from. A woman is really cooperative with a man if he is courteous, but when the guy is coming on too strong she can get bent out of shape fast. If he's talking to her on a respectful level, there shouldn't be any reason for her to be all wound up, and looking crazy. Women get like that when they are put in an uncomfortable situation, and they get uncomfortable when the guy is being forceful and slyly putting them down. Women are a group, full of passion, laughter, temper, and a generous, welcoming nature. They enjoy relationships with all kinds of people and love life. They take emotional risks and put themselves out into the world. Yet, all women don't fit this description. Some act as very small children; hiding somewhere deep behind their emotions. They are afraid of what everyone else thinks of them, and afraid to be who they should be. They take refuge in a job, and finances. They have only a few friends, and date none at all. A lot of guys try to think like men when it comes to figuring out women and that's where they mess up. Men are physical creatures who are more intrigued by what they see. It's all in the male's eyes. Men will date a woman solely based on looks. She could be on drugs and working on the block, but if she has a nice shape and cute face guys will try to be with her.

13

Surgery Without Pain

> *"And he was teaching in the synagogues on the Sabbath. And behold there was a woman that had a spirit of infirmity eighteen years, and was bowed together, and could in no wise lift up herself. And when Jesus saw her, he called her to him, and said unto her, Woman thou are loosed from thine infirmity. And he laid his hands on her: and immediately she was made straight, and glorified God."* (Luke 13:10-13)

Physical deformity assumes many shapes, size, and forms. Each one is hard and painful to look at. The first surgeons of the world had to guess who was sick by looking at the outside of the body. Much progress has been attained in treatment of disease since the crippled and sick were laid along the streets of ancient cities. But all the medical and surgical skills in the world will never sever the oldest disease, which hang on the human race, for the worst deformity of mankind is spiritual deformity. What the world want is surgery without pain, and to receive a bill that doesn't anesthetizes them. The world has not seen but one surgeon who could straighten crooked limbs, put sight in blind eyes, put sound back in the ear drum, make a patient stand up without falling down, and all of this was done without pain before or pain after. That surgeon was Jesus Christ. He loves chronic cases. Jesus sees all of our troubles and he is ready to heal. Jesus was in the house of God on a Sabbath day when he performed a miracle on this woman in the gospel of Luke. She had an evil spirit of infirmity that by divine permission had been put on her, and had bent her almost double for eighteen long years, but her spirit was bent as well. The evil spirit had her so bound and bowed together by strong convulsions that she could not stand, and in no way could she lift herself up. People called her the "bent over woman" naming her by her disability, and calling attention to that which was broken, not whole. No one remembered her real name. Her back and body had been bent, sore, and twisted out of shape for nearly twenty years. She couldn't even remember what it had been like to stand up straight, laugh, and breathe. She couldn't run or move very quickly, and walking was uncomfortable. She saw mostly the ground in front of her, and had to twist her neck to see where she was going, or even look around. It was hard for her to look someone else in the face. Her illness was seen by some as a punishment from God. Women avoided her, because they thought that she must have done a terrible sin, had a curse, or did something that caused it. In the temple of worship she sat near the other women on the far side of the synagogue, but she sat on the edge, toward the outside to avoid being ridiculed.

There are women that are bent with bones and muscles

There's Enough Woman Left to be Your Lady

twisted out of place from bending over to pick up after someone else. Some are bent from physical back breaking labor. They have to work, even when their bodies ache, just to put food on the table for their families. Some are bent not on the outside, but on the inside from great responsibilities. These are married and single parent mothers struggling to be both mother and father to their growing children, grandchildren, aging parents, and sometimes grown children at the same time. Others are bent from verbal abuse from spouses who constantly criticize and put them down. These women have compromised so many times to save their marriages they no longer know who they are, and have nothing left to give. Some are bent from experiences in the church. These women sometimes blame God and themselves. Some are bent from childhood experiences. These are women bent out of frustration, needing others to care for them. All of us have known and have been at one time or another bent over with a burden of sorrow. The break-up of a marriage, death of a child, or numerous other pains may have doubled us over with grief. A "spirit of infirmity" could refer to social and economic conditions such as poverty and oppression. These are conditions that cause men and women all over the world to stoop in city garbage dump searching for something to eat. Such conditions break people's backs and their spirits. A "spirit of infirmity" can also refer to a moral problem, such as guilt or shame, or an emotional burden, such as sickness of heart like depression or grief. The infirmity of this woman was not only physical, but also mental. She was bent double in her body, and was bowed down with sadness and depression of the mind. Her outward appearance showed sympathy between her body and her soul, which it's not always so plainly seen as in her case. This disease was incurable, and had caused her to look deformed, which made her an object of charity. Imagine this woman who had lost all of her natural beauty and brightness. Just to move may have been painful to her, yet she went to church on the Sabbath day. In church on that Sabbath morning this poor woman may have been the least noticed by the other members, because she was bent over to half her original height. She was bent so low that she could have come in and gone out and not been noticed by anyone. But Jesus had noticed her while worshiping in church. He saw her for he always occupies a place where he can see those bowed down with heavy loads. This woman no doubt use to be a young girl with a beautiful smile, sparkling eyes, and the beauty of youth that walked erect. Like others of her time she used to be able to see the sun, moon, stars, and people rejoicing all around her. She once found life to be a joy; but there gradually crept over her an infirmity, which dragged her down, probably a weakness of the spine. Satan caused either the muscles and ligatures to began to tighten or the woman had developed scoliosis. She was bound together so that tight that she was drawn towards herself and the earth. The demonic spirit bowed her towards that which was depressing. All she ever saw was the ground. Her entire life revolved around constant stooping. She had bent lower and lower as the weight of the world, years, and age pressed upon her. Her looks and her thinking was downward, nothing heavenly and nothing bright ever came before her eyes. Her view was narrowed to the dust and the grave. The closer she walked with the Lord, the more she physically seemed to grow downward. There are church members who like this woman go to church every Sunday. Then there are those that have not have not gone to church for twelve years or more, and have not prayed for eighteen years. Their thoughts sink evermore like lead and their feelings run in a deep groove. Some people will go to church depressed, bent over with sin, and can't even rise to stand on their feet when praise is being given to God. They return home in the same state of mind. Where some leap for joy when the Gospel is preached, others stoop under grief. If a preacher reads a scripture or thunders a portion of it in a

There's Enough Woman Left to be Your Lady

sermon, some people believe that he was talking about them. They allow something said in the sermon, or said by a church member to cause them sadness that binds them up for a long time. They are forever bowed down in some form or another. They can see nothing but the ground, but no one can glorify God that has not been set free. If a woman hasn't really felt the power of God in her life, and her nature hasn't been changed from sin unto righteousness, when she's in church on Sunday morning dressed in finery and shouting the name of the Lord, she's just another devil imitating holiness. When the right sinner shows up and influence her she will run right back into the mud hole of worldliness. A hog also can be shaved, deodorized, and have a ribbon tied around its head, but just a soon as the hog see mud it will run right to it. Why, because it's in its nature to wallow in filth and dirt. There's no use in blaming anyone for his or her shortcomings because like the Bible says about the bowed woman, *"She couldn't lift herself up."* When the Devil binds a soul he binds it so tight that it can't break free. It's in bondage. The remedy for spiritual bondage is to endure, no matter what it takes. It's only Satan's way of trying to scare a person back into sin. We must remember that it's the Devil's duty to steal, kill, and destroy our joy. The scripture did not say that Satan possessed the bowed woman. That was good because possession means ownership. However, in this woman's case Satan had only made a knot that held her. A knot binds up a person and slowly chokes the life out of them. The Devil's chief aim is to make people and society as miserable as possible in this life. Some people have never had much sorrow in their life until he or she started living for God. Just as soon as they put on holiness the Devil started tearing things down in their life, bending them over with despair, and keeping their mind always down in the gutter. He dispenses broken spirits at will. A broken spirit is like a puzzle. There are many pieces to it and sometimes the person assembling it don't know where to start, but you have to pick a place to start in order to bring forth the picture that's hidden within. We are all pieces of a puzzle that fit together to make a beautiful picture. If we are constantly trying to be someone else, struggling with who we are, what we look like or comparing ourselves with others, we will not "fit" into the spot that has *"our"* name on it.

Accepting Yourself

We live in a time when accepting who we are can be difficult. Most women set themselves to unrealistic standards. What they fail to realize, is that oftentimes these standards are too high. They represent a "front" with no real substance. Women that have issues have often tried to bring forth the woman that's hiding under the surface within them, but have been bound by their own prejudices and fears. Some of God's women are all about themselves. They are looking for a self-only blessing. They come to church driving Mercedes Benz, Lexus, and Cadillac's, styling with their Liz Claiborne outfits, gold necklaces, diamond rings, Rolex watches, sculptured nails, and weave hair. They look good but they are still bent over. Some are bent over looking for praise. They are the one and only thing that they see. Their only thought is their own condition in Christ. This "Bless only me" mentality has caused the Spirit of God to withhold blessings from the entire church, because the person asking for a blessing and the church were not all on one accord. These actions and thoughts bind the spirit of God. Those type women are bent towards themselves, and no matter who feed them the Gospel or send them water from the river of life they will never lift their heads no higher then themselves. Some of these women are not happy and don't want to see no one else happy. Women must be careful of what they desire, because many times what they think that they are running to, is often what they are running from, and it can carry mixed emotions. We all come into this world as blank canvases waiting for the various colors of life to be painted or splashed into our world. As children, our first knowledge of who we are comes from our parents. If our parents continue to feed us positive affirmations of our worth and value, we tend to grow with a positive self-esteem. However, if we are told over and over again that we are nothing and that we won't amount to much in life, we will begin to believe that it's true. We must be careful what we say to others, especially children. As a child I used to hear people say, "sticks and stones may break my bones, but words will never hurt me." This is not true. It's amazing what you accept as truth when you hear it enough times. The Bible tells us that the tongue can both cut and heal. Some people will say that you are stupid and ugly every single day. Don't believe them or you will lose confidence, and your self-esteem will wither away. It will cause you to stop smiling, talking, and you will dread meeting people. You will become convinced that you are worthless, and you will stress over every thing. You will try to be invisible as possible, thinking that you can't get hurt if everyone forget about you. In a desperate attempt to get away you will find that running away don't solve your problems. When you awaken to life you awaken to the importance of loving and promoting yourself. You realize that it's time to stop hoping and waiting for happiness, safety, security, and for something to change in your life. You come to terms with the fact that your man isn't Prince Charles, and you are not Princess Diana or Cinderella. You also realize that in the real world there aren't always fairy tale endings or beginnings, and that any guarantee of "happily ever after" must begin with you. You stop complaining and blaming other people for the things that they did or didn't do to or for you. You learn that the only thing you can really count on is the unexpected, and that people don't always say what they mean or mean what they say, and that not everyone will always be there for you. You stop judging and pointing fingers and you begin to accept people as they are and to overlook their shortcomings and frailties. You begin to sift through all the junk that you've been fed about how you should behave, look, and how much you should weigh, what you should wear, what you should do for a living, how much money you should make, what you should drive, how and where you should live, who you should marry, and the importance of having and raising children. Slowly, you begin to take responsibility for yourself. You begin reassessing and redefining who you are and what you really stand for. So, you learn to stand on your own and to take care of yourself. In the process you learn that it's not all about you, and that you don't know everything, and it's not your job to save the world. You learn the difference between wanting and needing and you begin to discard the doctrines and values you've outgrown. You learn that your body is your temple that deserves to be treated with love, kindness, sensitivity, and respect. You won't settle for less. You distinguish between guilt and responsibility, and you learn to say NO and set boundaries. You stop trying to control people, situations and outcomes, and learn that being alone does not mean being lonely. You make yourself a promise to never betray yourself and to never settle for less than your heart's desire. Maybe you have considered suicide, but suicide is something you can't take back. This type action causes little respect for yourself. The world is a scary place when you stop liking yourself. Insults can stop at any time, but you still have to face yourself. You must realize that you matter to God and suddenly you will have value, and something to build on. That's when your healing begins. *"I have chosen you and have not rejected you. So do not fear, for I am with you; do not be dismayed, for I am your God. I will strengthen you and help you; I will uphold you with my righteous right hand."* (Isaiah 41: 9-10) Words are powerful things, but God's words of love are the most powerful of all. God can still make up for your silent years, and you will no longer walk around with your head hanging down, and eyes on the floor. If you are ever going to accept who you are to be in the future; you must know who you are at present, and understand where you have come from to determine where you want to go. It's important for you to know your meaning in life, so that you can prepare your message to society, in order to carry out your mission. When you know and understand your purpose and why you are here, it's much easier for you to accept who you are and the person that God has made you to be. You should make up your mind that you are not going to let the past control your future. Don't concentrate on negative things. Holding on to pain and hatred causes anger and bitterness, which can cause stress and anxiety. These emotions can cause a variety of other health problems. You can learn to break down the walls of hurt and pain that hinder you from forgiving others and living unfulfilled lives personally and professionally. At the proper time you must learn to confront the people in your life that has hurt you. Pray for those who have hurt or abused you because it's very difficult to hate someone that you are praying for. Once you have confronted and released your past and its pain, then you have to learn to let it go by employing forgiveness. Forgiving and grace is a big step in the healing process. Each of us knows the parts of ourselves in need of healing. Some of our wounds are visible to others, but most of them are not. For some it is physical or mental illness or disability. Others suffer from broken relationships, yet it's possible to embrace happiness, experience joy, and have success. If you count all your blessings, it will be hard to be depressed. Live life now. Don't wait until tomorrow because tomorrow is not promised to you. With courage in your heart and a deep breath you should take a stand, and begin to design the life that you want to live as best you can, with the help of the Holy Spirit. Never underestimate the gifts that God has given you, to make you unique. The choice is truly up to you!

Jesus could have finished his spiritual lesson and gone home and no one would have even thought about this woman, but he stopped and called her. Jesus stops in the middle of his teachings and looks out at the throng and says, "Woman, come here." And there is a shocked silence. The people in attendance crane their necks around to see whom Jesus is talking to, and then they realize that he is talking to the woman from the streets who had been bent-over for such a long time that no one hardly noticed anymore. Nonetheless, without warning or explanation, He took the initiative and made an issue of this woman's depressed condition, but that was against the law! What happens next is quite amazing. Jesus didn't ask her about her disease, and she didn't ask Jesus to heal her, but in the bowed woman's case Luke said, *"And when Jesus saw her, he called her and said to her, "Woman, you are loosed from your infirmity."* (Luke 13:12-13) She was still bent as she was before, but Jesus did not say that she was going to straighten her up right at that moment. He was preparing her for the blessing to come. He meant the physical power of Satan to make her bow was broken, and he no longer had control over her life. Jesus breaks another rule when he reaches out and he touches her. At his touch, a miracle occurs! This woman, who everyone in town has seen or looked past that was completely bent over for eighteen years, begin to stand up. Like someone awakening from a cramped position in a long, hard sleep, she begins to straighten. She uncurls slowly, like an opening flower, until finally the woman is lifting her head, looking into the eyes that had seen her, and recognized her need. A hush falls on the crowd. Everyone is staring at the woman. Then suddenly, she shouts out with words of joy and there is gleeful pandemonium in the crowd. It was _only_ when Jesus laid His hand on her and poured His _life_ into her that she was made physically and spiritually straight, and from that moment on she began to praise God. By Jesus putting His hands upon her, the electrical energy that flowed from His infinite body gave her a vitality that boosted her bent body, and the broken pieces in her life were also restored. The woman had suffered from lack of strength. His touch quickened her spirit so that she not only had the physical, but also the spiritual strength to lift herself up, and to get out of any position that she was in. No pressure or force was put upon her. She lifted herself up. When Jesus gives a person spiritual life, he also gives him or her physical activities to move away from things that has caused hurt and sorrow in their lives. The woman probably moved around just to be sure that she was not imagining things. When she was sure that a miracle had been worked the one with no voice found her voice and praised God. The one with no name was carried from anonymity to the place where she received a new and precious name, and discovered herself to be a child of God. She was called "Daughter of Abraham." She knew herself to be a child of the promise. Jesus brought her from the margin of isolation to the center of the community. He transformed her from a broken body to one that was whole, and from silence to praise. On that Sabbath day, Jesus brought her the gift of rest. She had asked for nothing, promised nothing, and she had not cornered Jesus or forced his hand. God had put His divine protection around her just enough to let the afflicting spirit come in contact with Jesus the intercessor of our faith. The worse point about this woman's case was that she had borne a chronic disease for eighteen years. Terminal diseases do not start overnight, it evolves and festers for months or years, and then sometimes without warning it violently explodes on the scene with little time to treat it. Sin also doesn't just start overnight. Some sins in the lives of people have been ongoing for years, and it becomes a cancerous disease that has spread all over the body. This could be considered a stronghold where the Devil has entrenched his forces to smite, bind, and deceive a person, but he cannot kill him or her. If the devil cannot hit you with lightning bolts he will try to scare you with thunder. As Satan had bound Job, he had also bound this woman, but he could not take her life without God's permission. Yet, God says that the sinner is bound by the infirmity (sickness) of sin and cannot lift himself up. Many people have been bound by Satan, and in their attempt to get away from him may have gone to a Christian person seeking prayer. They may even have started going to Church or reading their Bible more, but the Devil still had them bound. When saints of God are bound they are hindered, but there's a limit as to what the Devil can do. It's only when Jesus draws sinners towards the cross that they straighten up. For he said, *"If I be lifted up I'll draw all men unto me."* Jesus had the power to draw the bowed woman's curved and misshapen bones of sin back into their proper places, and he can also put yours in its proper place, but the Lord must have all the glory even to the point of death. If believers could stop mourning their lost, thinking of themselves, looking down on other people, and start thinking about Jesus, then a change could come over them also. Intercessory Prayer can tear down strongholds. It's the only weapon that can be used effectively against the Devil's authority. We intercede by encountering the Devil with fasting and warfare prayer.

The ruler of the synagogue was indignant because Jesus had healed the woman on the Sabbath. He said to the people, "There are six days on which work ought to be done; come on those days and be healed, and not on the Sabbath day." Unfortunately, Jesus' sermon was lost on the leader of the synagogue. He was so concerned about decency, good order, rules, and regulations that he failed to see the miracle, and he missed the moment of God's grace while troubling the waters of infirmity. All of us have done it. We expect God to answer our prayers in a certain way, and we miss the unanticipated blessing while he is working to restore our lives. We have received and invested so much in the way things are that we miss the opportunity to discover the way things can be. The leader of the synagogue may not have understood Jesus, but the bent over woman did. His statement caused Jesus to become offended enough to say something about the Sabbath day and what it meant to keep it holy. He also had something to say about the hypocrisy of the synagogue leaders who watered their oxen on the Sabbath, but get ticked at him for healing a human being on the Sabbath. *"You hypocrites! Does not each of you on the Sabbath untie his ox or his ass from the manger, and lead it away to water it? And ought not this woman, a daughter of Abraham whom Satan bound for eighteen years, be loosed from this bond on the Sabbath day?"* Jesus understood not only the letter of the Law, but also that the Sabbath was made for man, and man was not made for the Sabbath.

Jesus also had something he wanted to say about women. If the only point Jesus wanted to make was the point about doing well on the Sabbath or the point about the hypocrisy of the leaders, he could have simply said, *"Ought not this woman whom Satan bound for eighteen years be loosed from this bond on the Sabbath day?"* But that's not all he said, He called her a daughter of Abraham. *"Ought not this woman, a **<u>daughter</u>** of Abraham be loosed from this bond?"* Those words, "daughter of Abraham" are intended to carry a message to the synagogue leaders. The message was similar to this: "On top of all the other reasons why you should care more about a suffering person than a thirsty ox, is the fact that this woman is a fellow heir of the blessing promised to Abraham and she is your sister. You pride yourselves in saying, "We are the children of Abraham. She too has Abraham as her father and is a child of Abraham and the Kingdom." The message of Jesus to the synagogue leaders was a message not only about their Sabbath keeping and their hypocrisy, but also about how men and women ought to relate to each other as fellow heirs of God's promises. He was saying to men in the synagogue then, as he is saying to men in the church today, *"The believing women in your midst are heirs of the promises of God. They too are the meek who will inherit the earth.* (Matthew 5:5) *They too are the righteous who will shine like the sun in the kingdom of their Father."* (Matthew 13:43) As he said this, all his adversaries were put to shame, and all the people rejoiced at all the glorious things that were done by him. Jesus has done more than anyone has ever done to bring purity and harmony between men and women. Therefore, we must do the same. Jesus is calling us to love even the unlovely. In this wicked and perverse generation, He puts people in our paths that have no hope, so that they can see the Jesus in us.

Jesus sees, calls, and responds to each of us. His love brings us out of isolation and places us in the presence of others. He challenges us to take off our blinders, to look at one another, to see and be seen. What does this mean for husbands, wives, brothers, sisters, boy friends, and girl friends? It means that all of us should relate to each other as men and women of God. It means we should learn to look at each other through the lens of God's word, and not our own prejudicial thoughts. Women cultivate "seeds" of thought either deliberately or spontaneously. These thoughts grows into a seed that will be sown and produce its own pattern of belief that will bloom into joy or suffering. That's why it's so important that a woman cultivate her mind toward perfecting pure thoughts. It will keep her mind free from weeds of doubt and anger. A woman's mind can bring forth good or evil manifestations that will cause her to learn by either blessings or suffering. If negative thoughts are allowed to fall into her mind and take root, it will germinate into a life of consequences. A woman can become mentally chained or trapped by her inner emotions and thoughts, which can either free or imprison her. She's literally what she thinks. The way any woman feel about herself is a reflection of the way society sees her. She can make or break herself by right or wrong choices that she makes and the application of thought. There are some Christian women, who have been destroyed by the charm of good-looking men, whom they thought would make a good husband.

Sin has done a great and awful work in the world that has grown through all ages. The whole world is poisoned in body, soul, and mind. Many women have been poisoned by the jagged edge of unreturned love, affection, and unforgiveness to themselves. They have allowed the venom of envy to creep into their system. There are times when revenge motivates women to envy other women who find happiness, when they should be happy for them. Suffering and pain is on a whole scale, but a woman suffers and fails because of mental overload. Her fuse box of emotion has been overloaded with unstable thoughts and relationships, which causes her to fail at marriage, parenting, ministry, and relationships. Some women carry around issues of wretchedness, bitterness, and revenge. Perhaps some may have been exposed to past sins that still haunt them more times than they would have liked. Every condition and circumstance of a woman's life embraces the whole of her being. Women that are plagued by circumstances are continually seeking relief by way of improvement in earthly or heavenly things. Most women who don't seek to improve themselves spend most of their time beating up on themselves or having a "One woman pity party." They wallow in self-pity, longing for things that they used to have, but can only dream of now. A woman has to give up something that's valuable to her before she can claim her blessings to something that has greater value than what she gave up. Women that want to lose weight cannot do it by exercising alone. They must give up their craving for larger portions of food and sweets in order to gain the size that they desire to be. When looking for a soul mate, if a woman is continually frustrated with a man that will not commit himself, and she thinks that all men are no good or dogs, her spiritual communication, and the negative thoughts of her mind and life, will always attract those type men. She must learn to think positive and stay on task. Women that want to meet good men must stop looking for certain type men that meet all of their outward approval, and puts envy in the eyes of other women. When a woman is worn out, envy not only gets a foothold; it puts a foot in her mouth as well! Women should take all the time and emotional energy used to waste on jealousy and put that energy into doing a better job for the Lord. Jealousy, resentment, and anger ultimately lead to self-pity, and self-pity usually comes from feeling powerless. You can't control God's actions. Your eleventh commandment should be: Thou shall not whine. Be patient. If you're not in the spotlight, count your blessings. Scripture tells us, "From everyone who has been given much, much will be demanded." (Luke 12:48) Sometimes having less is enough to worry about!

Women eventually produce fruit of one kind or another. Therefore, they should always be alert to the seeds that they allow in their heart. They should watch the fruit in their own life, and in the lives of others. The fruit gives them away. They should be slow to speak especially words that sow negative seeds about another, quick to listen, and guard their heart every day with Holiness. Ephesians 4:29-30 states, *"Do not let any unwholesome talk come out of your mouths, but only what is helpful for building others up according to their needs, that it may benefit those who listen. And do not grieve the Holy Spirit of God."* The simple question to ask before opening your mouth is: "Will this lift Jesus higher or will this lift me higher?" Yet, no matter what decisions a woman makes in her life whether it's spontaneous, rebellious, reactionary, or coincidental, she will always be judged and compelled in one way or another to be a "lady." A physically and mentally weak woman who aimlessly walks around thinking without purpose cannot grow divinely strong. She is oppressed. Her thoughts and conditions have enslaved her, but she must gather strength within her mind to alter her condition. Until she stop accusing and blaming other people for her condition, and mark a straight path to Jesus, build herself up, and move toward a spiritual healing, she will never be able to walk upright. In order for a woman to be a role model for people to emulate she first must look up to herself. In a bent condition of despair she can't sit upright, sleep right, walk right, see right, and in some cases love right. She may feel like she is an embarrassment to everyone she may come in contact. She can't look anyone in the eye, because most people don't know how to make conversation. She must cause herself to be virtuous by lifting up her thoughts. Soon her mind will become so expanded that her thought pattern will no longer be able to contain her. Her mind will be an open door that will exit an anointed, inspirational account of God's blessings. When a woman's thoughts are impure she will quickly fall back into walking around bent over, murmuring, stooping under persecution, and looking ever downward and depressed.

Clinical Depression

Depression strikes women with regard to no single ethnic group at twice the rate of men. It can be caused by one or a combination of triggers including environmental and biological factors, genetics, negative thinking patterns, physical health problems, and some medications. Untreated depression is the No.1 cause of suicide. Many African-American women don't get treatment often because of a lack of insurance and the widespread belief in the African-American community that depression is evidence of personal weakness, not a legitimate health problem. The signs and symptoms of Clinical Depression are sleeping too little or sleeping too much, reduced appetite and weight loss, or increased appetite and weight gain, persistent sadness, anxiousness, worry, fatigue, difficulty concentrating, remembering, and making decisions. Depressed people also feel guilty, hopeless, worthless, cry a lot, withdraw from friends and family, and have thoughts of death, sickness, or suicide.

If you are a person who has lost hope on life, or may have already planned to end your life or may even tried to please read on. You may say, "I do know why I am a failure. My husband or wife left me. My children hate me. I'm in debt. Someone died. I'm unemployed. I'm lonely." Though you have many problems and struggles, most likely, you are also struggling with depression. Your feelings and your depression cannot be trusted, because your feelings are not the true you. Thinking about killing yourself is to believe lies about life, and about the future. You must have the courage to go on, and believe that your life and future can be different, and that you can make a difference in someone else life. You are a person of value. Therefore, it's time to challenge your thinking, and see your life from a healthy perspective. You are important and you can change your thinking and behavior and improve your life! No matter how hopeless you think your life is, someone understands the burdens you carry or the emotional turmoil you are experiencing. You should give life another try. You need to move in another direction, away from the self-destructive thoughts that have plagued you, and try to understand why you are depressed.

How Can You Get Help For Clinical Depression?
The first step is to talk to your doctor or to a qualified

mental health professional. You also may be able to get help through a pastoral counselor, guidance counselor, or local mental health association, but most people with clinical depression often don't have the motivation or energy to seek treatment for him or her self. It's often necessary for friends and family to help them seek treatment. Building and maintaining a strong support network of friends and relatives can help prevent clinical depression and aid in recovery. You can also make a difference! Lifestyle factors including diet and exercise can impact depression. Regular exercise such as walking, running, swimming, or other aerobic activity causes the brain to produce more of the chemical serotonin, which combat depression. Increasing the amount of omega-3 in the diet also has been found to bring relief from depression. Omega–3 is the key building blocks of the brain. Good dietary sources of omega-3 include oily fish such as Salmon, Tuna, Sardine, and Herring. Eating chicken, dried peas and beans, whole grains, and seeds also seem to help ward off depression. Seeking help from a spiritual source also has proven helpful for many. People with a strong spiritual faith have a lower risk for depression. People in church have access to healing of deformities; yet, some has never sought Jesus by way of prayer or deliverance. Talking with Jesus can help teach people how to better handle problems, change negative styles of thinking, and change relationships that can cause or worsen clinical depression. When a woman let God do the selecting of a partner he will send a good man into her life. It may not be what she wanted, but it will be what God knows that she need. Sometimes it's easier to believe that miracles will happen for other people, "but not me." Or maybe you just forget in the moment of your most challenging crisis that the Lord really will deliver you. You panic, plead, worry, and beg, when all along he intends to see you through. Sometimes you can almost hear the Lord rebuking you saying, "Oh ye of little faith." When

Jesus comes into your life, he does some cleaning and improving that can feel uncomfortable or even painful at times. As he cleans out your body and mind, sometimes it causes an earthquake around others. Spouses, family members, or friends may not be happy with the changes in you, and may feel uncomfortable sinning around you. They may wish that Jesus hadn't cast those habits out of your life because it disrupts theirs. There have been many moral earthquakes that have gotten people into a terrible twist, and have left them with burdens to lift. But in life there are some things that are difficult to remove. In some form or another we have always carried around back breaking, heavy loads of guilt, shame, and nakedness. In all of our lives there are crooked things that need to be made straight. Sometimes they come down on the shoulders, sometimes they come upon the head, and sometimes they come upon the heart. Conflicts rage in some men and women, conviction grow, and they cannot get the problems out of their lives, which causes them to walk around bent over. There are many women who have been hunched over for years carrying around burdens of guilt. They strained at a gnat and swallowed a camel. They are deformed and disfigured by past relationships, and are struggling with personal hang-ups. Some of the nicest women have been thrown together with some of the meanest men, and some of the nicest men have been united with some of the most worthless women. Over the years some women have developed coping strategies using substances and activities to ward off the pain. Still others use dope. When they found the strength to face one addiction, another would soon pop up in its place. They drank too much, ate too much, shopped too much, and worked too much; all in an attempt to keep themselves numb, in addition to denial to keep the loss at a distance. It didn't work. First, of all addictions are ingrained habits that are hard to break. If it were that easy to quit it wouldn't be called an addiction. One might say the same thing to a young prostitute who is addicted to crack cocaine. Once so full of bright hopes for her future, her life has now become a vicious cycle of degradation and misery. She doesn't remember much of what happened after smoking crack. She doesn't remember changing her clothes, taking a bath, or where she left her children. All she remembers is waiting for the drug dealer to come out with the crack. Crack cocaine can have a woman laughing, crying, or just hanging out on the block waiting for the dope dealer or a hustle, no matter the temperature. Some women stand on the street in zero weather shivering and hugging their elbows because they have sold the coats off their backs to the dope man for little of nothing to get drugs. They could use the coat indoors because their houses have no electricity, gas, phone, or luxuries. A woman crack addict's life is an empty place. A crack house is nothing more than a temporary site with one sole purpose: making money. On those occasions where it's somebody's home, it's almost empty and on its way to being shot up, robbed, or raided by the police. The female occupant may be beaten, prostituted, raped, or evicted. It's only a matter of time. Some women will float for years through a confusing existence, ruled by a dependence on drugs, and the responsibilities of motherhood. Some women only wake up when it's their next hit. They have no need for clocks. Others may be sick every morning from using drugs, and every night they will pray for death. Many things that have been done to straighten up those type women have caused them to be more crooked. Some women just sit down in despair and give up. To us, it seems so ridiculous to throw one's life away like that, but it's because we don't understand the power of sin. Or do we? We often lack compassion for others who are bound up in some sin that doesn't affect us. It's easy to look self-righteously at someone committing sins that don't interest us. What these women need is understanding, caring, love, and the all-consuming passion of God. No intake counselor can help them, but God is able to take them in. He's the only one able to save their lives. They need assurance that God still loves them and that Jesus will bring peace into their lives. Their main coping mechanism was continually moving and changing all the outer circumstances of life. It never occurred to them to look inward for peaceful resolution. The kingdom of God can come to a broken-down crack house because Jesus takes on a face and a name for prostitutes, pimps, and addicts. In spite of some women lifestyle, a lot of them are in denial. They believe that they don't need Jesus. The woman, who comes to Christ with years of bondage to overcome, will take some time before she can learn to live in the truth of that statement. Jesus said, *"Come unto me all ye that labor and are heavy laden, and I will give you rest."* An interesting corollary passage to this is Hebrews 4:11-16. In this passage Paul say, *"Let us labor therefore to enter into that rest."* Any woman seeking peace, rest, and Heaven gates, must labor in order to enter into the Lord's rest. It takes effort and work on a person's part to do all that he or she can do. When anyone first set out to take Jesus' yoke upon them and "learn of'" him by studying God's word, their true motivations and intent of heart are often ugly and distasteful. As they begin to labor toward becoming the person that God wants them to be, they begin to feel heavy laden. The word of God causes them to become keenly aware of the burdens that have been placed on their back through environment, poor choices, or willful sinning. They learn the "why's and wherefores" for their sins and psychological burdens. A common example might be that as a child they were taught to be concerned about what others thought about them, and so they started to do things for praise or worldly popularity. Later in life they may actually be doing good works, but they are doing them for the wrong reasons. As they study the scriptures they might learn that they aren't doing them because they care about others, but because you want to look good to others, and they want to gratify their need for praise, pride, and vain ambition. As they become more aware of their true motivations, the words of the Apostle Paul will become more visible to them. *"The word of God is quick, and powerful and sharper than any two-edged sword, piercing even to the dividing asunder of soul and spirit, and of the joints and marrow, and is a discerner of the thoughts and intents of the heart." "Neither is there any creature that's not manifest in his sight: but all things are naked and opened unto the eyes of him with whom we have to do."* (Hebrews 4:12-13)

God sees everything. There's nothing that's hidden from his sight. As you steadfastly come unto Christ, he shows your weaknesses so that you may humble yourself and allow him to help you. Once you realize that God see all that you do, you will feel totally disgusted with yourself and heavy-laden, but until you give the reigns to Him, you cannot be freed from the heavy load that you have accumulated on your back. When you come unto Christ and give your burdens to him, he promises to make them light. Only He can lighten your heavy load. Jesus is not an abstract God who doesn't feel your pain. He is intimately aware of your feelings of worthlessness, loneliness, foolishness, fear, guilt, and infirmity. Yet, he also knows how to conquer them, because he has already conquered them in that great atonement which he performed in your behalf. Because of Jesus Christ you shall find rest to your soul and you can, *"Come boldly unto the throne of grace, that you may obtain mercy, and find grace to help you in time of need."* (Hebrews 4:16)

Jesus is your one and only hope of freeing yourself from the burdens that have been packed on your back through time, circumstances, and poor choices that you've made or others around you have made. Don't panic or give up when you become aware of the load that you carry. Instead labor diligently to meet Jesus. Do your best and He will make up the rest and take the load from your back. This is his mission, *"to bind up the brokenhearted, to proclaim liberty to the captives, and open the prison to them that are bound."* (Isaiah 61:1) Don't just believe in Christ, but believe on him when he says he can free you from your most haunting sense of loneliness, your most annoying weaknesses, and your most sensual desires. I testify to you that He lives and He loves you. He died for you so that you would not have to suffer under this heavy load. You must trust him and "hold fast" to your faith and not give up because he is there and will help you if you let him. *"Seeing then that we have a great high priest, that's passed into the heavens, Jesus the Son of God, let us hold fast our profession. For we have not an high priest which cannot be touched with the feeling of our infirmities; but was in all points tempted like as we are, yet without sin."* (Hebrews 4:14)

Can you imagine eighteen years of dependency, and yet there was an escape out of it. The toils of life had left its impression upon this woman. Perhaps she had been bent by the worry of a child. Children can cause parents to stoop before their time. No amount medicine can cure the heartbreak of a mother over the death or ruin of a child. Many women have suffered for a child. They have gone through long struggles in which sometimes their loss were greater than their gain to support a child. They were tired in the body and mind, yet they would never tell the child of the sacrifices that they had made. In times of trouble mothers' are a refuge for a troubled or bereaved child's heart. The quickest sympathy anyone will ever receive will come from his or her mother. Sometimes even in adulthood when confronted with problems some people may say I will call "Mom or Dad" and then realize that, "I no longer have a mom or dad, they are gone." They may be gone, but, Jesus your comforter is still around and he will never leave you or forsake you. Blessed is the broken heart that Jesus reaches out to heal.

Men if you were the bowed lady's husband what would you see? Husband's what do you see when you look at your own wife. The answer to that of course, depends on what type glasses your peering through. What you see will be very different depending on whether you look through the lens of the Bible or a pornographic magazine. If you look through the lens of God's Word you too will see a daughter of Abraham. If men learn to see Christian women the way Jesus saw this woman in the synagogue they will see them as heirs of the King of glory, and that will have a deep effect on their relationship with women. As daughters and sons of Jesus and heirs of all God's promises we are destined together for unspeakable glory. Jesus came to help us recover what God created us to be as male and female in the image of God. Jesus helps us recover the purity and harmony of how men and women relate to each other. Women are just as likely to be disappointed with their husbands as men are to be disappointed with their wives, but women are less prone to speak negatively of their husbands. They want to believe that their husbands are all the things that they dreamed he would be, but a woman also must learn to look at her husband through the lens of the Word of God. Any believer of God knows that given the choice of having their sight or memory, they will choose sight because they would rather see where they're going, than to remember where they had been. As believers in Christ women must help steer their husbands with all his imperfections toward salvation, so that he will someday be changed in the twinkling of an eye, and shine like the sun in the kingdom of his Father. Every sin will be gone forever, and he will receive a glorious body like Christ's. When we suffer pain and loss, sometimes we ask the question why has all of this happened to me and sometimes we go so far as to question God. Complaining can hinder God's work. The alternative to complaining is to give God an opportunity to create a new body in us, and in our circumstances, even if our circumstances don't change. Old Testament Scriptures tells of the account of how the Israelites had murmured against God and against Moses, and God sent fiery serpents among them. The people were dying by thousands from the snakebites. When Moses called unto God for a remedy, God instructed him to make a serpent of brass, and put it upon a pole and then God said, "And it shall come to pass, that every one that's bitten, when he looketh upon it, shall live." (Numbers 21:8-9)

Brass speaks of divine judgment as in the brazen altar described in Exodus 27:2. We know from Genesis 3:14 that the serpent is a symbol of sin. The brazen serpent was a figure of Christ in the image of sinful man. What healed the dying Israelites? Was it some power in the brass? Was it the healing virtue of the pole upon which the brazen serpent was placed? Was it the Israelites' ability to look upon the serpent of brass? No, it was none of these things. God's servant Moses had called upon God for a remedy for the dying people. God told him what to do, and Moses obeyed the Lord's command. He made the serpent of brass and lifted it up on a pole, which symbolized the foreshadowing of Christ being lifted up on the cross. (John 12:32) He then gave the people God's command that they "look and live." Those who believed God did what Moses said, they looked and were healed. They did not ask for an explanation. They did not say, "Moses, I don't understand how looking at a serpent of brass lifted up on a pole can help me." They simply believed the Word of God and did what God's man told them to do, without asking for any explanation. The healing power was not in the pole, nor in either the brass or the serpent. Faith healed the Israelites, the same kind of faith that will today keep a sinner out of hell. It was in their believing. "Believe on the Lord Jesus Christ, and thou shalt be saved." (Acts 16:31) It made no difference how near death the Israelites were, if they looked at the serpent of brass they were immediately healed. In contrast, it makes no difference how deep in sin anyone may be, if a person will look to Jesus and believe on Him, he or she will be saved. During His earthly ministry Jesus declared that one day instead of a snake, that he would be lifted up to draw the poison of sin out of mankind. (John 3:14-15) He would repeat the act of being looked upon on a pole. You may say, I don't understand how that believing on Jesus could help any of us, but it's for sure that you can't change your condition from a drunk, a liar, a thief, or harlot to that of a refined lady or man of honor without the aid of Christ. Until you surrender your life fully to Christ at the foot of the cross, and trust him to perform the miracle that your life need, you will never comprehend how anything so simple as looking upward and believing on Jesus could change you. This woman had obeyed God's command, *"He that believeth and is baptized shall be saved: but he that believeth not shall be damned."* The woman believed, and she was baptized with the Spirit of Christ. Unlike the man at the pool of Bethesda where miracles took place only when an angel stirred the waters, and then only the first person to get in the waters was healed, this woman knew that she had discovered everlasting waters. She also knew that she did not have to wait by a pool expecting some sign or wonder to be healed. The method of waiting to see or to feel something great has caused many people to loose out on their blessings. They did not know that the cure was in their face. Jesus had not just seen this woman with the physical eyes, but he had seen all of her emotions, frustration, doubts, anger, bitterness and turmoil of soul through the spirit. In one minute his spirit had read her life history and diagnosed her case. Everyone has subluxations (partial dislocation) or pinched nerves of the spine. Because of the everyday stress of life some are never corrected, but they can be improved with adjustments (remove interference) to relieve pressure on the nerves. Jesus knew that nerve interference had caused the woman's problem. Therefore his touch manipulated her spine to bring her vertebrae back in line. He sent a signal to the body to heal itself naturally. The best surgeons of this generation perhaps would have prescribed braces or surgery to stop her progression of bending from getting any worse. Yet, Jesus the Surgeon General of the world only put both of his hands on her, and from that doubled up posture she begin to rise to the heights God had intended for her to be. Her spinal column began to adjust itself, her neck began to supply more blood to the brain, and then the muscles began to relax from years of inactivity and stress. Now the eyes that could only see the ground before, looked straight into the eyes of Christ with gratitude because she was now straight. She had been restored back unto the gracefulness, charm, poise, and beauty of a healthy woman without the use of drugs. When people are sick, the belief is embedded deeply inside of them that they will recover. Most of the time the odds of the person recovering is very great. It's belief or just the confidence within a person that bring out the results. A person's reason for believing is that God commands them to believe. "He that believeth and is baptized shall be saved." That's the law of the Gospel. That command includes permission to come forward unto Him. "He that believeth in Him is not condemned." This states that Satan cannot call the shots on when to tear your temple down. Your soul has witnessed that there is already a saving change within you, because you trust in Christ. When there is no communion with God saints and sinners alike will have no peace, little joy, and no comfort. They will always be leaning toward things that are depressing. When a person has put trust in Christ, he or she surrenders their own will and end rebellion. Peace is established within the mind, spirit, and body and cause spiritual warfare to end. Many people have postponed a meeting with Christ, and have fallen into mistakes that they never could straighten out without the help of Jesus. When the spirit of a person is very low all they think about is death, and the grave. On the other hand when a person who is living close to God is assured of their walk in Christ, and is on the straight road to heaven that person is full of joy, satisfaction, and love of life. He or she understands very well that if God helps them to live right, He will also help them to die right. When a person trust Jesus without looking for miracles, signs, or evidences they have a power within that will sustain them throughout eternity. There will be times where we all will have to rely on God alone and have to say like Esther, " If I perish let me perish, but I am going to see the King."

The devil has not bound everyone, but in this life everyone has had some trials, tribulations, and sad times. Women that are anxious to improve their circumstances, but are unwilling to improve themselves are bound and often will not back down from self-crucifixion. Women have to learn to trust God in everything that they venture into. They will have to trust Him in family matters, business, and various trials of life. There is nothing else to support them except the love of God. At the right time and the right place, God will heal them of any problem that may torment their lives. The true child of God realizes that no matter how long the Devil seek to control him or her, they were a child of God before Satan attacked, and will be a child of God long after he cease doing his worst. Although this woman was bowed down both physically and mentally, yet in her spirit she frequented the house of prayer. It was while in the house of prayer that this woman found her liberty, and you can find yours there too. The Devil took eighteen years to forge a chain to bind her, but it took Jesus only eighteen seconds to break it. Her heart was right with God. It had to be right because from the moment she was healed, she began to glorify her God. The praise that had been bottled up for eighteen years began to come out. This poor woman had been restrained from what her soul needed. She was like an animal, which needed to get to water, but the devil had tied her up so that she could only get so far. She knew God's promises, she read her Bible and she went to church every Sabbath. She had heard how Jesus had come to set the captive free. But she couldn't enter into the liberty because Satan had done all that he could do to this woman. Whenever Satan bounds a child of God he never spares his strength for he knows nothing of mercy. But where the Spirit of God is there is liberty. God's people when they have found mercy and favor in his sight will walk in the light of his countenance. The Lord permits those whom we love to suffer, and sometimes it appears that he doesn't pay attention to our prayers. Yet, all our deformities and weaknesses are only temporary. If you are in some way or another damaged by past abuse, feeling defeated by sin, or if you are feeling so inferior to other people that you are walking with your eyes to the ground; lift up your head and see what God has in store for you. Rejoice because all that degrades and limits is only temporary. Make what you can of affliction. It will soon be gone. Some of it sooner rather than later if you trust in Jesus. Adversity tests us and sometimes it's hard upon a person. There are precious few like the woman who walked around for eighteen years that can keep their moral, spiritual, and financial equilibrium while balancing on the strength of life. When adversity comes we have no choice but to stand up to it or fall down. Life is hard for everybody. For some it's harder than others, but our troubles don't take God by surprise. Some of our wounds may not ever heal; and some of our deficiencies may not be corrected during our lifetime. In fact they may even get worse. God doesn't alter the physical laws of the body nor the universe just because we are Christian. To a Christian, as well as a sinner disease and poison has the same effect. It doesn't discriminate. God has a solution for all of our troubles and wisdom to match its difficulty. For the wisdom of man is foolishness to God, and the world by wisdom neither knows God or his salvation. Some people pray only in a crisis. Their quick fix mentality sees God only as a problem solver. When a merciful solution comes, He is courteously thanked, then forgotten until another crisis comes out. Life's predicament can produce godly character within us, and cause us to grow spiritually, but the sinner must be able to say like Job, *"Tho He slay me, yet will I trust him and I am going to wait until my change comes."* However, for people to grow physically something animal or organic must give up its life. For believers in Christ to grow spiritually, the old habits, desires, and ways of thinking have to die. Many people are deformed and short in spiritual growth because of low self-esteem. Some are stooping because of criticism. Some are stooping low because of what they did in the past. And still others are stooping because they have never learned to stand up straight to anybody or anything. If a person doesn't stand for something they will fall for anything. Not only will they be bent over, but also some people will run over them. Some people are bent over because they are overanxious, overindulgent, overactive, overcritical, overwhelmed, overweight, and some have a hangover. But God will see to it that the devil don't *overstay* his welcome. He will make sure that you *overcome* and not come *over* to the side of the devil. We cannot maintain happiness all the time in this life, and those that seek to be happy must remember that the root meaning of happiness come from the word to **happen.** Things happen in our lives so that we may be led towards perfection in the Lord. Our joy is not dependent on our circumstances. We must make things happen in our lives. That's where our joy comes from. Joy is the fruit of God's spirit, and it's not affected by what has happened to us whether good or bad. Ever since God put man in the Garden of Eden good and evil have been two great forces at war with one another and in the world. Both of them are symmetrically powerful. The basic principles are that both operate using *mind power*. A person's life, the way he or she walk or dress, and his or her way of thinking are the result of mind power. When a person is bent over physically it shows an outward sign of depression and an "I don't care" attitude, whereas a person that has a straight in-line body shows outward signs of inward strength and confidence. People are a product of their own thoughts. Thoughts correlate with its object. What you believe yourself to be, you are. Thoughts determine character, careers, longevity of life, and draw upon the great source of power that lives within you. Whatever a person thinks is about to happen to them will happen whether good or bad. That's because thoughts are magnetic. They attract positive and negative results. It creates after it's own kind. Some thoughts are upsetting and weaken self-confidence. These types of thoughts can turn a person away from trying to achieve a high purpose. Your situation in life depends on how high you want to go in God's grace. Your attitude determines your altitude. You alone have the power reserved in you to get back on your feet. Jesus was so effective in controlling the devil and healing those that sought healing, because the person seeking the healing had to be on the same wavelength as Jesus was. Jesus often asked those that sought a cure from Him the question of "How great is your faith?" He asked that question, so that the person seeking the cure would reach down in their subconscious mind, to see if he or she really believed that He could cure them. The mind, especially the subconscious, also control a person's age or how old a person act. If a person think they are old they will act old for what a man think of himself so is he. The power of belief is that if you want something you can have it according to your faith. If you believe you can do something, you can do it. Belief is a motivating force that enables a person to achieve a desired goal. The opposite of belief is fear. Sin causes anxiety and fear to come into a person's life because of the guilt that plagues them. Some fears become realities from a person's imagination. It's fearful thoughts that bring about hard times, sickness, economic failure, and anxiety. Nothing comes through a person body or mind unless emotionalized thinking first creates them. People are not only created in the image of God, but every person is a creation of himself. He or she is in the image of his or her own believing, and thinking. The Bible says, "Where there is no vision, the people perish." To achieve anything a person must see it in the mirror of their soul. They must have vision along with a camera-ready view of themselves doing what they believe they can achieve. Without imagination or visualization people cannot attain that which they long to have whether it's a job, wealth, relationship, or health. Many people have allowed themselves to cut off the flow of God's blessing because they were influenced by negative thoughts of themselves and others. Some people wear themselves down trying to fight negative forces by will power. They never realize that it's their own minds along with suggestive influences that are causing all of their troubles. People have to sell themselves on the idea that they too can receive God's blessings, and can do anything somebody else can do. When a person has confidence in himself or herself, it brings out magnetic energy, which draws either the things that they covet, or bring into focus a person or thing that can cause them to move in that direction. That's why Jesus said, "If I be lifted up I will draw all men unto me." The Bible speaks of times where people were healed just by a touch of Jesus' hand. Maybe it was because certain impulses were flowing from Jesus' finger or His mind.

Whenever He laid his hands on anyone, Jesus gave off electrical vibrations. Those vibrations were pitched at a much greater frequency than what normal people were accustomed to. When He touched a person and used the power of his hands, a form of electrical energy flowed from His fingers and sent a ripple effect through the person that he had touched. The energy that flowed from Him caused static electricity to interfere with the forces at rest in that person whom He touched or whoever had touched Him. That's how He knew that the woman with the issue of blood had touched Him, because His energy had been drained to give a boost to her low life cell. The degree of consciousness, concentration, and the strength of the lady's faith show the intensity or the degree of power that Jesus sent forth. She was at her lowest state of mind and depression, therefore when she touched Jesus he had to send healing from the crown of her head to the sole of her feet.

    Look at this woman. She had abundant faith that Jesus could heal her. Everything that she hoped for must come out of Jesus. She was a not a woman of great wisdom, but her chief quality was energy. You must have energy to arouse yourself to come near to God and the church. Whenever a sinner gets near the mercy gate and begins knocking, the noise of faith knocking is heard in Hell, and the Devil get off his throne to drive the person away from the gates of hope. People shouldn't say I can't do this or I can't do that. When people use their imagination they bring into actual existence things that they have pictured themselves to be or to have. No one will ever be healthy, wealthy, or wise until they get out of wishful thinking, and go into positive thinking. It's desire that generate the power of all human action. It's by your own intentional, voluntary, indisputable, and distinct touch of faith in the Master that you will receive healing. The act of believing is the generating power that leads to accomplishments. This woman was a mass of physical and spiritual disease, but Jesus can take a mess, and turn it in a monumental testament for God. She believed that she was going to be healed, and she received a lot of healing. You also may be defeated, crawling around in the dumps, and bent over with every issue of life flowing from you, but you are the only one who can declare, "I will get up, from my bed of affliction, and I will rise from my oceans of despair." It doesn't matter who you may be, what you have done, or where you have been, when you come into contact with Jesus he brings deliverance. Preachers, deacons, and evangelists are not the only ones that God has given power to heal, and restore lives. You have it also, but you must act upon your faith and submission. There are, of course, problems with the principle of submission. Misplaced submission involves submitting to the wrong authority at the wrong time. There are multiple levels of authority in life, and sometimes this creates tension in the one who is trying to please conflicting authorities. There are other biblical commands that take priority over the command to submit to authority ("we must obey God rather than man.") Peter appended this command with the idea that wives should win their husbands "without a word." Selfish refusal to obey this command on the part of those called by God to submit doesn't mean that she should give her husband the silent treatment. Rather, when her husband is "disobedient to the word of God," she must cease from certain forms of speech that would further antagonize him. For instance, she should never nag, argue, manipulate, debate, or use devious schemes on him with the gospel. Rather, she must lovingly submit to him, and then he will be won over by her behavior.

Christian women must be careful taking all of their personal or marital business to Pastors. The Word of God doesn't state that the pastor suddenly becomes your head if your husband or wife is unsaved, backslides, or die. After all the Pastor is also in the flesh, and sometimes he or she is only giving his or her own personal opinion regarding your problem.

While I readily agree that a saved woman should not submit to an unsaved husband in ways that are contrary to God's word, it should be remembered that he is still her head. Being the head doesn't mean that he is always right or in charge. It just means that the wife is giving him the chance to be responsible and respected in the family. The husband is not to lord over his wife by demanding that she jump at his commands and do whatever he says. This is clearly shown in Scripture, with the reasoning that the wife may somehow bring her unsaved husband to Christ through her prayers, submission, and actions as a sanctified wife. As an anointed woman of God you must be careful of what you pray for. First you must be sure that you're praying for something that's rightfully yours to have, and then the spirit will agree with your subconscious mind. Sometimes we pray for things that we already know the answer to, but we think that we're the exception to the rule. "Sure, I know the scriptures teach that, but my case is different. I need the Lord to tell me specifically what to do in my situation." But the truth is you are not an exception. Sometimes your cry for help drown out the still small voice that's speaking the answers. Have you searched the scriptures for your answer? For example, if you are struggling with whether you should forgive a person who has seriously offended you, and you pray to the Lord for guidance in this; you may feel you aren't getting an answer, but in reality, the answer has already been given to you. It's found in (Matthew 18:21-35). You need to be willing to act upon the Lord's commands first. Then, as you act, you will feel a confirmation that your decision is the right one. You will have feelings of peace and contentment that following the Lord's commandments is truly the best course for you. Similarly, in our frantic state, we are often too stressed to open our spiritual eyes and see answers that are in plain view. Relax. Try to emotionally detach yourself from the situation, and look at it objectively. Find a quiet place to pray and really listen for answers. Within the scriptures are advice and direction in the way that we should live. Because the Lord has an eternal perspective on your existence, He knows best about what you need in your life. Sometimes, in your own best interest, the Lord tells you "No" even when you pray for something that seems like it should be perfectly acceptable in His sight. It takes faith to believe that our Heavenly Father knows best, and that if He says "No" it's still an answer, and one that will be best for you in the long run. There are other factors that can play a role in whether our prayers are being answered, but they are always on the end of the communication channel. Is your heart right? Are you pursuing His course for your own honor or glory? Did you receive an initial answer from the Lord? Are you staying true to God's initial message or are you working and reworking the situation to serve your own purposes? If you seek His help, be sure your life is clean, your motives are worthy, and you're willing to do what He ask, for He will answer your prayers. The Lord always listens. He is your loving Father, and you are His beloved child. He loves you perfectly and wants to help you. It's up to you to keep the channels clean by being obedient to the Lord, listening, learning to recognize His voice, and being willing to accept His will instead of your own. When your prayers involve the intercession of others, you must be especially patient. No matter how many times you ask, or how many sacrifices you are willing to make, the Lord's answer doesn't change because of you. The Lord will never force anyone to see the light or to choose His will in answer to his or her prayers. He may gently persuade, lead, and guide them until they eventually see the light, but He will not force Himself upon them. Patience is critical when your prayers involve the conversion of others. You may have a believing spouse, but he may not be as committed, interested, or as humble in spiritual things as you would like him to be, but you can't go into all this with a "holier than thou" attitude that says you're so much better than your husband is, and that he's bad and evil for wanting to continue a destructive lifestyle or a life without God. You must let your husband know that serving God is something important to you and that you realize it may not be important to him, but that you can still love and respect him unconditionally. Every woman doesn't need a major catastrophe in her life to feel forgiveness, or to be a servant of God. Selfishness, fear, and betrayal destroy marriages and none of these come from God. Many wives cannot get prayer through to God for their husbands because they don't believe in what they are saying. They only go through the ritual of praying. Prayer is reconciliation to God. Secondly, a wife must be able to ask for what she can specifically handle.

The only way to have a happy and fulfilled marriage is to put God at the center, and the only way that's going to happen is that one of partners must take a stand. Many times through faithfulness, prayers, and example, your mate will come around. If he or she doesn't come around as quick as you desire then you will have to wait on the Lord to do a change in him or her. The Lord often asks us to wait a while. Why does God put you in a waiting room instead of the emergency room? God puts you in a "waiting room" because He wants you to stop looking outward and start looking inward. He wants you to develop a relationship with Him so that you can learn what He wants to teach you. It's a control issue. He knows that you want to control your situation, but you have to learn to give Him the control. Normally in an "emergency" or crisis situation there is chaos. There is no time to waste, but when you have to wait you get frustrated and impatient, and you beg and plead for

God's sympathy. You bargain with the Lord trying to get Him to let you move on and make things work the way you think they ought to, but when God puts you in a "waiting room," you have to stay there. Your waiting room can be a confirmation for marriage, to be healed of a disease, to get a job, get out of financial bondage, to sell a house, for a child to come around, or a spouse to see the light. God knows that you don't really need to be "patient," you just need to have "purpose." There's a purpose for your waiting and you need to ask God to help you discover what that purpose is. Waiting isn't idle time; it's a time to work purposefully. God wants you to work through serious challenges so that you can grow in wisdom and faith. Waiting purposefully is a blessing. It's a very solitary, unique, work that will secure a permanent partnership in God. He will never show up early or late with your blessings. Waiting is the time that God is giving you to run and walk in Him. It's not a time to sit, twiddle your fingers, and get frustrated. You must renew your strength, and grow closer to Him. *"But those who wait on the Lord shall renew their strength; they shall mount up with wings as eagles, they shall run and not be weary, they shall walk and not faint."* (Isaiah 40:31) Pay attention to your history, improve your present, make your future infinite, for God has nothing but time in his hands. Your past isn't there just to fill up history books. It's an endless spring of self-knowledge if you will drink from it. Before you go forward, you must look back and see what worked and what didn't; what made you happy and what didn't; and what brought you closer to God and what didn't. The past will prepare you for the future if you will listen to those lessons. One of the reasons you spend so much time stalled and waiting is that you failed to learn what God tried to teach you in the last similar circumstance. The signs are there, but you refuse to read. If you continue to find yourself frustrated in a certain type of relationship, job, or other situation, perhaps it's because it's not who you are, but who God means for you to be. You continue to put yourself in the wrong places, and then refuse to see the unwelcome results as a call for change. Then you wait through the pain, loss, and confusion while God is waiting for you to find a purpose for it all. Your frustration mounts, and you can't overcome it because you won't stop long enough to pay attention and trust what God is trying to tell you; even though God lets you ask all the questions you want, and will never lie to you. So He sits you in the waiting room again and again until you have been delivered from your oppressions. Finally you get it. Remember that you are not in this wait alone, even though it may feel that way at times because you are broken in spirit and it hurts so much. In some form or another we all are broken, and in need of forgiveness. We will be effective servants offering love only to the degree that we embrace not just our own broken humanity, but also the grace of God that teaches us that we are more than the broken pieces that's connected to our lives. Like the woman who bathed Jesus' feet with her tears, her story has much to teach us about giving ourselves away and accepting grace. Only when we allow ourselves to be claimed by God and given away as instrument of his peace will we see blessings spring forth in our lives. When a woman desires something she should fully concentrate on what her desires are, and let nothing or no one cause her to deviate from her way of thinking. She may have to walk a long way, and like the Israelites she may have to hunger and thirst for a while to achieve her goals, but in the long run it will be worth it. However, to ensure that she gets what she desires, and have spiritual blessings in her life, she should never reveal to anyone except God, what her wishes or desires are. To do so may cut off her blessings before they are given. Jesus told some people that he healed *"Go and tell no man."* His reason for saying that was because the oneness of Christ with that person was attached in a positive flow. If the person told anyone about his or her prayer request they would be guilty of being disobedient. A disobedient spirit break the flow of contact with Jesus and causes envy, jealousy, pride, rage, or some other spirit to crop up in another person; who may try to put doubt in the mind of the blessed person. When a person tell everybody what they are going to do, or how they have asked God to bless them they scatter forces, and that connection with Jesus, and their subconscious will be broken. The subconscious is the power source that's connected unto the generating impulses of Jesus. It's a universal sending and receiving station that can communicate with the spiritual, mental, and physical world that are past, present, and future. The power associated with the subconscious is the ability to deduce and imagine. If people continually speak things that they believe, it will come to fruition, because they have spoken it into existence. A mind is like a door. Whatever comes through it dominates you by its positive or negative thoughts or emotions. The thoughts that are strongest will control all of the other thoughts. To draw upon the power of God families should spiritually pray together. The Holy Spirit draws upon the power of prayer and the subconscious mind and it awakens into action to break the yoke and shackles that bind children, spouse, finances, or marriage. The subconscious will not work if a person doesn't believe that it will work. For if a person believes little, they will receive little. If they believe much, they will receive much. That's why Jesus told everyone that sought to be healed, *"Go it's already been done, but sin no more."* He was conveying to the person that it must be in their spirit to feel and to know that they were healed. Then they must patiently wait while God was permanently fixing the problem, but should they return unto sin while waiting on the cure their sickness would return in greater portion. People should always think on positive things and surround themselves with positive thinking people. Unless a person utilizes his or her mode of thinking they will forever have to do physical work. To seek success a person must have initiative. Never say, "I wish I had." Make it happen by faith. We should call things as if they are already ours, and indeed they are. For God will not hold back anything good from those that loves him. To succeed in anything a person must concentrate only on what they seek to obtain. They must think on that one subject until they have put all of their common sense, strategy, energy, wisdom, and acumen in that one direction. That's called faith. However, concentration without enthusiasm leads to failure. If a person desires a new computer, car, or for that matter a new house that cost an astronomical amount of money, they can have it. By repeatedly telling themselves that it's possible for them to have what they want, and do it with emphasis and anticipation, they will usually get what they want, but it should also be reminded that faith must have action for, "faith without works is dead." People are dominated by their own fears and thoughts. Whatever our mode of thinking entails either bring about good or bad vibrations. When people walk around thinking that they are sick or are going to die it will soon happen, because they have they have thought about it so deeply with emotionalized thinking, that it has upset the chemical balance of their body. Everyone is the image of his or her own thinking and believing. *"For as he thinketh in his heart so his he."* (Proverb 23:7) We should never approach anyone or a critical situation unless we have first convinced ourselves that we can convince someone else of our belief. Whatever we fix our mind on or continually focus on is what we attract. Aren't you happy that Jesus loves you no matter how messed up and deformed that you are? Some women will never find rest in this world. They will always have constant struggle and toil, but God has a healing deliverance along

There's Enough Woman Left to be Your Lady

---

with a crown and whenever a teardrop falls from their eyes it's another diamond set in the crown. After all tears have been wiped away and the crown cannot hold any more diamonds God say to the angels, *"Her crown is finished, let her come home that she may wear it."* Women will have great rest in Heaven! No more sitting up waiting on drunken staggering bodies. No more slaps in the face. No more critical, jealous friends. No more curses being hurled at them. No more lies being said behind their back. The Queen has gone home! The Queen is the woman that has come up out of great tribulations. Jesus knew that she had to get out of this world some day. He kept her near the cross and gave her a precious fountain that had a healing stream that flowed from Calvary's mountain. He kept her until her raptured soul found rest beyond the river. Jesus has spread a banquet on the table with twelve manners of fruit from the tree of life waiting for her arrival. Waters from the rock will cascade down the street. Christ will point out the celebrity of the hour and it will be woman. When Christ consummates his love for her she will feel the earth move beneath her feet, and feel his heart so close to hers that it feels like the trembling heart of a captive bird. No longer will women bodies restrict or pain them, nor will their testimony in Christ be backbreaking daily labor that damage their body, and wound their spirit. Their broken bones, crushed spirits, and spiritual bondage will be set free to allow them to move with ease to dance in the spirit when Jesus touch them with healing grace, and speaks the word of hope, "You are set free. Go and sin no more." There is enough woman left to be His lady. He's already paid the price. Accept the gift!

14

Drinking From Deeper Wells

✤

In the New Testament all of the stories that we read about involving women showed that they were called daughter. This let's us know that Jesus affectionately looks upon women with a fatherly love. When a woman needs love or affection Christ is there to dispense of himself. Such was the day that Jesus and His disciples arrived at a hole about 150 feet deep called Jacob's well near the city of Sychar. Jesus being weary and tired sent the disciples into town to purchase some provisions, and then he sat down on the top stone edge of the well that served as a seat for weary travelers. While Jesus was sitting there a woman came to draw water from Jacob's cistern. The woman's coming to the well was no accident. There are no chance meetings in the world that are not presided over by the living God. Jesus was purposely waiting for her. This woman at the well had nothing going for her. She was a notorious member of a race of people called Samaritan who had inherited the general area. She could scarcely get anything lower than a Samaritan. Bitter hatred existed between the Jews and Samaritans. During those times it was very unusual to see a woman come to draw water alone; it was the custom for women to come by two, three, or even as many as a half-dozen at a time. But this woman came to the well alone. In a spiritual sense all sinners are alone, *"Without Christ strangers from the covenants of promise, having no hope, and without God in the world."* (Ephesians 2:12) This particular woman was alone because she was sinful and had a bad reputation in the community. She was an aging prostitute whose own people shunned her. Inside herself, she was hard, bitter, evasive, and deceitful. She was addicted to her desires. She was driven by the emptiness of her life, and alienated from her own heart. She was a home-wrecker that did not have a friend that would be seen in her company. According to John 4:28 it seems likely that her only friends were men. She had wasted her life in immorality. Perhaps the other women in the community had turned on her, or it may be that they had even threatened her; but whatever her reason, she came for water at a very unusual time. It was the custom for women to come to draw water in the early morning, but this woman came in the heat of high noon, when she knew that other women were in prayer and no one else would be near the well. The woman had come with her rope and leather bucket to draw water. Jesus always seeking lost souls and never one to let an opportunity pass to show himself as a friend, struck up a conversation with her. After five centuries of hostility and hatred between the Samaritans and Jews, Jesus broke the hostility that afternoon with a simple request, *"Give me a drink."* A Jewish rabbi would never have spoken to a woman in public, not even his wife, daughter, or sister. Moreover, the Jews would not drink from a

Samaritan's vessel for fear of becoming ceremonially unclean. It was a religious thing with them. Jesus knew that this Samaritan female was an adulteress and a fornicator, yet he still talked with her, because he valued and respected her. He saw deep in her soul a lost person who needed to come home. By speaking to her Jesus had crossed religious and cultural barriers. He tore down ancient religious prejudices and subdued her stubborn will by appealing to her kindness. The woman was amazed and bewildered. *"How is it that you being a Jew, ask drink of me, which am a woman of Samaria? For the Jews have no dealings with the Samaritans."* (John 4:9) Jesus answered and said, *"If you knew the gift of God, and who it's that smith to thee give me drink; thou would have asked of him and he would have given thee living water."* The woman's response to his quest for a drink is quite interesting, in verse eleven she states, "Sir, You have nothing to draw with and the well is deep; where then hast thou that living water?" The woman is so preoccupied with the deepness of the water and the size of the pot that she didn't listen to God. Some women are only concerned with the deep sins that are hidden in their lives; those sins that almost drowned them when they fell in the water far from the peaceful shores of salvation. Empty water pots in the lives of burdened individuals are banging, and clanging all around us. It distracts us by the noise that it makes. Some women have filled their pots with water from wells of pleasure that were poisoned with desire. The water that they drank while seeking pleasure slowly choked the life from them. A leaking "water pot" in your life simply keeps the soul preoccupied with trying to find "fulfillment" so that you will not have the time to concentrate on the presence of God. Christ gets crowded out of your inner life. Satan will use anything to keep us from Christ. He will even use religion. If he can get your mind off your efforts, merits, and religious convictions by using distractions, rather than

Christ, he will keep you occupied with everything but Christ. Satan will try to cause you to put limits on Christ. *"Sir, You have nothing to draw with and the well is deep; where then do you get that living water?"* We say to ourselves, "If you only knew how deeply sinful I really am. How can God possibly save me? It's raining outside I can't go to church tonight." These are leaking water pots filled with excuses that keeps going into our pots and then spilling out. We go from one extreme to the other. We either excuse our lack of remorse by insisting that we are too far-gone as a sinner, or we deny the depths of our depravity and thus excuse ourselves. Hurting women must learn that water of lust, infatuation, and adultery cannot quench love, nor can floods of indiscretion, deceit, and harlotry drown it. The devil uses wells of pleasure and buckets of material things that you need and depend upon to keep you in his grip. He makes them your duty and obligation. He uses pleasure to keep your mind occupied so that you will not listen to God when He speaks. These are not necessarily evil things that the devil uses to distract us from God. Most of the time they are good things, well-intended things that our families need. However, we should draw deep within ourselves as to our obligations, reputations, pleasures, and amusements to see whether making a good living for our family outweighs our living good for Jesus. God wants to plugs the holes in your life so that He may fill your spiritual pot until it runs over with blessings. That's what he wanted to do with the woman at the well, but she doesn't yield. Things are heating up and she tries to side step Jesus. She had a religious background, and she tries to throw Jesus off onto religion and denominations. *"Are greater than our father Jacob, which gave us the well, and drank thereof himself and his children and his cattle?"* Jesus refused to be drawn into an argument. He answered her, *"Everyone who drinks of this water shall thirst again."* Jesus did not answer the woman's question as to whether or not he was greater than Jacob was, nor did He take time to explain to her how he would draw the water. He instead focused on her need of salvation. In order to be saved, a sinner must believe that Jesus is more than a prophet. He laid before her a need for this living water. He had already told her that if she would ask, he would give her living water; and he was trying to get her to ask for it. His greatest task was not in producing the water, but rather in creating within the woman's heart a desire and a thirst for it. The hardest thing soul winners face today is getting sinners to stop long enough to hear the Word of God, and to try to keep them from comparing churches and preachers. Soul winners must create within a sinner's heart a desire for a thirst of the living water, salvation, and a love of people.

The woman at the well said to Jesus, "Sir, give me this water, so I will not be thirsty again, nor will I have to come all the way here to draw." She is thinking of worldly things. Her mind drifted back on physical needs. Perhaps she was thinking, "Man, if you give me this water. I won't have to work so hard. I will have it made in the shade. I won't have to keep making this long journey, coming back and forth to get this stagnant water." Like the woman we take off in the opposite extreme involving religion. We ask questions such as, "How then shall we gain eternal life?" "How can there be three Gods?" "How can God have a son?" "How can a man die for my sins?" The well is too deep for our short ropes; therefore we ask questions to deflect attention away from our own shortcomings, but you have got to face reality. God wants you to lower yourself down into the well of faith and deal with it. The woman is confused, but Jesus is patient with her. They talked some more about theological issues. Jesus helped her to see her spiritual thirst with its deep needs, but she kept talking about material things. Many are ignorant of God's wonderful salvation, and ignorance has relegated many poor lost souls to Hell. Many people have been talking when they should have been listening to Jesus. They were silent when they should have been talking for Jesus. We all have been idle when we should have been carrying the good news that Jesus saves. Indeed everyone who drinks from the water wells of pleasures in this life will keep on getting thirsty. It will never quench, or satisfy a thirsty soul seeking deliverance from sin. It can't because it won't satisfy. Water alone doesn't have what it takes to solve problems. It can't get to the soul of man. Only an intimate loving relationship with Jesus Christ will satisfy the deep longings of the soul. Nothing but the "living water" that Jesus offers will quench a dry, parched, thirsty soul. Sinners will forever keep on drinking at an old broken religious fountain that issues forth putrid water, but if they drink of the water that Jesus gives they will never thirst.

What was the woman at the well's thirst? Was it money? Finding the right man? Getting a larger house? She had gone through life making excuses, and blaming other people for her troubles rather than facing up to the reality of her depravity. Jesus removes her mask. He takes this woman, in her pain and confusion, and helps her see her spiritual need and God's solution. In every person there is there is a nameless unsatisfied longing or thirst in his or her heart that only Jesus Christ can satisfy. The woman at the well had a history of burning passion that involved men and it was still unquenched. Jesus knew it. Therefore he said to her, *"Go call thou husband, and come hither."* Jesus exposed her sordid past. She became shameful. She said, "I have no husband." When the woman admitted her life of sin, Jesus told her exactly how many husbands she had in the past. Jesus' reply was devastating, *"Thou have well said, I have no husband for thou have had five husbands, and he whom you now have is not your husband, in that saidest thou truly."* She had been married five times and the man that she now had was a live in mate who perhaps did not think that she had enough morals for him to marry her. The Samaritan woman is the image of love gone wrong. Traditionally, she has been pictured as a seeker after love in all the wrong places. The five husbands are just a way of saying that. Jesus was pointing out to her that she couldn't quench her thirst by giving her soul to somebody who only wanted her body. Some women hide their true beauty of temperance, love, and devotion under a cloud of suspicion and shame. They've had a Jezebel spirit of whoredom that was hid under tons of mascara and unrequited love.

The woman at the well immediately realized that she was in the presence of a very unusual man. One who could see into her heart and know every hidden secret of her soul. There is no holding out on God, for he knows our every secret. When Jesus made known to this woman the secret sins of her dark life, she immediately exclaimed, "Sir, I perceive that thou art a prophet." When a sinner is willing to come clean with the Lord, that sinner is ready to be saved. *"For with the heart man believeth unto righteousness; and with the mouth confession is made unto salvation."* (Romans 10:10) The Word of God will likewise convict anyone of sin today. Before anyone can be saved, he or she must be willing to confess to God, not to man that he or she is a sinner. Jesus' words drove conviction deep into her heart. She again tried to change the subject. She knows she has to do something here, or its going to be too late. So, she makes one last grasp to hold on to her illusory world. She pretends that she is fine, respectable, and totally all right just the way she is. Suddenly she became very religious, and asked Jesus where he thought was the proper place to worship. This poor woman was not ready to worship; even though she knew she needed salvation, she only asked that question to try to take Jesus' attention away from talking about her sins, but Jesus would not be sidetracked by would be religion. He kept on pounding at her heart, convicting it until she was softened in her way of thinking. Jesus told the woman in a nice way that she was ignorant. He told her frankly that she did not know what she was talking about, but that God must be worshipped in spirit and in truth. Jesus tells her what she needs is not religion, but Truth, and the life transforming, life giving Spirit of God. That's when she breaks. Her mask just won't stay on. All the masks of her lies, fornication, adultery, and hard and deceitful ways slip away. She admitted that she knew the Messiah would come, and that He would "Tell us all things." At sometime in her life perhaps in childhood, someone had instructed this poor, sinful woman that Jesus the Messiah would come to save his people, and she had not forgotten the story of his coming. God wants more than a story told about the goodness of Jesus; he wants you to know by experience about Jesus.

Jesus compelled the woman to face herself when He brought her sins out into the open. He had cut to the heart and core of her spiritual problem. Spiritually she was bankrupt and. poverty-stricken. Jesus confronted her helplessness and awakened within her a sense of spiritual wealth. He tenderly and patiently led this sinful woman, step by step, touching her heart, searching her conscience, and awakening her soul to a conviction of her desperate need for spiritual water. She was so overjoyed to be delivered from sin that she forgot that she was thirsty, and she ran off without her precious water pot. She went through the community shouting her testimony, *"Come see a man who has told me all things whatsoever I have done!"*

The devil is still using those same old tactics today. Thousands of people are joining churches; they may even attend church faithfully each week, but they have never trusted in the shed blood of Jesus for the remission of their sins. There are also some in churches that say women should be silent. They should not give testimonies. They should not teach or preach. Is that the way that Jesus Christ, the king of kings and Lord of Lords treated this woman? Even in Samaria, this woman had no credibility as a person because she was a woman. Even worse, she had no credibility because she was a sinful woman, yet God used her. The first preacher to the Samaritans was this woman. She brought others to meet Jesus. When they met him, they also believed. Many of the Samaritans from that town believed in him because of the woman's testimony of, *"He told me everything I ever did."* So when the Samaritans came to him, they urged him to stay with them, and he stayed two days, and because of His words many more became believers. They said to the woman, "We no longer believe just because of what you said; now we have heard for ourselves, and we know that this man really is the Savior of the world." Jesus alone was perfect, yet he showed kindness to this immoral woman, and made no attempt to stop her ministry. He built on what she did. This poor Samaritan woman had been strapped with fear and humiliation. She was thinking in terms of buckets and ropes, the kind that she had lowered herself into, which were the buckets and ropes of sin and limitations. This woman did not promise to quit her sin, she did not promise to "turn over a new leaf," she did not promise to join the church and be baptized, nor did she promise to "do the best that she knew how." She simply believed the Word, and by doing so she was born again. By the power of the Word she believed and was delivered from her transgressions. Her conversation with Jesus changed her from a home-wrecking harlot to a house-to-house missionary. The water in Jacob's well was good water, but it could not satisfy one's thirst indefinitely. There are no cut-off points for God when it comes to souls. God desires that all of us come to the waters of life. God will stand persistently, patently, unrecognized, despised, mocked, and rejected to ceaselessly invite us to the "Living Water" of eternal life. The "living water," that Jesus talked about is not a wage to be earned, but a gift of God. Our "thirst" is too deep for the waters of this earth to satisfy. They are shallow and muddy. The "thirst" in man's soul is a spiritual thirst. It makes no difference how far in sin you may have gone, how wicked you may be, or how long you have been living a sinful life; if you will simply believe on the Lord Jesus Christ you can be saved with the power of the Holy Spirit. There was something new that Jesus promised with regard to the Holy Spirit. He said that He was going to be poured out in a way that had not previously happened. He spoke of this in the Spirit, of whom those who believed in Him were to receive. When Jesus was lifted up in the glory of the cross he said, "I thirst." His enemies raised a branch of hyssop with a sponge dipped in vinegar. He drank from it and said, *"It is finished."* He had drank of the bitter cup of death and finished the work his father sent him to do. He bowed his head and gave up his spirit. That spirit is what we should present to thirsty, gossiping, villagers who run out to slake their thirst for rumors about the number of times that a woman may have been married, divorced, or caught in sin. We should skip past crucifixion and go on to resurrection. God repeatedly showed in the Old Testament that the whole family paid for the sins that their forefathers committed, as well as those who sinned in the "camp." Family, groups, or even a church can have sin in the camp. The sins of the fathers passed to the third and fourth generation. Guess what? They continue on as each successive generation continues in those sins! If it stopped and didn't occur after the third and fourth generation then it would be broken, but that doesn't seem to happen. Those curses are carried out by Satan due to legal rights of breaking God's laws. The ironic thing is that Satan will attack and kill one of God's servants when given the chance through legal rights by God, who will lift His hand and allow destruction to fall on someone, but God Himself will not harm anyone. That is why so many of Satan's servants have the curse of adultery, fornication, barrenness, homelessness, insanity, cancer, diabetes, adultery, perversion, bondage of drugs or alcohol, lying, stealing, and other stuff. He will take them to hell if given the chance! Generational curses are the most complicated of all curses. This is why we see families passing down sickness, whoredom, obesity, alcoholism, and other problems. Doctors believe there is a "gene" that passes this on. That isn't always true. Pastors who don't understand the reason blame it on the sick persons "lack of faith." Many who were not healed from diseases do have faith, but if someone in the camp has sins, the camp suffers. Many times happily married families have joined churches where the pastor or leadership was into adultery. Without repentance many members of the church fell into that also! These are the reasons so many people in the ministry are dying young or before their time! Words and curses spoken by others, yourself, or your parents such as: "He'll never change..." or "She'll be just like her mother." "She'll never find a good man." "Nothing ever goes right for me!" "I'll never find someone to love me!" These are curses that need to be broken to be free. God limits the enemy for a time on how much affliction is allowed, but unless the person finds out why they are being cursed with sickness, poverty, fear, and much more it will continue getting worse. But there's a fountain flowing from the cross with water breaking forth that heralds everyone's new birth. It's a spring gushing up with water so living that there is a torrent that drowns you. Jesus is that Pump of Living Water. The water of Jesus flows through clay pipes to the world. We are the clay pipes, and we aren't even good pipes. Some of us are cracked and broken, but water can still flow through us to those who are thirsty. We just cannot add anything to the water, nor make it any wetter than it already is. The best we can do is to try not to clog it up. Do you have any water pots in your life?

Are you so occupied with water pots clanging (sound of sin) that you cannot hear the still small voice of God? Then you need to fill your rattling buckets with the smooth, quiet, sound of water from the Rock. Jesus' water of salvation muffles every noise of sin that rob you of your joy in the Lord. When Jesus came into this world, he came to an earth torn by war, disease, racism, and the subjugation of women. He healed diseases, and treated women, people of different races, and sinners with dignity and respect. Jesus did not see a person with regard to race, or of an inferior gender. God loves women, sinners, and people of all races. He wants to save them and use them to further his kingdom. Jesus was not a racist, and there is no room for racism, sexism, and a holier-than-thou attitude among the people of God.

15

What Good Am I without You?

There are Spirit-filled Christians all around the world that has the distinctive fragrance of the presence of Christ filling them. The oil of the Spirit compounded with different fragrances of grace saturates them. When we have been around Christ we begin to smell like Him. Those who walk along in the presence of Christ are emitting everywhere about them the sweet fragrance of the knowledge and love of Jesus. The Gospel of Jesus Christ brings a sweet fragrance to those who are saved. It has the aroma of victory from death to life. Christ has an unmistakable fragrance because he is the Rose Of Sharon and the Lilly of the Valley. You can smell it on someone who is genuinely Christ-like. Genuine Christianity is always emitting a fragrance that's pleasing to God. Its scent permeates every crevice in life. We are a glorious fragrance of Christ to God. Our attitudes and motives of service come from a pure fragrance of heart. We do it so the exceeding abundant greatness of the power of God may be manifest, as coming from God and not from ourselves. Paul writes, *"But we have this treasure in earthen vessels, that the excellency of the power may be of God and not of us."* (2 Corinthians 4:7) Paul is pointing out that God's valuable treasure is contained in weak, fragile, and valueless containers. God has chosen to put His valuable and expensive treasure of precious fragrance in clay pots. He doesn't use beautiful bottles, or the fine china of man's making to house His fragrance. As born again believers our old, fragile, earthly bodies of clay possess this priceless treasure of the fragrance of the Gospel of Jesus Christ. God takes our simple clay pots and fills them with His glory, so that He alone can get the honor. God loves pots that are sealed. Most of the time sealed pots has to be broken before they emit the sweet fragrance of His grace. God breaks the seal of pride, selfishness, and immorality in human pots through the pressures that come in people lives. It's amazing how one word can change your whole world by opening a crack in your plans for your life. What seemed like a nice, normal, ordinary life with everything in its place including God, in a little compartment called religion, can suddenly show serious flaws. A single word from the doctor like "Cancer" can open up a huge crack in your lives. A word from a spouse or just the mere mention of the word "Divorce" can open a huge crack. A word from the boss "Fired," or if you receive traumatic news about one of your kids or your parents can have serious consequences. It will cause us to see that our lives are built upon sand. The ground begins to shift and the cracks appear. Fragile, flawed, cracked, and leaky clay pots are His choice. God enters through those cracks in your life. He can enter through serious illness, death, financial problems, or through someone close to you. Some people think that life

There's Enough Woman Left to be Your Lady

isn't fair. They want a trouble free life full of joy and happiness, but in life there are domestic fights and natural calamities such as earthquakes, mudslides, fires, flash floods, tornadoes, hurricanes and blizzards. The wrong people get sick, robbed, killed in wars and in accidents. Some people see life's unfairness and decide there is no God; to them the world is nothing but trouble. But we know there will always be sickness and death. The fact is that we hurt, but we don't comprehend pain and suffering. Like pottery we want to be glazed, polished, painted, displayed, and put on a safe shelf. But that's not God's way of producing His precious fragrance. He releases the sweet fragrance of His grace only by taking the pot off the shelf. He drops the pottery to crack or break it, and then he pours out the fragrance. He does this through the pressures that come in our lives. God press' us hard on every side by putting trouble all around us. When this pressuring takes place through affliction we feel the constraints of a confined space, and then the pain that it causes. There are times when that pressure takes the form of persecution, and we are left at a loss and perplexed. We feel like we are being hunted down like a wild animal, but we are not deserted, fully destroyed, and left behind by the Lord. We are crushed, perplexed and bewildered, but we are not despairing for we still have breathing room. When things are going smoothly and well, we tend to live as if we don't need God. It's as if we can handle things without his help. But the cracks show us that God is sovereign, and we are not the lord and ruler of our lives. God wants to be lord of our lives, and not in just the little areas that we are willing to give him on Sundays. He wants to rule our lives completely. We have to decide what we are going to do about problems, and about how much we are willing to let God carry us through them. Often we want to just close up cracks in our lives as quick as we can. We want to get some putty and paint to patch it, so that it looks all right again. We want to get things back to normal the way they used to be. When illness strikes, our first reaction is to immediately pray for healing, "Fix it, Lord. Take away the disease. Put things back the way they were Lord." But if God does that without us making any spiritual changes in our lives, then that illness was for nothing. Sickness is sometimes used to make us turn our face to God in prayer. Paul also writes, *"We are troubled on every side, yet not distressed; we are perplexed, but not in despair; persecuted, but not forsaken; cast down, but not destroyed."* (2 Corinthians 4:8-9)

Perhaps you are someone who feels as if your rope is about to break. In your Christian walk you feel that you aren't getting anywhere with God. Things just aren't happening. Around and around the wheel of God' justice and mercy goes, and around and around your body of clay goes with it. It seems the wheel is going nowhere, just around and around. You get a little impatient. You want God to use you for His glory, but you aren't seeing any results. If you want God to make something out of your life you must stay on the wheel. If you decide that the potter isn't working fast enough and jump off the wheel, you will become an old, useless, shapeless, ugly, lump of sinful clay again. When you stay on the wheel people smell the fragrance of God's grace in your life. They suddenly realize that there is not anything significant about the vessel, but it's what's inside of you that count. A lot of people are uncomfortable with the teaching that God is in control of all things, but when people see us die in the flesh to lust, pride, envy, and despair this death in us changes them. They suddenly realize God can use them, too. When God wants to do an impossible task He takes an impossible person and crushes or breaks him or her. God heals us of our brokenness by sealing the cracks in our lives with the power of the Holy Spirit. The Lord is trying to get in to our lives. God has a purpose in every bad thing that happens. Don't miss the spiritual

There's Enough Woman Left to be Your Lady

purpose behind all the crisis of life. We are constantly being delivered to the point of death so that God's message will leak out. Don't hide the cracks in the clay. That's the only way to let out the fragrance. It's amazing how often God honors a weak, broken piece of pottery-and how seldom He uses the fine china. The fact is fine china usually doesn't like being used.

The Bible and Jesus is a woman's best friend. It's a woman's emancipation, her eulogy, her joy, her heaven, and her strength. When she is troubled she will go to the Bible. The verses will explain to her "Let not your heart be troubled" for "Weeping may endure for a night but joy come in the morning," because "All things work together for the good." Look at what Jesus did for women: Jesus broke down barriers! He healed and fellowshipped with them at a time when most Jewish rabbis showed their righteousness (ignorance) by totally avoiding them. Jesus welcomed them to participate in God's kingdom. He had women among his disciples. (Luke 8:1-3) He chose women as the first witnesses of the Resurrection (John 20:10-18) He ministered to the Samaritan woman who had three strikes against her. First, she was immoral. Second, she was of the wrong ethnic group. Third, she was of the wrong gender, but look at what women did for Jesus: The Samaritan woman evangelized her village. Women gave to him financially. (John: 4) Women stuck with Jesus when it became unpopular to be his friend. (Luke 8:1-3) Danger didn't keep them away from the cross. (John 19:25, Luke 23:27-49) Women followed to see where his body was laid. (Luke 23:55) It was women that took the good news of his resurrection to the other disciples. (John 20:10-18) The Holy Spirit also empowered and enabled women in the upper room when it had descended. Jesus said the purpose for receiving the Holy Spirit was to give power to saints to witness. Women were not disqualified from this awesome experience! Women received the power too. When Paul wrote of the gifts of the Spirit in Corinthians he didn't restrict them to men. Paul ranked prophecy as a top gift. (1 Corinthians 11:5 and 12:29) The Holy Spirit is not afraid to use women!

The woman with the issue of blood, the raising of the dead twelve year old girl, the Syrophonecian woman asking Jesus to heal her daughter, and the straightening of the woman with the bowed back was all done because they believed that Jesus could heal them. What's within the reach of some is out of reach for others! Healing was out of reach for the woman with the issue of blood. Life was out of reach for the Jarius' daughter and the family of Lazarus. Living a moral life was out of the reach of Mary Magdalene. Deliverance was out of reach for the Gadarenes demoniac. Walking was out of reach for the cripple! Seeing was out of reach for the blind man! Hearing was out of reach for the deaf and dumb! Cleansing was out of reach for the lepers! Heaven, forgiveness, mercy, grace, love, and adoption was out of reach of us all, but Jesus brought them within reach through the cross! In the world people are going to have setbacks. Yet, most people would not have become Christians if it were not for their setbacks. Everyone living has forces inside of him or her that will come to their rescue if they would just believe in them and call on them. Jesus said unto a follower, *"If thou shall believe, all things are possible to him that believe."* (Mark 9:23) Have you been disappointed with yourself? Most believers, while generally striving to live a positive productive life, reach a point at which they are disappointed with themselves in one respect or another. Although we are living an obviously blessed life, there are disappointments. When you are troubled you need shut down your Internet of fear and go on line to Jesus at faith.com. We experience self-disappointment whenever we fail to do that which we think we should do, in the way we should do it. Dealing with self-disappointment is a private war, an internal struggle that's not seen by others. Unless we tell someone else, other than God himself, the only other person who knows about our self-disappointment is the man or woman in the mirror. The man or woman in the mirror reminds us of what we are. The face that keeps changing in the mirror keeps pointing out the size of the gap between our ideals and reality, and that disappoints us. We lied when we promised ourselves, we wouldn't lie. We lost our temper when we promised we would be in control. We cheated when we said we would be faithful. We have lit up another cigarette after telling ourselves that the last one would be the last one. We drank more whiskey, wine, or beer when we promised not to. Today, there are many believers who are frustrated over their inability to stay on the right path. They accept Jesus' moral standard, but they're simply angry and frustrated with themselves. As Christians, we struggle daily with our self-disappointment. Our only redeeming grace is the knowledge that, while the God we serve is not happy with our personal failures, he is forgiving and merciful. Despite our flaws and shortcomings, he blesses us continually. We let others know that we are blessed because it comes out in the wave of our hand, and the praise that falls from our lips. We said we wouldn't tell anybody, but we just could not keep it to ourselves.

16

I Am Working My Way Back to You

The Word of God often talks of angels (Hebrews 13:1) and how that even today they may come to our assistance. If God created an angel for everyone that has ever lived (Psalms 34:7), then we could figure the number of angels is at least a trillion or their innumerable. Jesus had twelve legions of angels waiting to assist him (Matthew 26:53.) When Satan fell from heaven, he took one third of heaven with him. Those have become evil spirits. Imagine the number of evil spirits that exist in the world today. If we could look into the spirit world we would be able to see all the spirits that are there to attack us. Jesus encountered and cast demons (evil spirits) out of a man in the country of the Gadarenes (Mark 5:1-19.) The devil called himself legion to signify that there were many demons attached to his domain. There were enough demons in that one man to cause two thousand hog's to run off the cliff and kill themselves. (1 John 4:1-3.) These are the same spirits that we war against today. It's no wonder that we experience so much trouble in the church and the world in general. We are being attacked spiritually as well as physically on every side. Children are being abused at alarming rates from assaults and physical abuse from both sinners and preachers. Violent earthquakes are rocking subcontinents and causing havoc among inhabitants. Greedy businessmen are selling contaminated food and swindling people out of money. Scientists are trying to imitate God by duplicating clones of people and animals. Guns, drugs, and violence have become a way of life. Uncontrollable diseases are running rampant, and symptoms of depression now vary among different age groups. Everyone worries excessively about life in general. Fear has taken hold of sensibility. The U.S. is adamant about warring with Iraq, and building a missile defense shield to protect itself from missiles fired from rogue nations. Defensively that can be done, but what can we do to stop the terror that invades our infrastructure? When terrorist suicide plane hijackers are bent on mass destruction and mayhem within our nation, what can we do? States and nations that practice democracy are a diverse society predicated upon respect for other cultures. However, on the eventful date of 9/11/2001 Americans and nations from all walks of life, and religious persuasion saw how beastly man can be. As if on cue the date of the casualty 911 signified a distress signal. America was wounded. She was delivered a crushing blow while her back was turned, because cowards didn't have the nerve to attack her face to face. The world saw the unsteady movement, and swaying of the democratic icon named the World Trade Center buckle to nothingness, as terrorist plowed domestic assault weapons (commercial airlines) into its interior. The plane left an ugly gash that caused the twin towers to implode. It fell so hard that reverberations were felt across oceans and continents, prompting other nations to share in our sorrow. For just a moment etched in time the Statute of Liberty had sat down on its pedestal, bowed its head and wepted with open shame and sorrow. As its trembling frame tried to stand against the assault, smoke, flames, anguish, and moaning sounds of death billowed from the inferno. She was in distress and calling on all of God's creation to help her as she reeled and rocked from the blow. All she could do was to blink back the tears, and watch in horror as thousands of her sons' and daughters lost their lives. What had been a testimony of life, liberty, and the pursuit of happiness, was now a monument of death, bondage, and sadness. The USA and the world have not faced a greater crisis than the terrorist assault on the World Trade Center in New York and the Pentagon in Washington, DC. No other crisis in history has resulted in the grounding of air traffic worldwide, the halt of trading on Wall Street, 24 hours commercial-free coverage by the media, cancellation of all sporting and entertainment activities, and much more. It was a time of unprecedented crisis. The cowardly act of sneak attack has not only destroyed a landmark, but also our sense of invincibility was destroyed. The attack brought with it a new style of geographical gangsterism. Unprovoked and uninvited guest had invaded our shores, and they have left a calling card of fear. For many people, the events that had been played and replayed on the TV screen looked unbelievable. Sporadic fires, ash sooted, dazed Americans, and some of its visitors were panic stricken, and tranquilized into a twilight zone of terror. Thousands lost their lives because of the actions of fanatical, evil madmen whose agenda and image is forever seared and etched in our minds. Our souls has also been scorched and scarred. In such a tense atmosphere we must tread cautiously through the rubble of burning hatred, and vengeance.

Many people are still trying to process the incident that has left everybody in a state of shock, grief, and anger. We really don't know what to do. We mourn, and we try to figure out what to do in times of crisis, but the unintended consequences of our practices include human suffering and environmental degradation. Human loss is always immeasurable in numbers, but it's irrevocably damaging when it's in such large numbers, that has claimed our brothers and sister's in our homeland. In the wake of the terrorist attacks, everyone is on guard. We have essentially lost our security blanket. Our homeland as we once knew it as having safety and security; has unfortunately conjured up emotions that show's there's something dark and sinister hovering in its background.

America: a blessed, proud nation based on Democratic rule, the protection of God, and built by the integral efforts of all nations whether foreign or domestic has had "collateral damage" invoked upon its people and soil. It should not have been such a great surprise that it happened. We are teeming with richness of freedom, money, resources, intellect, and intermingling of race, religion, and culture. That along with possessing the title of the only super-power has caused some countries to hate us, especially in the poorer segments of the world. We occupy two camps in the world that have been recognized: Terrorist and Capitalist. Both can be scary. Terrorists say that the world should worship as they do. The capitalists say that money is the answer to all things, but many countries pray for America's downfall. To some it's easier to drop out than to live with the tension of participation in any political or religious ideology, but to live in this world and to be a part of it is called life. All of us are together in the "Internet" of this world. Our cultural worldview and experiences shapes how we think. These are the assumptions that influence the emotional responses and truth that make us feel that we live the "good life." It's our common sense, but things seem to be coming apart. Our way of living, and our affluent lifestyle, seems to be out of our control. The way we live is creating more problems than it helps to solve. To know how to live, understand, and to simplify life seems to be an elusive, complex puzzle, for all of us are both "in" the world and "of" it. We try to refrain from self-deception, denial, and wishful thinking. We try to understand the world and its surroundings, and we call ourselves to participate in it with integrity, vision, and justice, but still at times we get hoodwinked.

The world today is broken and fractured by conflicts about racial differences, ethnic groups, nationalities, different lifestyles, philosophies of life, different cultures, and religions. The inability to deal with differences except with hostility and violence is destroying families, cultures, societies, and indeed the planet itself. Before this crisis America was fast sliding into the depths of religious indifference. To call on the name of God, pray in a public place, open a Bible, or to wear a cross in the classroom was almost a crime. The American spirit as "one nation under God was laughed at and its flag blatantly burned." But all this suddenly changed since disaster struck. It's now vogue to be patriotic, churches are filled, and flags are waving everywhere. However, these are reactions that are hypocritical. Why must it take a disaster of such apocalyptic proportions to bring America back to its Christian religious origins?

Like the terrorist that has claimed this to be a holy war, we as a nation have a duty, almost a holy responsibility to honor those who have fallen in death, and to protect those that are living. We should wrap our arms around the living and grieve for the fallen, and record and honor those unseen or unsung heroes whose random acts of kindness prevail. Even when an unprecedented calculated act of evil so threatens to disrupt ordinary lives, we must invoke the cry, "Lord I lift up my soul, not to vanity, but to thee. So Lord lift us up where we belong." We must have a holy contempt of the world and the things in it. We need to place God ever before our face and in our hearts, because we were tempted to abandon our sensibilities relating to brotherhood and fair marketing when soon after the attack some merchants doubled and tripled the price of gasoline, and some Americans attacked innocent people of Arabian or Muslim descent or religion. People of different American ethnic persuasion should try to hold their anger in check, until the right culprits are identified, and even then we must be patient with those Americans whose race or religious persuasion will be identified with the attackers. While justice demands that guilty people pay for their misdeeds, fairness demands that no innocent persons be held responsible for what they did not do. If not unrestrained, lawless, Americans will take out their anger and frustration on any person or group of people who look like the suspects who come from suspected countries that support terrorism, or on those that belong to a certain religion. Yes, terrorists have killed innocent Americans, but if Americans respond by killing other innocent people, how then can Americans show that they are more civilized than the terrorists? I would hope that we don't sink to the level of the attackers by seeking out those who are ethnically connected to the attackers. The enemy that has to be destroyed is faceless, because it involves lots of other people as well as those who lend them support. If this is indeed a "Holy War" as has been proclaimed by the enemy, then Satan is the architect and chief instigator directing the enemy whomever it may be to carry out his diabolic plans of destruction. As people of God all these emotions in our hearts causes our faith to struggle to make sense out of senseless catastrophe done in the name of God. What the world need are people who have come alive out of insight for human condition and love for God, rather than for religion, power, or prosperity. When we peek inside ourselves there is some aspect of adolescent, and

There's Enough Woman Left to be Your Lady

there is usually a response in gratitude for life. Sometimes there is a tear, smile, or embrace for those of us that somehow have not been afforded the peace, tranquility, or material things that life has to offer. It cannot be refuted that we have lost angels among us. We may never see their wings, but we will feel a stirring breeze every now and then from the wounds of a brief life for young, old, rich, poor, black, white, red, and yellow people of a mighty nation. It's a past life that we seek to mask, which borders on darkness and madness. It's the darkness that comes from the death, loneliness, and brokenness of our brothers and sisters in Christ. May we ever see their brightness and, in God' good time, may we see the angels who surround us with folded wings, open them to help us to open our hearts, minds, bodies, and souls to those who seek to know God's welcoming love. Since the events of September 11th, we have been telling each other that the world is now different, and that the world has changed forever. At the same time we wish for things to get back to normal, but we are not sure what normal really is any more. Therefore, it's only the world of Americans that have changed forever. We are only experiencing what other nations have gone through for decades or centuries. Our lifestyle will definitely change, because our enemy's ways of conducting war has changed. The Geneva conference is a joke to our enemies. This enemy infiltrates all the cultural aspects of American life. He is trained in our schools, eats at our restaurants, drives on our roads, dresses like us, shops in our stores, attends our games, and may even be sitting or standing next to you in the mall or at a grocery store. Is our world different? Of course, for those immediately affected by this catastrophe, the world is vastly different. Their world is infused with profound sorrow and grief, and no matter how much money, sympathy, and recognition the victims or their families receive the pain and loss of a loved one will remain. Sunrises and sunsets, sunny days, and dreary rainy days will be their forecast, but life goes on. There is terrorism in the world. But there has always been terrorism in the world. Terrorism is not new to black folks. Black folks have known, and experienced terrorism on America's soil for hundreds of years. Domestic terrorists murdered, raped, lynched, and systematically destroyed the very fabric of the black family. But through it all African-Americans learned the deeper meanings of faith. Those whose ancestors were not fully included among those covered by the Declaration of Independence, and wouldn't be full partners in the American dream until the Civil Rights Act; for them patriotism and religion has always been a part of black worship. Black people know that you have to put your trust in God when your whole world is crashing down about you and the earth is shaking beneath your feet, and you have no hope, choice, or desire. They know that you put your trust in God when you literally have nothing. Yes, Black people are suffering emotional anguish along with every American, because they also died in both the airplane and towers disaster and the sniper shootings too. Yet, black people have learned through all their years of trial and pain that God still sits high and look low, and that he can be trusted in all conditions. In times in which the very foundations of our lives seem to be shaken, all creation needs to remember that God is still on the throne. Religious fanaticism has not just been let loose in this millennium. Human history has been steeped in bloodshed, poverty, and misery of religious madmen. It has churned out thousands of madmen whose ultimate aims were to promote their own cause. They run the gamete from wanting to be world dictator to avenging angels of God. It has always been that way starting from Cain and Able, Peter of the Bible who cut off a man's ear, Jim Jones, Saddam Hussein, The Ayatollah, The Taliban, or John Brown of Harper's Ferry notoriety. The succession may not ever end. However, good, kind, and noble people outnumber all deranged and misguided people by a million to one. Each of us is totally vulnerable to destructive human and natural forces that are always waiting to be unleashed: whether by terrorists, or acts of nature. Each moment of our lives is just one breath from eternity. We live in a dangerous world, but we have always lived in a dangerous world, even when pursuing peace. Society's culture and life can radically change in the blinking of an eye. We discovered that when the space shuttles Challenger, Columbia, and Endeavor disintegrated before the world while seeking answers to enhance our existence. We also discovered our fragility again when the nation was held captive by gun wielding thugs, who sought to cease our existence by inciting fear, and committing murders during three weeks of random shootings in the Beltway Sniper attack of October 2002. We should take courage because the Lord said that he would lift up a standard in us against these types of attacks. (Isaiah 59:19) God is an Ark of protection. In the Old Testament the ark was a symbol or token of God's presence. It came with the mercy seat. (Joshua 3:11) God's mercy is ever with this nation. He has the keys of not only of hell and death, but also of heaven and life. We all sometimes feel rejected by God. In our pain of feeling abandoned, and in darkness we sometimes cannot muster the strength to pray, but in Psalm 24:7-8, it states, "Lift up your heads oh ye gates; and be ye lift up, ye everlasting doors; and the king of glory shall come in. Who is this King of Glory? The Lord strong in battle the Lord strong and mighty, the Lord mighty in battle." The doors and gates of this country should thrown wide open to give God entrance. God should be let in our hearts continually as a nation, not just when a national calamity befalls. He continually stands at the door and knock. He is ready to come in. God is an everlasting door. He is the Lord of host. He is more durable than any missile defense system or strategic planning for military readiness that the nation can employ. He can also be our destruction if we don't let him in. America needs to go back to the Christian principles of her founding fathers. There are battles taking place in the spiritual world that spills over into the natural, but we can only war against Satan by speaking out and praying in the spirit. We are given authority to act against the Devil. *"Whatsoever we bind in earth is bound in heaven."* Would God give us something that we don't need today? Everything that he has given us is needed to live in victory today and tomorrow. Jesus has shown us that he has given us power over all evil spirits in this world, and that He also gives us protection. No matter how religiously fanatical any group acts, Satan cannot prevail against the true universal church of God. The Universal Church is comprised of all true believers in Christ. We have the authority to bind and loose things in this earth. Whatsoever we bind in the natural on earth, will be bound in the spiritual in heaven.

In the American spirit of patriotism, will the crisis tear Americans apart or bring them closer together as a nation? Only time will tell. Probably after the tears have dried, the dust has settled, and time has healed all wounded, collapsed, and condemnatory hearts and houses, we will see how Americans respond to their Christian heritage. The side effects will be costly as the nation grapples with restoration and healing. It may take one citizen at a time, but to sustain what we have fought so long to achieve means that we have to sustain our losses, and gather strength to get through this. The American public always rises to the challenge of protecting its own, and the heroism, generosity and self-sacrifice shown in the rescue effort shows that this crisis has not broken, but has rather strengthened the American spirit of togetherness. It will be another chapter in our long list of historical casualties, but for those that witnessed the early morning raids, history will never be able to reveal the imposition, anger, fear, and total distrust Americans feared on that eventful date. It will be forever imprinted in their minds and hearts. These are the darkest hours in American history, but God blesses America and all other countries whose faith is based on the God of Abraham, Isaac, and Jacob. Although darkness surrounds us on every side it's now the time to lift our souls to God. There we will find solace, comfort, and light at the end of a long and winding corridor of confusion. The world is still filled with people who care, and when called on can behave with profound courage, self-sacrifice, beauty, and love. The events of September 11, 2001, October 2002, and February 1, 2003, has reminded us that people of faith are of every religious persuasion. We need solidarity with people of good will from all of these faiths. Out of all of this maybe God is trying to tell us something. Maybe he is trying to show the world in an indiscreet way that we all intrically linked in some way or another, and what happens to one happens to us all, that we are all in the same ship drifting towards eternity and judgment. Maybe people will learn to truly love their neighbor. Maybe we will learn to appreciate each other more and value life more. If there is a motion towards a reformation, God will move in our direction to heal our grief. God wants to work in our life, but we must speak (pray) into being those things that we need (Matthew 21:21-22.) God spoke and things came into existence. He has so ordained it that He will answer those who call on him the same way. This is the reason we can ask for things by faith. By praying, we give God authority to operate in our lives and in our nation. It also helps us to relieve circumstances of others. What any terrorist dead or alive doesn't understand is that whenever Lady Liberty is knocked down, her torch's flame has not and never will by the grace of God be extinguished. The light of freedom will forever shine in the hearts and minds of those who live on to secure the dreams of all oppressed people. Empowerment and liberation are consistent themes in democracy and God centered preaching. We all must see these crises as a time of great danger and opportunity, as well as a chance to get back in touch with God. Although her back was bent, there's still enough women left in the United States to be God's Lady.